# TASTY™
# ULTIMATE

# TASTY™

# ULTIMATE

### how to cook
### basically anything

CLARKSON POTTER/PUBLISHERS

*New York*

Copyright © 2018 by BuzzFeed, Inc.
Photographs copyright © 2018 by Lauren Volo

All rights reserved.
Published in the United States by Clarkson Potter/Publishers,
an imprint of the Crown Publishing Group, a division of
Penguin Random House LLC, New York.
www.crownpublishing.com
www.clarksonpotter.com

CLARKSON POTTER is a trademark and POTTER with colophon
is a registered trademark of Penguin Random House LLC.

TASTY is a trademark of BuzzFeed, Inc., and used
under license. All rights reserved.
Some recipes originally appeared on Tasty.co.

Library of Congress Cataloging-in-Publication Data
Names: Tasty (Online store)
Title: Tasty ultimate: how to cook basically anything / Tasty.
Description: First edition. |
New York : Clarkson Potter/Publishers, 2018.
Identifiers: LCCN 2018012828| ISBN 9780525575863 |
ISBN 9780525575870 (eISBN)
Subjects: LCSH: Cooking. | LCGFT: Cookbooks.
Classification: LCC TX714 .T388 2018 | DDC 641.5—dc23
LC record available at https://lccn.loc.gov/2018012828

ISBN 978-0-525-57586-3
Ebook ISBN 978-0-525-57587-0

Printed in China

Book and cover design by Stephanie Huntwork
Book and cover photographs by Lauren Volo
Photograph on page 262 by Marshall Troy

10 9 8 7 6 5 4 3 2 1

First Edition

To our Tasty community—the choppers, measurers, spillers, grillers, food testers, mess makers, and photo takers who have brought Tasty to their kitchen tables

# CONTENTS

# WELCOME TO OUR TABLE

**DEAR READER: YOUR LIFE IS ABOUT TO GET A WHOLE LOT TASTIER.**

Whether you're an aspiring chef or you just want to be able to make yourself dinner without ending up on a BuzzFeed list of kitchen fails, you're in good hands with Tasty. We want to be the wind beneath your buffalo wings, the Watson to your Sherlock home cooking, the Hall to your overnight oats. From tips and techniques to envy-inducing recipes, this book will be the beginning of a beautiful friendship between you and your kitchen.

The world has proven its insatiable appetite for all things Tasty by watching the step-by-step tutorials from start to finish a bajillion times, collectively. And since the only thing we love more than making you hungry is helping you make the recipes that turn any meal into a good time, we're giving you all the Tasty you can eat, right here in book form. For anyone who has ever emerged—both hungry and inspired in equal measure—from a rabbit hole of Tasty videos, this is the next step in your culinary education.

This isn't just a book of recipes—it's a Tasty production, which means we're going to guide you through all steps of the kitchen gauntlet. We've selected the recipes here to give you a mini-but-mighty culinary crash course. This book is the ultimate handbook for anyone who wants to learn to cook like

the Tasty team. We can't guarantee internet fame, but we're certain that while you cook your way through this book, you'll get something more lasting: a love for creating meals as deep and profound as your love for eating them.

As you whip up your Tasty creations, you'll also be learning to poach with panache, blanch like a boss, and fry famously. Learning the fundamentals of cooking gives you endless options. Those caramelized onions you learned to make for French Onion Soup (page 32)? Why not add a few of 'em to a pot of cooked rice to make some magic! The pan-basting skill you picked up when you made Honey Mustard–Glazed Ham (page 282)? That knowledge is fully transferable to chicken, fish, and pretty much any kind of protein your stomach desires.

The only thing better than wowing your friends and family with your newfound culinary prowess ("Oh, this old homemade pan pizza with all the toppings? I just thought it would be easier than ordering in!" you'll say smugly) is treating yourself to incredible cooking every day. The question "What's for dinner?" will never make you break out in a cold sweat again. No one breaks down the steps you need to tackle any recipe like Tasty does. Whether you're cooking a lazy breakfast for one or a fancy AF feast for twenty (side note: can we come?)—we've got you covered, chef!

# ESSENTIAL INGREDIENTS

It's amazing how much easier cooking is when you're not trying to whip up a meal using sprinkles, ketchup, coffee filters, and half the sandwich you had for lunch. Every good meal starts with good ingredients, and stocking your pantry with these staples will make tackling any recipe less daunting. "Shelf stable, dinner on the table," as the saying (we just made up) goes! This list of ingredients includes everything you need to make the recipes in this book, but feel free to accumulate what you need as you go—you'll have the full complement of basics before you know it. Think of your pantry as your edible toolbox for quality cooking, dish after beautiful dish.

## THE PANTRY

### Fats

#### Olive Oil

Liquid gold, as far as we're concerned, olive oil comes in two basic types: **regular** and **extra-virgin**. Regular olive oil is great for everyday cooking, sautéing, roasting vegetables, and other recipes with a Mediterranean profile. It has a high smoke point, unlike its finicky sibling, extra-virgin olive oil. Extra-virgin (which refers to the acidity level of the oil—the lower the better) can be used to dress salads, drizzle on vegetables, and generally add finishing touches to your dishes, like a very fancy chef person. Unlike the neutral oils below, olive oil has a distinctive (and delicious) flavor, so keep that in mind when you're cooking.

#### Vegetable Oil

Neutral in flavor, vegetable is a workhorse you can use in every kitchen situation, from pan-searing and sautéing to desserts. It has a fairly high smoke point so it's a good choice if you're frying or sautéing on high heat. Other neutral oils great for cooking are grapeseed, sunflower/safflower oil, and corn oil (the last of which is great for deep frying, thanks to its very high smoke point).

#### Grapeseed Oil

A neutral-tasting oil with a high smoke point, grapeseed oil can be used for pan-frying and sautéing, as well as in salad dressings.

#### Sesame Oil

Sesame oil has a similar smoke point to grapeseed oil. There are two types: Regular sesame oil is relatively neutral in flavor and can be used like canola and vegetable oil. If you have a bottle of this stuff on hand, your sautéing, pan-frying, and roasting needs are set. Toasted sesame oil is made from roasted sesame seeds; it's the dark red kind that has a very heady aroma. It is primarily used in other recipes with Asian flavors because it has such a distinct flavor/smell. It can be cooked with, but often times, it will be used at the end of cooking to keep its flavor unadulterated by heat. A little goes a long way!

#### Avocado Oil

Packed with good fats and boasting one of the highest smoke points of any plant oils, avocado is a pantry all-star that can shine as a high-heat cooking fat or in place of olive oil as a dipping sauce for bread or tossed with salad.

#### Coconut Oil

Coconut oil has a relatively low smoke point, so it's good for searing and sautéing. It's white and solid at room temperature, but melts pretty easily (and becomes clear).

#### Butter

Made by churning cream until it solidifies, butter is the fairy godfat that elevates everything it touches. Go for pure butter in bar form rather than anything squeezable or spreadable (chances are these have added

## 101

## Smoke Points

In order to select the right oil to take your food from rawsville to flavortown via the fryway, make sure you choose one that can handle your heat. Smoke point refers to the temperature at which oil starts to smoke and burn—and in some cases, even turn rancid. Make good oil choices! Don't worry—we're here to help.

stabilizers, fillers, and colors). Butter has a surprisingly long shelf life—about six months—so don't stress if you don't use it right away. If you open a stick, wrap it in plastic so it doesn't absorb refrigerator odors. (You can also keep it in the freezer.) Unless otherwise specified, the recipes in this book call for unsalted butter; it gives you more freedom to season your food to your exact tastes. But if you end up with salted butter, don't sweat it—just keep it in mind when figuring out how much actual salt to add to a recipe.

### Mayonnaise

We get it, mayo is divisive! But it's essential for so many dips, salads, and sandwiches that it's a must in the Tasty kitchen. It's typically made with with egg yolks, oil, lemon juice, and mustard. You can sub light mayo for full-fat if you like, but we'd recommend staying away from fat- or sugar-free varieties—they're shadows of the glory that is mayo (and won't work as well or taste as good).

## Sauces and Stuff

### Dijon Mustard

Spicy with a gentle tangy kick, Dijon mustard, which has roots in the region of France with the same name, contains touches of horseradish and white wine (yeahhhh, it's pretty French). Great in salad dressings, sauces, and—of course—on sandwiches.

### Spicy Brown Mustard

The classic deli mustard, spicy brown has a coarser texture than Dijon because the bran is left on the mustard seeds used to make it. It's also less acidic and (duh!) spicier than either of the other mustards listed here. Perfect with pastrami (or whatever Sally was eating when she met Harry).

### Yellow Mustard

Made from yellow mustard seeds and turmeric (hence that crazy yellow color) and other seasonings, this is the classic hot dog topper. And bonus: It lasts forever.

### Ketchup

A staple in American cooking, ketchup is made from tomatoes, vinegar, sugar, salt, and spices. You probably already know it's the perfect tangy sidekick for fries, but it's also delicious in a sauce, a glaze, or even a salad dressing (we see you, Rémoulade, page 109).

### Vinegars

Vinegar is perfect for adding a burst of bright tanginess to a dish. It's the black sheep of the booze family; yes, it's made from alcohol, but that alcohol has fermented into acid long before it hits your grocery store shelf. Vinegar won't get you drunk, but it will take your food to the next level. **Distilled white vinegar** is used in brines and pickling liquid (and it's also handy for cleaning). It has a strong smell and a harsh flavor—it's made from grain alcohol—so you'll probably want to stick to something gentler for your improvised salad dressings, like, say **red** or **white wine vinegars,** both of which are great in vinaigrettes. Red wine vinegar is more robust (and its color is more dramatic, if that's what you're after), while white wine vinegar is milder. **Apple cider vinegar** is relatively mellow and pleasantly tart, which makes it a good choice for dressings and marinades. Distilled from rice (go figure), **rice wine vinegar** (aka rice vinegar) can add a sweeter acidic element to a dish. It's great in dressings and as a counterpoint to rich dishes like our Salmon Pokē Bowl (page 127). And of course, sweet, sticky **balsamic vinegar**—which is not made from alcohol—is perfect as a dip for bread, a salad dressing (particularly with olive oil), or for drizzling over finished dishes, both savory and sweet.

### Soy Sauce

Ubiquitous throughout Asian cuisine, soy sauce is a salt lover's dream. It's made from fermented soybeans, is dark brown in color, and can add both savory and umami flavors to marinades, sauces, and roasted veggies. We recommend cooking with low-sodium soy sauce so you are always in control of how much salt goes into your food—you can always add more salt, but you can't take it away. Though many soy sauces contain wheat, gluten-free varieties are also widely available. **Tamari** is a great gluten-free alternative as well!

### Hoisin Sauce

This deliciously thick condiment is made with fermented soybeans, vinegar, garlic, and a variety of warm spices, including Chinese five spice, a blend that contains star anise. Its salty-sweet richness is perfect in a marinade or glaze for meats, a sauce for stir fry, or even on its own as a dipping sauce. Yeah, it's that good.

### Fish Sauce

Fish sauce—salt, anchovies, and water fermented in wood barrels—is integral to the flavors of Vietnamese,

Thai, and Indonesian cuisines. It may be stinky in the bottle, but once added to a dish, it deepens the flavor and adds an unparalleled pow of umami.

### Sriracha

Originally hailing from Thailand, this smooth, spicy hot pepper sauce is a mainstay on restaurant tables—Asian and otherwise. It adds great heat to recipes—not to mention a real punch when squeezed on top of dishes like our Traditional Vietnamese Beef Pho (page 51). It also plays well with other sauces—sriracha mayo, sriracha ketchup . . . the world is your (sriracha-garnished) oyster!

### Gochujang

A fermented chili paste and one of the key elements of Korean cooking, this stuff lasts forever in the fridge—and that's the least of its charms. Use it in our Korean Fried Chicken Wings (page 72), but also go freestyle and swap it in for other hot sauces, or to add some extra heat and complexity to sauces.

### Honey and Maple Syrup

Liquid sweeteners like honey and maple syrup are ideal for adding sweetness to savory or sweet dishes where their unique tastes also add complexity and depth of flavor. In savory dishes, their earthy sweetness complements other savory flavors better than granulated cane sugar, so it's good to use those there. Honey and maple syrup have very distinct, opposing tastes, so don't substitute one for the other without adjusting for the strong flavor each one brings to the party. But from a consistency point of view, maple syrup is slightly thinner than honey, but both can be substituted for the other in most recipes that call for the sweeteners in measurements of less than ¼ cup.

### Nut Butter

You know peanut butter as the constant lifelong friend who'll never leave your side, but these days, there are lots of other nut butters vying for your affection. Any nut or seed can be made into a "butter" by processing it with a little oil and, if you like, sugar, until it's completely smooth and spreadable. Almonds, cashews, and even sunflower seeds are just a few of our favorites, but even tahini is technically a nut butter since it's made with ground sesame seeds. For the most part, you can substitute one for the other, keeping in mind the obvious difference in flavor.

## Dry Goods

### Pasta

Most standard pasta is made from wheat and water, and can go from dry to daaaaaamn in just a few minutes. Pasta is a pantry MVP: It can chill for years on your shelf without going bad, it's wildly versatile, and it's perfect for feeding a crowd. It's also delicious. Quit bragging, pasta! Most pasta boxes have cooking instructions printed on them, and you'll often see the phrase al dente to describe the ideal finished product. Italian for "to the tooth," al dente means slightly undercooked with a tiny bit of chew. (If you're going to be cooking the pasta again—think mac and cheese or a soup with pasta in it—you'll definitely want to aim for al dente.) It's easier than ever to find a pasta that suits your tastes and dietary restrictions. Many grocery stores carry rice-, millet-, chickpea-, and quinoa-based varieties. (Just keep in mind that texture and cooking time varies depending on the main grain.) You can also experiment with fresh pasta—either homemade or from the refrigerator section of your grocery store. Just remember that it cooks much more quickly than its dried counterpart—it only takes around three minutes. *Mangia!*

### Rice

Much like it's carby cousin pasta, rice can really pull a meal together. It comes in a number of varieties. **White rice** is the basic long-grained rice you'll find in every grocery store. **Basmati rice** is another white, long-grained rice and is often used in Indian cuisine. **Brown rice** can come in long or short varieties—it's simply rice that retains its outer shell (and the heartiness and nutrients that come along with it)—and can be substituted for standard white rice in most cases. **Spanish** and **arborio rice** both absorb liquids like delicious little sponges, so they're perfect for paellas and risottos, respectively. **Jasmine rice** is an aromatic long grain rice that's native to South East Asia, so it's an easy choice to serve with Thai curries, stir-fries, and other Asian dishes. Cooking times vary for all these varieties, so make sure to check the packages.

### Other Grains

Rice is great and all, but sometimes you want to switch it up with a new grain, especially now that there are so many on the market to choose from and explore! **Quinoa** and **couscous** have been around for quite sometime, but both make great substitutes for rice,

whether it's for the pleasant chew they bring to your dish or their ability to mimic rice in soaking up all the wonderful juices from whatever you place on top of them. But don't just stop there: **Farro, wheatberries, millet, bulgur,** and even **sorghum** are grains that everyone is chatting about lately. Each has a different cooking time, so be sure to pay attention to the package directions. Pro tip: If measuring water and standing nervously by the pot to watch the grain cook to make sure it doesn't burn or stick on the bottom is not your idea of a great time, simply cook any grain like pasta instead of like rice. Bring a large pot of water to a boil, stir in your grain, season the water with salt, and cook, stirring when you can, until the grain is tender or just as chewy as you want it. Then drain it and use. This is the best way to cook grains if meal-prepping, too; just make sure you rinse the grain in cold water afterward to stop the cooking and wash off any excess starch that could cause it to get sticky when refrigerated.

### Bread Crumbs

Bread crumbs are so much more than just a messy by-product of toast! They can act as a binder (think meatballs), a crispy coating (chicken cutlets, anyone?), and an element of texture (especially when you toast them with a little butter). If you have some leftover stale bread, it's easy to make your own—just toast the bread and either pop it in a food processor or place it in a bag and go to town with a rolling pin or wine bottle. You can also find many varieties of pre-made bread crumbs at the grocery store. **Panko** are Japanese bread crumbs that are extremely low in moisture, meaning they crisp up like mad when fried or baked, making them perfect for breading. You can experiment with swapping in some of these for regular bread crumbs in some recipes—just remember that they take a little longer to moisten.

### Corn Starch

Flour is our go-to thickener for sauces and stews, but sometimes, like if you want a slightly cleaner and less murky appearance to your sauce or pie filling, you can turn to cornstarch instead. It thickens liquids slightly stronger than flour, so use a little less than a recipe calls for of flour if substituting it. Unlike flour, though, which needs to be cooked or mixed with fat first to help keep it lump free, cornstarch is best mixed with cold liquid first, then stirred into a hot liquid. If you've ever heard the word "slurry" used in a recipe (see box, page 289), this is what they're referring to. It helps keep the cornstarch from creating lumps when it hits the hot liquid, a saving grace when it comes time to get that gravy ready at the last-minute on turkey day.

## Seasonings

### Salt

Salt is one of the most important ingredients in almost any recipe. Used correctly (we're here to help you with that!) it acts as a flavor intensifier and makes delicious things even more delicious. The standard salt our recipes call for is **kosher salt.** Flakier than table or sea salt and with a less concentrated saltiness, chefs love it because you can easily pinch it between your fingers for more precise seasoning. Your average salt (the kind you'll find in restaurant shakers) is **table salt** or **fine sea salt,** which is often used in baking. Because it has such small grains, it dissolves more quickly than kosher salt. Fine sea salt is a tad pricier, but a container will last you for ages, so we recommend spending the extra dollar or two. One thing to remember about seasoning is that you should be doing it throughout the cooking process, not just at the end. Salt needs time to dissolve and work its magic with a dish's flavors, so if you only add it at the end, your dish will be missing some oomph. However, you can add **flaky salt** (like Maldon) for a tasty finishing effect.

### Pepper

Freshly grinding whole peppercorns is a game-changer. The pre-ground stuff just doesn't have the same zip as the freshly ground variety. You can go two routes here: Buy a pre-filled pepper grinder that you throw away once it's used up, or buy whole peppercorns and a reusable grinder, and refill at will. Either way, you come out ahead. If you really want to buy ground black pepper, look for something less dusty—

### 101

## Season to Taste

Though we call for specific amounts of salt, pepper, and spices in most recipes, feel free to season more or less. A bit of extra salt, pepper, herbs, or spices can help coax extra flavor from a dish, so be creative and feel free to jack up—or down—the seasonings to your taste.

anything labeled "butcher's pepper" is a bit more coarsely ground.

### Spices and Herbs

As a group of five wise women once said, "People of the world / Spice up your life"—and who are we to disobey the Spice Girls? A properly outfitted spice rack is a beautiful thing; not only does it prepare you for the recipes in this book, but it also encourages you to experiment. Try to keep spices away from heat sources—don't store that paprika right on top of the toaster oven!—as warmer temperatures cause their flavors to dull faster. Though conventional wisdom holds that dried spices should be used up within six months, we think they're good for up to a year. That being said, give them a whiff to make sure they still actually smell like they're supposed to.

This isn't an all-inclusive list by any means—think of this as the foundation of your spice cabinet. As you expand your cooking repertoire, you'll discover even more spices that you want (that you really really want).

Most spices used to be herbs, and can add incredible depth to the flavors of your dishes. Dried herbs like **sage, basil, thyme, parsley,** and **oregano** will make your marinara or Bolognese sauce sing. These will be all-stars to level-up your salad dressings, or to add a little freshness to any dish.

**Garlic powder** and **onion powder** are great for rubs, seasoning bread crumbs, and adding flavor to all kinds of dishes when fresh onions and garlic aren't available— or even when they are.

One big category is things that come from peppers: For spice, nothing beats a pinch of **chili flakes**—the seeds of whole dried hot peppers, with a little skin thrown in for color) or **cayenne,** a powdered dried chili. **Paprika** comes in several varieties: sweet (which isn't really sweet; it's more neutral), hot (which can pinch-hit for cayenne), and smoked, which adds a delicious— you guessed it!—smoky flavor to dishes (think bacon or smoked meat, but without the meat). **Chili powder** is actually a blend of cumin, paprika, garlic, and other spices and isn't as hot as you might think; it's named for the dish it goes into (duh, chili) rather than what's in the powder itself.

**Cumin,** with an earthy, spicy flavor, and **coriander,** a nuttier spice made from ground-up cilantro seeds, are both widely used in Mexican and Asian foods. They're both delicious on their own, but together, they're an unstoppable duo.

## 101
# Fresh vs. Dried Ground vs. Whole

When going dried, you want to buy whole spices whenever possible and grind them when you need them because once they're ground, their flavors will start to dissipate. Consider grinding black pepper fresh from a grinder versus using the pre-ground stuff; it tastes better and is more potent. Spice and coffee grinders are the most efficient ways to grind quickly and are cheap, but you can also go old school and use a mortar and pestle. Regardless, the rule of whole-to-ground spices is usually ⅓, meaning whatever amount of whole spices you have, you'll get about ⅓ of that in ground spices (i.e., 1 tablespoon whole black peppercorns will yield 1 teaspoon finely ground pepper).

Warm spices are perhaps the most hygge of pantry staples: Think of anything that would be good in a glass of hot cider and you're on the right track. **Cinnamon,** in both dried and in stick form, may be a dessert workhorse, but it also enhances dishes like the Vietnamese soup called pho (page 51) and Slow Cooker Honey & Spice Lamb Shanks (page 54). **Cloves, cardamom,** and **allspice** fall into this category as well, and come in both whole and ground versions.

## Canned Goods

### Tomatoes

Canned tomatoes deliver the flavor of tomatoes picked at their peak, all year long. Never let the winter freeze prevent you from enjoying the everyday magic of tomatoes. Usually peeled and canned in juice, **whole canned tomatoes** are ideal for making sauces. They've got a ripe, fleshy texture and lush, tomatoey flavor. Use a pair of kitchen shears to snip them into smaller chunks right in the can. **Diced tomatoes in juice** are just what they sound like: cubes of tomato in their own liquid, ready to be used in place of fresh—and they're often preferable if ripe options are lacking (or lackluster). Made by pureeing canned tomatoes mixed with tomato paste, **tomato sauce** lends a rich, concentrated flavor to soups, stews, and chilis. If you're watching your salt intake, do some label-checking, since canned tomatoes can vary widely in salt content. You can buy them without any added and season it yourself. You'll find **tomato paste** in a small can or a tube, and it doesn't take much to add a major pop of concentrated tomato taste to your dish. The paste caramelizes when sautéed, which adds complexity to your flavors. Look for pure tomato paste without added dried herbs or seasonings so you can customize it to your dinner's delight!

### Beans (Dried and Canned)

Healthful, filling, and packed with protein and fiber, the humble bean is a culinary powerhouse and a great thing to have on hand at all times. If you can't find the exact variety a recipe calls for, feel free to swap in another variety, like pinto for kidney or black beans, or navy for cannellini, and vice versa. Though we mostly call for canned beans in this book, dried chickpeas (also known as garbanzo beans) make a few appearances as well. While it's not strictly necessary, many people prefer to soak dried beans for a few hours or even overnight to cut down on cooking time. If you're using a canned variety, just give them a quick drain 'n' rinse.

### Broth

Broth is more than just something to slurp when you're under the weather—it's a key ingredient in soups and well as some sauces and basting liquids, and it's also a great way to add flavor to lentils or grains. Broth should, ideally, have as few ingredients as possible. Go for low-sodium brands to help you control the salt in the recipes. **Chicken** and **vegetable broths** can be used pretty much interchangeably in most recipes, while **beef broth** has a heartier flavor. At the store, you'll find liquid broth in either cartons or cans, or you could use bouillon cubes or paste, both of which need to be diluted in boiling water before use.

### Coconut Milk

A staple in many Southeast Asian and Caribbean cuisines, coconut milk will add creaminess to both sweet and savory dishes, from puddings to overnight oats to curries. In some recipes, it can even be used as a nondairy, vegan substitute for heavy cream. Make sure to use canned coconut milk, not the kind that stands in for regular milk for drinking or eating with cereal. That stuff is watery and tasteless. The canned stuff has the fat (or cream) on top that is often skimmed off and used in recipes, too. Look for brands that are just coconut and water, no stabilizers.

## FROM THE FREEZER

### Frozen Spinach

Take the spinach out of its bag, put it in a colander, and run cool water over it until it's fully thawed. Then squeeze out the excess liquid (there will be a fair amount) so your food doesn't drown in Popeye water.

### Frozen Peas and Corn

Defrost these with cool water in a colander. In some cases they can be added, still frozen, to a bubbling stew or casserole at the end of cooking.

### Frozen Berries and Cherries

Berries are fragile little babes, so you should defrost them gently—ideally in a bowl of cool water in the refrigerator. If you're using them in baked goods, though, no need to defrost at all; the oven will do all the work for you.

### Frozen Puff Pastry

Thin, deliciously flaky puff pastry dough can be used to make treats like croissants as well as sweet or savory tarts and pies (see page 144). You can find it in the frozen foods section of your grocery store, but you'll need to thaw it in the fridge before you get to work. It can be tricky to work with, because its individual layers are very thin and dry out easily, so keep it covered with a damp cloth as you work, removing one piece at a time (for more information, see page 288).

## FRESH INGREDIENTS

### Produce

Buying produce should be a hands-on experience. To find the best apples, plums, zucchinis, and avocados, don't be shy: touch them, smell them, hold them! Try to buy loose produce that you can inspect yourself; pre-packaged produce is often a way to hide the less-than-perfect items out of sight (sneaky, sneaky!). Seek out unbruised items that look fresh, smell good, and seem heavy for their size, especially when it comes to fruit (this means they're not dried out or old). If you're buying bagged lettuce, make sure there are no wet-looking leaves inside; a few bad ones can quickly spread and ruin the whole package. And believe it or not, spraying produce with water may make it look fresh, but it makes it expire faster, so look for fruits, vegetables, and alliums (onions, shallots, garlic, scallions, and more) that are dry on the surface.

For the most part, produce should be stored in the refrigerator—leafy greens, cucumbers, cauliflower, carrots, broccoli, green beans, apples, grapes, and berries in the drawers, and beets, asparagus, bell peppers, summer squash, and citrus on the shelves. Garlic, onions, shallots, potatoes, and winter squash prefer a cool, dark space like a pantry or a cupboard (but be sure to refrigerate any unused portions once you cut them up). Tomatoes, bananas, pears, and melons should stay on the counter to ripen.

### Proteins

If you're buying packaged protein products—that is meat, chicken, and fish—make sure it looks fresh, with no grey or discolored blemishes. Seek out the packages with the latest expiration dates (they often get hidden in the back, since sellers want you to buy the oldest stuff first). If you open a package and it smells less than stellar, don't be afraid to take it back to the store. With meat, a good indication of freshness is a nice red color and not too many juices swimming around in the packaging. For fish, a good indicator of freshness for a whole fish is clear, bright eyes, reddish gills, an overall gleam and no discernable fishy smell (we know, it's counter-intuitive).

Striking up a conversation with your local butcher or fishmonger may seem like a scene straight out of a black-and-white movie, but having connections behind the counter is the best way to get a primo cut of meat or a swimmingly good fillet of fish—not to mention the best service. Shoping for meat and fish can be intimidating, but an open line of communication is the best way to gain some knowledge and sharpen your skills. Come armed with questions and an open mind. What's new? What's seasonal? What's local? If you want to eat the best foods, these are the people who will tell you what's for dinner, especially if you're open to trying something new: your fishmonger could suggest that if you like cod, give pollock a try or try swapping arctic char for salmon. Same goes for meat: if they don't have the cut your recipe calls for, ask for an able swap-in. These professionals can also help you cut down on dinner prep time: A good fishmonger can de-scale skin-on fish, make fillets, or butterfly per your request; a good butcher can cube meat for stew, trim off unnecessary fat, and give you the prime cut he reserves for the very best customers. If you don't use it within 3 to 5 days of buying, you can freeze meat and fish for up to 2 months if well-wrapped and handled. Thaw it completely in the refrigerator (this can take at least 24 hours), and use it that day. The longer you wait, the more the protein fibers start to break down, and going from frozen to thawed accelerates that process.

## THE DAIRY AISLE

### Milk and Yogurt

Unless you're a habitual milk-drinker, stock whole and one percent milk in smaller quantities (half-quarts). Sour cream makes a delicious topping on chili or stew, and also lends richness to baked goods and dips; and

The Ultimate
Chocolate Cake,
page 183

both Greek and plain whole-milk yogurt add tang and moisture to recipes. If you're watching fat content, you can swap out whole milk products for low-fat replacements—just stay away from fat-free options, which often have gums and added fillers.

You can often use dairy-free versions of these ingredients—coconut, soy, almond . . . pick your poison! As long as it's not real poison—just be sure to check their sugar content, as they're often sweeter than their dairy counterparts.

### Eggs

Filled with golden treasure (or yolks, if you're feeling less whimsical), eggs are the crown jewel of the fridge. You can use them in pretty much every meal, and they give you great bang for your buck. The standard egg size for our recipes is large, so your results may vary if you go for extra-large or medium. Try to buy farm-fresh eggs when you can, but don't stress if your only option is the grocery store variety—they'll still be delish.

### Cheeses

If you're a fan of Tasty videos, you've probably noticed that we have kind of a thing for cheese. In fact, there's a whole chapter of cheesy recipes here. Call it a fetash, but we think cheese is pretty dang gouda. When in doubt, we always gruyère on the side of cheesy. And look, we're not saying people who don't like cheese are muensters, we're just saying that if you're a cheese fanatic, you're not provolone—we're right there with you. Anyway . . .

Fresh refers to white cheeses with a soft, spreadable consistency. These cheeses—which include **chèvre** (goat cheese without a rind), **cream cheese, cottage cheese,** and **ricotta**—have more moisture than the hard stuff, and less complexity of flavor. Which doesn't mean they're not delicious! Just that they tend to taste more like the milk from whence they came, which could be cow, goat, and sheep.

Unlike fresh cheese, hard cheeses have been processed or aged. They're perfect for slicing and melting—think **cheddar, gouda, gruyère.** Quality can vary a lot based on where the cheese comes from (is it imported? Domestic? Or some kind of drifter?), and how long it has been aged. One indispensable hard cheese is **Parmesan,** aka the perfect pasta topper. You can go two routes here: Invest in a wedge of Italian Parmigiano Reggiano cheese—which is aged for up to three years and packs a lot of flavor into each bite—and grate it yourself, or a container of pre-grated cheese. (Note: We recommend steering clear of the dusty, pre-grated stuff that comes in

a can—it's an imposter!) If you can't find real Parm (which is recognizable by the cheese's distinctive golden rind marked with little indented dots), ask for Grana Padano, a cousin of Parmigiano Reggiano that has a similar flavor profile (and a slightly lower price tag).

Don't let spoiled cheese get your goat! Store it in the refrigerator, in a plastic bag or wrapped tightly in plastic wrap or wax paper once opened. Fresh cheeses should be eaten within 1 to 2 weeks; hard cheese like Parmesan will keep for about 3 to 4 weeks.

## BAKING ESSENTIALS

### Sugar

With all due respect to sugar-abstainers, we think it's pretty magical in all its forms. **Granulated sugar** is pure refined cane sugar and is the most standard sugar called for in desserts. **Confectioners' sugar** is cane sugar that has been processed to be fluffy and easily dissolved, and is often used in cake frostings; it usually contains a bit of cornstarch, too. **Light brown sugar** is granulated sugar with the addition of molasses, which provides moisture and warm flavor notes; the only difference between it and **dark brown sugar** is that the dark version contains more molasses, which makes it a little more moist. We'll always specify which you should use in a given recipe, however, in small amounts (let's say, less than ½ cup) they're pretty interchangeable.

### Chocolate

So many types of chocolate, so little time! How do you pick? It's all about the amount of sugar and the amount of cacao paste—one of the two main ingredients in a chocolate bar. **Unsweetened dark chocolate,** often known as 100% dark chocolate, contains no sugar and is used exclusively for baking. **Bittersweet** and **semisweet chocolates** generally contain between 50 and 65 percent chocolate and are essentially interchangeable, though bittersweet chocolate generally contain less sugar. **Milk chocolate** is simply semisweet chocolate that has milk added for softness and creaminess. **White chocolate** is cocoa butter, devoid of cocoa solids, with added milk solids and vanilla to give it a more distinct flavor. They both typically have the same percentage of sugar in them, around 35 to 40 percent. We'll always specify which type to use, though.

### Cocoa Powder

No offense to the dusty instant hot cocoa packets in your office pantry, but the cocoa powder we're talking about is in a different league. It's unsweetened, intensely chocolatey, and essential for many chocolate desserts. There are two main types of cocoa powder: **natural** and **Dutch processed.** Cocoa is naturally acidic, so natural cocoa powder has a lower pH and reacts with baking soda to make those treats rise. Dutch processed cocoa, on the other hand, has been neutralized (which sounds much scarier than it is). It has a mellower flavor, and won't give your desserts that height unless you use baking powder as well. Got it? No? Don't worry—most recipes will specify the kind of cocoa you should be using. Phew!

### Vanilla

As a flavor, vanilla has been unfairly synonymized with "boring." But vanilla extract (either pure or imitation will do the trick) is the unsung hero of countless baked goods. Even when it's not the star of a recipe, vanilla enhances the flavors around it (proving that there are no small parts, only small ingredients). Some recipes will call for fresh vanilla bean pods, which you'll either soak in a liquid to infuse it with flavor, or slice open and scrape out the delicious, seedy paste inside. You can also substitute the paste inside one pod for one teaspoon of vanilla, if you want your dish to have those beautiful speckles of beans.

### Flour

If you've ever loved a cookie, a cake, a pie, a dish of pasta, a slice of bread, a stew, or even a humble cracker, you have flour to thank. **All-purpose flour** (bleached or unbleached) is the most widely used and available variety, but you'll also encounter **cake flour,** which has a lower protein level than all-purpose, making it good for more delicate cakes, and bread flour, which has a higher protein level. The standard varieties of flour are made from wheat, but gluten-free options (made from rice, almond, and millet, to name a few) are becoming more and more ubiquitous, which is a great thing, because no one should be deprived of the magic of flour! Gluten-free flour mix, such as **Cup 4 Cup,** is a great substitute for and can be used in exact place of regular all-purpose flour. However, non-wheat flours have entirely different properties from wheat flour and therefore cannot be substituted one-to-one.

### Baking Powder and Baking Soda

The dynamic duo of baking science, baking powder and baking soda both help leaven baked goods, helping to give them a delightfully fluffiness. Baking soda is a ground up mineral that, when combined with an acid like buttermilk or lemon juice, creates carbon dioxide, which bubbles up to give your pastries a lift. Baking powder, on the other hand, already contains acid, in the form of baking soda, so any kind of liquid—acidic or not—will trigger the same delicious chemical reaction. Both have a long shelf life, so buy them now and thank yourself for cookie-filled months to come.

# ESSENTIAL EQUIPMENT

You wouldn't go on a camping trip without a tent and a sleeping bag, so don't set off on your grand kitchen adventure without the appropriate equipment! There are countless kitchen gadgets that claim to be essential—and, hey, feel free to try any that appeal to you along your culinary journey—but this list includes all the tools you need to cook the recipes you'll find here (and plenty more). You can find them all at big box stores and online, but many supermarkets also stock them.

### Nonstick Skillet

Whether you're frying eggs to sunny-side-up perfection or sautéing veggies for a weeknight feast, these pans make for easy cooking and cleanup. These come in a variety of sizes, but a standard 10-inch will be able to handle most of your stovetop creations. Make sure not to use metal cooking implements on these, as it will scratch off the nonstick surface.

### Cast-Iron Skillet

Cast-iron skillets are sturdy and relatively cheap cookware that lasts for generations. You can do almost anything in it: sear a steak, bake some rolls, or simmer a batch of chili—the properties of the cast-iron ensure that your food cooks evenly and gets a golden brown crust all over. If taken care of, the skillet becomes more nonstick the longer it's used, can be used in place of any other skillet called for in a recipe, and can even go straight from stove to the oven.

### Saucepan

You'll use this kitchen workhorse the most, to heat up virtually everything you cook. Liquid will evaporate from it more slowly than from a wider skillet, so it gives you more control when you're heating up sauces, soups, and grains. A 1- or 2-quart saucepan is considered small, 3 is medium, and 4 is large. Once you get into the 5-quart zone, you're talking soup pot or even a small Dutch oven (see below).

### Dutch Oven

Its name may be misleading, but think "big-a$$ pot" and you're on the right track. Heavy and sturdy, Dutch ovens take a "slow and steady wins the race" approach: they take some time to heat up, but once they do, they're second to none in terms of cooking evenly. These enameled or plain cast-iron pots are perfect for items that require "low and slow" preparation, like stews, brisket, and roasts (and as a backup pasta pot).

### Rimmed Baking Sheet

You'll use this for sheet-pan suppers, roasting vegetables, broiling meats—the list is endless. Invest in a good-quality, 13 x 18-inch model made of sturdy stainless steel; otherwise, it could burn and warp during cooking.

### Springform Pan

When you need side coverage during baking but then want to expose your cake in its full glory without having to invert or manipulate it too much (think cheesecake), use a springform pan. A hinged sidepiece clasps around a bottom disc during baking; once cooled, the sidepiece can be unclasped and removed for serving and slicing.

### Grill/Grill Pan

When you've got to get your char on, nothing beats an outdoor grill. If you've got one, use one! Clean the grates with a metal brush, or spray with grate cleaner and wipe clean with a soft cloth. If you don't have a grill, don't fret: that's what a grill pan is for! Look for a large model (10 or 12 inches) with a lot of surface area so you don't crowd your food. Make sure to preheat it well (about five minutes at medium-high heat). You will know the pan is ready if you hover your palm about 4 inches over the pan and feel the heat radiating off it. And if you hear a delicious searing sound when your food hits the pan, you know you're in for some searious deliciousness.

### Measuring Cups and Spoons

Invest in one nested set of measuring cups for dry goods like flour, sugar, and grains; two spouted liquid measuring cups—one 1-cup and one 4-cup—will help

## 101
# Cast-Iron Skillet Care

Most cast-iron skillets are ready to use at purchase—all you need to do is maintain the nonstick coating it comes with. To take care of yours, simply wipe the skillet clean with a damp paper towel after each use. For foods that leave lots of oil and bits of food in the bottom, simply wash and rinse the skillet like any other with mild dish soap and warm water. Dry it immediately with paper towels to remove all the water, which can rust cast-iron if left to sit. Pour a spoonful of vegetable oil in the skillet, spread it all over the inside surface of the skillet with a dry paper towel then place it in a 500°F oven for an hour, enough time for the oil to burn off and set the nonstick coating back on the skillet (you'll see the skillet go from shiny to matte in appearance during this process). Turn the oven off, let the skillet cool completely inside, then remove it and store it with your other skillets. If you want to ensure it doesn't get any unwanted dings or scratches to that coating, place a paper towel on the inside bottom of the skillet before stacking other pots or pans inside it.

you portion out wet ingredients; and a set of measuring spoons for spices as well as wet ingredients in small quantities. For all three types, look for numerical markings that are embossed or etched into the cups or spoons rather than printed or stamped, so they don't wear off with repeated washings.

### Mixing and Prep Bowls

Mixing bowls of varying sizes will help you with a wide array of kitchen tasks—from mixing batter to tossing salad— so it's a good idea to have a few. Look for a set of three nesting bowls (space-saving FTW!). A set of smaller prep bowls is an organizational life-saver. Look for bowls that have rubberized grippy bottoms, so you can rest them on the counter and whisk with one hand instead of two if you're busy with another kitchen task (or 'gramming your handiwork).

## Cutting Board

Get at least one that's generous in size so you can get your work done without your food finding a new home on the counter or the floor. 18 x 24-inch is ideal; 12 x 18-inch will do the trick as well. You can certainly get away with one good cutting board, but since they can be porous and absorb odors, you might want to opt for a set of equal-sized boards in different colors. That way, you can designate one for meat and poultry, one for vegetables and smelly aromatics like garlic and onions, and one for fruit and other sweet things.

## Heatproof Silicone Spatula

Great for stirring pots and mixing batters. Since silicone is a flexible material, it's great for getting into corners of bowls and pots so you don't lose a single delicious drop. And since it's heat-resistant, you can walk away from a saucepan with the spatula inside and it won't burn or melt.

## Metal Spatula

These are generally wider than silicone spatulas, so they're great for tasks that require surface area: flipping pancakes, meats, or fish in skillets or grill pans, or removing them from said pans altogether. We recommend a slotted spatula, which will let you remove the solid while leaving liquid behind in the cooking vessel.

## Whisk

Essential for whipping egg whites and heavy cream into lush peaks and stirring and thickening sauces and dressings. We like to use a balloon whisk, which has the benefit of being the most widely-available variety.

## Bulb Baster

The bulb baster (commonly known as a turkey baster) immediately connotes Thanksgiving, but this tool is an all-star when it comes to roasting or barbecuing meat. Use it to suck up the delicious juices in your pan (by sticking the tip into the liquid and squeezing the bulb up top) and redistribute them over the meat as it cooks, keeping it moist and adding flavor.

## Tongs

Like an extension of your hand, tongs allow you to flip proteins, toss pasta, move veggies around in a pan, pretend to be a crab and pinch your friends and family—okay, maybe not that last one, but trust us, you'll find yourself reaching for these time and time again. Look for a locking pair (for easy storage) with scalloped tips (the better to grab slippery food).

## Graters

A standard box grater, whose four sides each are perforated with different sized holes, is a workhorse that will do everything from grate carrots to slice cucumbers. A fine grater or zester works better with smaller quantities of foods—it will help you create fine shavings of cheese, chocolate, or citrus zest, and can be held right over the bowl or pan.

## Vegetable Peeler

The most important qualification for this invaluable veggie prep tool is that is feels good in your hand and won't slip when you're hard at work de-skinning. Our favorite style is the so-called Y-peeler, which has a wide handle and a blade is at the end, so you can peel in an up-and-down motion with ease.

## Citrus Juicer

Citrus juice can add an irresistible freshness to a dish, so we recommend keeping a juicing tool on hand. You can opt for either a Mexican-style juicer, in which fruit is clamped into a small handled bowl to release its juices, or a reamer—a handheld wooden or plastic tool that you stick inside the halved fruit and rotate. Of course, you can just squeeze really hard, too.

## Strainers

A standard colander, with larger holes, is great for straining pasta or rinsing salad greens and other vegetables. If you need to rinse rice or anything else with tiny pieces, go for a handled fine-mesh strainer or sieve. While plastic colanders are convenient, a metal one will be able to handle the heat better.

## Kitchen Shears

Unmatched for taking apart a chicken, cutting whole tomatoes right in the can, trimming kitchen twine, and countless other tasks.

### Thermometers

A shocking number of ovens are miscalibrated, so an **oven thermometer**—which costs about $10 and hangs off the rack inside your oven—is a good way to make sure you're cooking things at the right temperature. An **instant-read meat thermometer** gauges the doneness of different proteins. When using a meat thermometer, insert it as close to the center of the cut as possible without hitting bone—bones get very hot and can yield a misleading and inaccurate read. A **deep-fry thermometer** clips onto the side of a pot and gauges the temperature of the oil to ensure even, efficient frying.

### Trivet

A heatproof surface that allows you to put those hot pots and pans on the table or counter without scorching the surface. Kitchen decor hack: Get one that looks cool when there's no food on top of it!

### Pot Holder/Oven Mitt

Underappreciated and overly important. Chuck those dog-eared, hole-filled specimens you probably inherited and invest in two thick, heatproof pot holders that will keep your hands cool when transferring hot-handled pots from skillet or stove to table.

### Kitchen Towels

Invest in a stack of absorbent towels you can use in place of paper towels whenever possible. Once you get in the habit of adding them to your kitchen repertoire, you'll love how easily they dispatch spills. Of course, their greatest advantage is that they're reusable—just throw them into a hot-water wash at the end of your cooking sesh. If you're using disposable paper towels, do the environment a favor and opt for ones made from recycled paper product. They're also good for covering rising dough because they let air in and out, but still give a protective covering for the bread. Plus they are basically nonstick, so they peel off from the dough easier than plastic wrap. Plain, clean terry-cloth cotton towels are the best.

### Storage Tools

Leftovers are precious—guard them with your life (or at least with your best bags, foils, and containers). **Heavy-duty aluminum foil** holds heat in better than the cheap stuff, and you'll be able to use less to achieve the same results. A better (read: slightly pricier) brand of **plastic wrap** is worth it—it will seal your food in and make it last longer. **Zip-top bags** come in handy for storage, marinating, and sending friends home with leftovers. They range in size from snack—great for leftover odds and ends of the nut, bread crumb, or chocolate variety—and sandwich-size to quarts and gallons, which make quick work of freezing leftover soups, fruit juices, vegetables, and more. **Glass storage containers** with tight-fitting lids in various sizes are good for saving leftover ingredients and leftovers themselves. Plus, they're reusable and good for the environment. Plastic works, too, but be careful. Many are dishwasher- and microwave-safe (just check the package to be sure). Keep a **permanent pen** and a roll of half-inch **masking tape** around to label leftovers. That way, when you come home starving, you'll know the difference between mac and cheese and cheesecake. Just make sure to include the date you cooked each food, so you never have to ask yourself, "How many meme life cycles ago was this chicken made?"

## ALL ABOUT KNIVES

Chefs can get pretty fanatical about their knives, and with good reason: A good knife is arguably the most important tool in a kitchen. Most recipes require the use of a knife, so it's worth spending a little time selecting your chopper of choice. But don't worry—we're here to help!

### What to Buy

Two essential sizes of knives can get any job done: An **8-inch chef's knife** for major chopping jobs, and a **paring knife** for finer work. The rule is simple: the larger the item, the larger the knife. The chef's knife is great for chopping large vegetables, smashing cloves of garlic (lay the flat of your knife over a clove, and press down with the heel of your hand), chopping piles of herbs, and cutting pieces of meat for stew—the big stuff! Your paring knife is ideal for cutting smaller vegetables—think radishes and snow peas—and for trimming small ends off of things like strawberry hulls and tomato cores. You can even use it to slice an apple in a pinch.

Look for knives that have a so-called "full tang"—a single piece of metal that starts at the base of the handle and extends all the way to the knife's tip. This indicates solid construction and will guarantee that your knife never snaps in two or goes all bendy on you! If you want to expand your collection, a **serrated knife**—one with toothlike edges on the blade—is great for slicing bread and tomatoes, as well as chopping chocolate.

## How to Store

Knives should be kept in a safe place, either secured by an in-drawer tray, a countertop knife block, a magnetic metal strip, or covered with knife guards, all of which are widely available online. The safest option is the magnetic strip because it gets the knife out of "tetanus drawers" and out where you can see them.It will also save your blades from getting dinged up and bent.

Never wash knives in the dishwasher—rattling up against other utensils can dull the blades—and dry them immediately after washing so they don't rust. It may seem counterintuitive, but the sharper your knives are, the safer they are to use. Dull blades require more pressure (danger!) and slip more easily (double danger!). A knife should glide through an onion with ease; if it doesn't, it's time to sharpen that baby up at your local kitchen store, or invest in a new one!

## Tips for Using

When using a chef's knife, grip the knife securely from its handle with your dominant hand. For smaller items (garlic, herbs, zest), use the so-called rocking motion, placing your non-dominant hand on top of the knife (near the tip), and using a see-saw motion to chop your ingredients without fully lifting the knife off the board. For larger items, use your non-dominant hand to stabilize the item you're cutting; curl the tips of your fingers toward your palm to protect them as you apply pressure to stabilize your victim—er, ingredient.

## Types of Cuts

**Rough Chop:** large pieces done in a freeform style, with pieces varying between ½ to 1 inch in size.
**Chopped/diced:** cut into ½-inch square pieces
**Finely chopped:** cut into small (¼ inch) pieces
**Minced:** Cut into very small dice—as small as possible
**Sliced:** Cut into thin strips; the width will usually be specified in the instructions
**Ribboned/chiffonaded:** cut into thin (⅛-inch), ribbon-like strips; this is used for delicate, flat-leaf herbs and leafy greens like basil and mint

**Julienned:** cut into thin, 2-inch-long matchstick-shaped pieces

When cutting, the more equal in size the pieces are, the more evenly they will cook. But don't worry if they're not perfect; if a few pieces of onion brown a little more during sautéing or roasting, they'll still taste delicious!

# COOKING TIPS

You've got the ingredients, you've got the tools, you've got the taste . . . you're nearly ready to get this food on the table! Before we move on to the main event, we have a few more hints to get you (and your kitchen) in tip-top cooking condition.

## Be Prepared

Let's be honest: it can be tempting to dive into a recipe immediately—as in, before you even finish reading it. We get it! Cooking is exciting! But we're of the opinion that it's even better when you're fully prepared. So spend a few minutes reading the recipe you've set your sights on. Make sure you have all the ingredients and equipment you need, as well as adequate time to prep and cook. Practice *mise en place*: roughly meaning "everything in its place," to help you stay organized and prepared to cook so you don't have to pause once you've pressed "play" on cooking to go get an ingredient or chop it, which could cause things to overcook or go bad in the meantime. It also makes cooking less stressful because there's no more prep work to do—just cooking.

## Get Organized

While you don't need to go full Monica Gellar on your cooking space, a little order will make your kitchen tasks easier and way more fun (seriously)! Having designated spaces for the tools you reach for again and again will seriously reduce the amount of time you spend ransacking your drawers in search of a spatula mid-sauté. If your kitchen space is limited, get creative with your walls: hang hooks for potholders, kitchen towels, and measuring cups, a mounted rack for pots and pans, and a hanging spice rack can all free up precious counter space. Take an honest inventory of the supplies you have, and stow away the ones you don't use as frequently. That breadmaker you've only used once? Stick it somewhere out of sight—hasta la-yeast-a, baby!

## So Fresh and So Clean

Flour-dusted countertops and pots dripping with sauce can lend . . . atmosphere to a cooking sesh, but if you're not careful you'll end up with a mountain of dishes and a countertop crime scene by the time you're ready to eat. Chances are, cleaning isn't your favorite part of cooking (if it is, please stop by the Tasty kitchen at your earliest convenience). That's why we love the "clean-as-you-go" method, which will make the final mess much less, well, messy. Keep a damp towel around to wipe down surfaces (just rinse it with a little warm water between uses), collect trash or compost in a bowl near your cutting board, and wash (or at least soak) those dishes when you have a free moment. The name of the game is containing the chaos!

# HOW TO USE THIS BOOK

It's no secret that cooking can be intimidating, and not just because it involves knives and fire. That's why we want this book to serve as a cooking demystifier just as much as a collection of recipes. Hey, you have to poach before you can Benedict! Throughout the book, we'll be giving you "the 101s" on the key culinary skills you need, from preparing cake pans and measuring flour to making garlic paste and crisping chicken skin. Don't worry: we'll never leave you (or your cakes) high and dry. The book is broken into two main sections. In the first, "Impress Yourself," you'll find classic, essential recipes organized by main ingredient. We start with recipes that teach you the basic techniques, then build up to more elaborate dishes. The second, "Impress Your Friends," is where you get to flex those newly built culinary muscles with holiday feasts, game day snacks, and a whole host of recipes designed for hanging out—and, of course, a little showing off. This section will challenge you with more advanced techniques and ingredients. And at the beginning of each chapter, we kick things off with a pair of "Versus" recipes, two dishes that tell a story through their comparison. They highlight how easy (and fun!) it is to switch up flavors for almost every dish you cook to make it your own—and how versatile the classic dishes we all love really are. Once you've mastered the meals in this book, use these "Versus" recipes as your inspiration to take your favorite dishes in a new direction that suits your tastes. We believe in you!

When it comes to food, we're all about sharing. And even if we can't actually taste your Tasty creations, we want to see 'em! Use the hashtag **#TastyUltimate** to post videos and pictures of finished products (and any of the steps along the way). Hey, it's not bragging if you've got the goods to back it up! We can't wait to see what you're cooking.

PART

I

# IMPRESS YOURSELF

neapolitan-style pizza vs.
takeout pan pizza 30
french onion soup 32
pepperoni pizza pull 34
cheesy spinach & artichoke
bread dip skillet 37
chili dog skillet 38

# CHEESY

baked pimiento cheese dip 41
cheddar & chutney puff pastry 42
slow cooker queso de cerveza 43
baked ham & cheese ring 45
clean-out-the-fridge cheese
& herb dip 46
chorizo fundido bread dip 47

# NEAPOLITAN-STYLE PIZZA

SERVES
1 or 2

1 teaspoon **extra-virgin olive oil,**
plus more as needed

1 teaspoon **sugar**

¼ teaspoon **active dry yeast**

½ cup lukewarm **water** (110°F)

1½ cups **"00" flour,**
plus more for dusting (see box,
page 179)

1½ teaspoons **kosher salt**

6 canned whole peeled **tomatoes**
(from one 28-ounce can)

4 ounces fresh **mozzarella,**
preferably mozzarella di bufala,
cut into 6 to 8 slices

10 **basil leaves**

**Flaky sea salt**

Pizza pizza: two kinds are better than one! When it comes to Neapolitan Pizza, think thin-crust with tender, bubbly dough and a middle that gets a little floppy on purpose—you may want to have a knife and fork handy, or perfect your fold-and-feed stance while this baby is baking. Italian "00" flour, made especially for pastas and pizzas, helps create the signature chewy dough that makes this pie so fly. This Takeout Pan Pizza is the pie of your dreams, doable in your kitchen—homemade crust and all. Make sure to check the date on your yeast when buying it—it's alive! Keep it in a cool cabinet, or even the fridge, to ensure its effectiveness.

1 Combine the olive oil, sugar, yeast, and lukewarm water in a large bowl and let stand until foamy, about 10 minutes. Add the flour and salt and stir until the dough comes together.

2 Turn the dough out onto a lightly floured surface and knead it until it is smooth and elastic, 8 to 10 minutes (see box, page 250).

3 Grease a large bowl with olive oil, then add the dough and turn to coat with oil. Cover the bowl with a kitchen towel or plastic wrap and refrigerate for at least 48 hours.

4 When ready to bake the pizza, preheat the oven to 500°F. Place a pizza stone or upside-down rimmed baking sheet in the oven to preheat.

5 Let the chilled dough stand, covered, for 10 minutes at room temperature. Turn the dough out onto a lightly floured surface. Press and rotate the dough to expel the yeast bubbles and stretch the dough into a 12-inch circle. Transfer the dough to a pizza peel or piece of parchment paper.

6 Crush the tomatoes in a small bowl with your hands, then distribute the crushed tomato pieces—leaving the juices behind in the bowl—evenly over the dough, leaving a 1-inch border around the edge. Arrange the mozzarella over the tomatoes. Brush the exposed dough with more olive oil.

7 Slide the pizza directly onto the preheated pizza stone or upside-down baking sheet. Bake until golden brown at the edges, 10 to 12 minutes.

8 Turn on the broiler and broil the pizza until the cheese is bubbling and the crust is lightly charred, 3 to 5 minutes (see box, page 57).

9 Scatter the pizza with the basil leaves. Drizzle with olive oil and sprinkle with sea salt. Slice and serve immediately.

# TAKEOUT PAN PIZZA

SERVES
4 to 6

1  Combine the flour, salt, sugar, yeast, and water in a food processor and process until a ball of dough forms around the blade, about 45 seconds (see box, page 173).

2  Turn the dough out onto a lightly floured surface and briefly knead it into a ball (see box, page 250). Grease a large bowl with olive oil, then add the dough and turn to coat with oil. Cover the bowl with a kitchen towel or plastic wrap and let the dough rise in a warm, draft-free area until doubled in size, about 1 hour.

3  Preheat the oven to 500°F.

4  Turn the dough out onto a lightly floured surface. Press and rotate the dough to expel the yeast bubbles and stretch the dough into a 12-inch circle.

5  Transfer the dough to a 12-inch round metal pizza pan or rimless baking sheet.

6  Stir together the tomato sauce, basil, and garlic in a small bowl and season with salt and pepper. Spread the sauce evenly over the dough, leaving a 1-inch border around the edge.

7  Sprinkle the cheese evenly over the tomato sauce, then arrange the pepperoni on top. Brush the exposed dough with more olive oil.

8  Bake the pizza until the dough is golden brown and cooked through, the cheese has completely melted, and the pepperoni are browned at the edges, 10 to 12 minutes.

9  Slice and serve the pizza hot with grated Parmesan, oregano, red pepper flakes, and garlic powder alongside for guests to sprinkle over the top.

2 cups **all-purpose flour**, plus more for dusting (see box, page 179)

1 teaspoon **kosher salt**, plus more to taste

1 teaspoon **sugar**

½ teaspoon **instant yeast**

⅔ cup lukewarm **water** (110°F)

**Olive oil**

½ cup canned **tomato sauce**

½ teaspoon **dried basil**

2 **garlic cloves**, minced

**Freshly ground black pepper**

2 cups shredded low-moisture **mozzarella cheese** (8 ounces)

15 **pepperoni** slices

Grated **Parmesan cheese**, dried **oregano**, crushed **red pepper flakes**, and **garlic powder**, for serving

# FRENCH ONION SOUP

*More, s'il vous plaît.* That's what you'll be saying after spooning up this rich concoction, which is basically an ooey, gooey cheese toast rested on top of the best soup you've ever tasted. Six—count 'em—cups of onions caramelize down to become the star of this dish. Swiss cheese works great, but if your grocery store has Gruyère—its nuttier, slightly more aged cousin—give that a whirl.

¼ cup plus 2 tablespoons **olive oil**

2 tablespoons **unsalted butter**

6 cups thinly sliced **yellow onions** (about 3 medium); plus ½ small **yellow onion**, grated (optional)

½ teaspoon **kosher salt**, plus more to taste

½ teaspoon **sugar**

3 tablespoons **all-purpose flour**

6 cups **beef stock**

1 cup **white wine**, such as sauvignon blanc

½ teaspoon **ground sage**

1 **bay leaf**

12 (½-inch-thick) slices **french bread** or **baguette**

3 tablespoons **Cognac** or brandy (optional)

**Freshly ground black pepper**

4 cups shredded **Swiss cheese** (12 ounces)

1 cup grated **Parmesan cheese** (4 ounces)

1   In a large pot, heat ¼ cup of the olive oil and the butter over medium-low heat. Once the butter has melted, add the sliced onions and stir to coat with the oil and butter. Cover and cook, stirring occasionally, for 20 minutes.

2   Increase the heat to medium-high. Stir in the salt and sugar and cook until the onions are brown and caramelized, about 20 minutes (the bottom of the pan will develop some browning—very important!).

3   Add the flour and cook, stirring, for 1 minute. Add 1 cup of the stock and use a whisk to scrape up the browned bits stuck to the pan (see box, opposite).

4   Add the remaining 5 cups stock, the wine, sage, and bay leaf and bring the mixture to a boil. Reduce the heat to medium to maintain a simmer and cook, uncovered, until the liquid has slightly reduced, about 40 minutes.

5   Meanwhile, preheat the oven to 325°F. Line a baking sheet with foil.

6   Arrange the bread slices on the prepared baking sheet and brush each slice on both sides with some of the remaining 2 tablespoons olive oil. Toast in the oven until golden brown and crisp, 20 to 25 minutes total, flipping once halfway through. Remove from the oven and set the baking sheet on a wire rack. Increase the oven temperature to 350°F.

7   Once the soup is done, remove and discard the bay leaf, stir in the grated onion and Cognac (if using), and add salt and pepper to taste.

8   Set six 12-ounce ovenproof bowls or ramekins on a rimmed baking sheet. Divide the soup among the bowls, filling each about three-quarters of the way. Top each with 2 slices of the toasted bread and sprinkle the Swiss and Parmesan cheeses generously over the top. Broil until the cheese melts completely and is golden brown in spots, 2 to 3 minutes (see box, page 57). Serve hot.

## 101

### Deglazing a Pan

You've browned some vegetable and meat in a hot pan. See all that good stuff stuck to the bottom? Don't wash that pan—deglaze it! Add water, wine, stock, or some combination to those golden brown bits clinging to the pan while it's still hot, then scrape as you stir. You create the base for a rich pan sauce or soup as the bits dissolve, releasing their caramelized flavor into the heating liquid.

## PIZZA DOUGH

1½ cups lukewarm **water**
(105°F to 110°F)

1½ teaspoons **active dry yeast**

3 cups **all-purpose flour**,
plus more for dusting (see box,
page 179)

¼ cup grated **Parmesan cheese**
(1½ ounces)

1 teaspoon **baking powder**

2 teaspoons **sugar**

1 teaspoon **kosher salt**

3 tablespoons **olive oil**

## PIZZA RING

2 tablespoons fine **cornmeal**

8 slices large deli-style **pepperoni**

8 slices deli-style **Provolone
cheese**

3 cups canned **tomato sauce**,
plus more for serving

3 cups shredded low-moisture
**mozzarella cheese** (12 ounces)

2 tablespoons **olive oil**

2 tablespoons finely chopped
**fresh flat-leaf parsley**

1 **garlic clove**, minced

# PEPPERONI PIZZA PULL

If you think something this ooey-gooey delicious can only come from your neighborhood slice joint, you've got another think coming. This triple-threat dish stacks three layers of dough with a three-cheese combo of Parmesan, Provolone, and mozzarella. It's basically an adult art project that you can eat. Gather your friends for a viewing—and a tasting—because this one calls to be oohed and ahhed over.

---

1  Make the pizza dough: Pour the water into a liquid measuring cup and sprinkle the yeast over the water (see box, page 173). Let stand until foamy, about 10 minutes.

2  Combine the flour, the Parmesan, baking powder, sugar, and salt in a large bowl. Whisk until evenly incorporated.

3  Pour the yeast mixture and 2 tablespoons of the olive oil over the flour mixture and stir until a dough forms.

4  Using a rubber spatula, scrape the dough out of the bowl onto a lightly floured surface. Knead the dough until it becomes tight and elastic, about 10 minutes (see box, page 250; if the dough is too sticky, sprinkle with more flour, a little at a time, up to ½ cup).

5  Form the dough into a ball. Grease a large bowl with the remaining 1 tablespoon olive oil. Place the dough in the bowl and turn to coat in the oil. Cover with a kitchen towel or plastic wrap and let the dough rise in a warm, draft-free area until doubled in size, about 1 hour.

6  Make the pizza ring: Preheat the oven to 350°F. Line a baking sheet with parchment paper and sprinkle with the cornmeal.

7  Turn the dough out onto a lightly floured surface and divide it into 3 equal balls. Working with one ball at a time, use a rolling pin and your hands to roll and stretch the dough into a circle about 12 inches in diameter, making sure to roll evenly so the middle of the circle is not too thin. Repeat with the remaining dough to make 3 circles total.

recipe continues

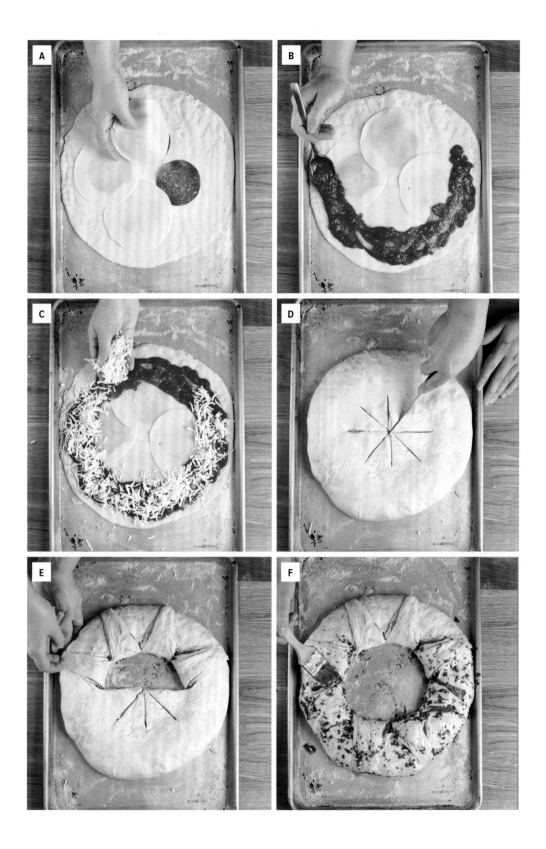

8  Place 1 dough circle in the center of the prepared baking sheet. Arrange 4 pepperoni slices in the center of the circle. Place 4 Provolone slices over the pepperoni **A** . Spread 1½ cups of the tomato sauce in a roughly 2-inch-wide ring around the pepperoni and Provolone, on the outside of the dough, leaving a 1-inch border (half the width of the sauce ring will overlap onto the Provolone and pepperoni slices) **B** . Sprinkle 1½ cups of the mozzarella over the tomato sauce **C** .

Place the second dough circle on top of the first, tucking the edges underneath the first layer of dough. Arrange the remaining pepperoni and Provolone slices as you did on the first dough circle, then top with the remaining 1½ cups tomato sauce and 1½ cups mozzarella. Place the final dough circle over the top and tuck the edges underneath, pinching them together to seal.

10  Using a small knife, make a 5- to 6-inch-long vertical cut in the center of the pizza, making sure you cut through all three layers. Make another cut perpendicular to the first, then make two diagonal cuts so you have 8 triangles to fold over **D** . Fold back each triangle, one layer at a time, over the outer edge of the pizza roll, creating an opening in the center **E** .

11  Stir together the olive oil, parsley, and garlic in a small bowl. Brush the herb oil all over the ring **F** , then transfer to the oven. Bake for 20 minutes, then loosely cover with a sheet of foil and bake until golden brown and the cheese has melted, about 40 minutes more.

12  Transfer the ring to a serving plate and slice. Serve warm, with a small bowl of tomato sauce in the center for dipping.

# CHEESY SPINACH & ARTICHOKE BREAD DIP SKILLET

SERVES
6

When your rolls are part of your bowl, you know you're in for a good time. Frozen dinner rolls frame a warm, melty filling that bubbles and browns as the rolls bake up golden and toasty. Make sure to squeeze as much liquid as you can from the spinach, and go for plain old water-packed artichoke hearts vs. marinated—you'll find them in the canned vegetable aisle.

Olive oil

12 unbaked frozen **dinner roll balls** (1½ pounds)

½ cup grated **Parmesan cheese** (3 ounces), plus more as desired

½ cup grated **pecorino cheese** (3 ounces)

½ cup shredded low-moisture **mozzarella cheese** (2 ounces)

¼ cup **sour cream**

1 teaspoon **dried basil**

½ teaspoon **crushed red pepper flakes**

1 (14-ounce) can **artichoke hearts**, drained and coarsely chopped

1 (10-ounce) package frozen chopped **spinach**, thawed and squeezed dry (about ¾ cup)

1 (8-ounce) package **cream cheese**, at room temperature

2 **garlic cloves**, finely chopped

Preheat the oven to 375°F.

Coat a 10-inch cast-iron skillet with olive oil. Arrange the dinner roll dough balls in a ring around the outer edge of the skillet. Cover with a kitchen towel or plastic wrap and let stand at room temperature until thawed, about 30 minutes.

Combine the Parmesan, pecorino, mozzarella, sour cream, basil, red pepper flakes, artichoke hearts, spinach, cream cheese, and garlic in a medium bowl and mix to incorporate evenly.

Once the dough has thawed, uncover it. Transfer the spinach-cheese mixture to the middle of the skillet, mounding it in the center. Brush the rolls with more olive oil and top with an additional sprinkle of Parmesan, if you like.

Bake until the rolls are puffed and lightly golden brown and the cheese dip is melted and golden brown on top, 25 to 35 minutes. Transfer the skillet to a wire rack and let cool slightly before serving.

# CHILI DOG SKILLET

2 (8-ounce) cans **crescent roll dough**

11 **hot dogs**, cut crosswise into thirds

1 tablespoon **vegetable oil**

1 small **yellow onion**, finely chopped

1 pound **ground beef**

**Kosher salt** and **freshly ground black pepper**

½ cup canned **tomato sauce** (4 ounces)

½ cup **ketchup**

2 teaspoons **chili powder**

½ teaspoon **ground cumin**

½ teaspoon **sugar**

½ cup shredded **Cheddar cheese**

¼ cup thinly sliced **scallions**

It's game day and you need a touchdown dish to make the crowd go wild. You prepare this chili dog skillet and instantly enter the hall of fame. Puffy, golden crescent dough covers hot dogs and cheese-topped ground beef chili like a tight end on a wide receiver.

1  Preheat the oven to 375°F.

2  Open the cans of dough and unroll the dough, separating it along the perforated lines into triangles. Cut each triangle in half lengthwise so you have 32 roughly 1-inch-wide by 5-inch-long triangles.

3  Roll each dough triangle around 1 piece of hot dog, starting with the wider end of the dough, to make "pigs in blankets." (You will have 1 piece of hot dog left over.)

4  In a 10-inch cast-iron skillet, starting on the outer edge of the pan, arrange the "pigs in blankets" standing upright in two tight, concentric circles, leaving an opening in the center of the skillet. Bake until the dough puffs up and becomes golden, 15 to 20 minutes. Set the skillet on a wire rack. Leave the oven on.

5  Meanwhile, in a large skillet, heat the oil over medium heat. Add the onion and cook, stirring, until translucent, about 8 minutes. Increase the heat to medium-high and add the ground beef. Season with salt and pepper and cook, stirring occasionally, until the ground beef is no longer pink, about 6 minutes. Stir in the tomato sauce, ketchup, chili powder, cumin, and sugar and cook, stirring occasionally, until the sauce has slightly thickened, about 10 minutes.

6  When the chili and the "pigs in blankets" are both ready, spoon the chili into the center of the skillet and top the chili with the cheese. Return the skillet to the oven and bake until the cheese is melted and bubbling on top, 5 to 10 minutes.

7  Transfer the skillet to the wire rack and let cool for 5 to 10 minutes. Top the chili with the scallions and serve hot.

# BAKED PIMIENTO CHEESE DIP

Chances are, if you've had this Southern picnic-basket staple it's been in the form of a cold spread studded with Cheddar cheese and sweet roasted peppers. We took inspiration from the original but turned it into a dip that's hot in more ways than one. Zingy olives and chopped parsley ensure that there's extra zip in your dip.

1 pound **sharp Cheddar cheese**, shredded (4 cups)

¾ (8-ounce) package **cream cheese**, at room temperature

¼ cup grated **pecorino cheese** (1½ ounces)

4 tablespoons **olive oil**, plus more for greasing

1 small **yellow onion**, grated and excess liquid squeezed out (1 to 2 tablespoons)

1 (12-ounce) jar whole **pimientos**, drained and coarsely chopped (2 cups)

¼ cup pitted **kalamata olives**, finely chopped

2 tablespoons chopped **fresh flat-leaf parsley**

2 teaspoons **Worcestershire sauce**

1 **garlic clove**, minced

**Kosher salt** and **freshly ground black pepper**

**Crackers**, for serving

1  Preheat the oven to 400°F. Grease a 1-quart baking dish.

2  Stir together the Cheddar, cream cheese, pecorino, 2 tablespoons of the olive oil, and the grated onion in a large bowl until evenly combined.

3  Spread the cheese mixture in the prepared baking dish, mounding it slightly higher around the edges than in the middle. Bake the cheese dip until golden, just melted, and heated through, about 15 minutes.

4  Meanwhile, stir together the pimientos, olives, parsley, Worcestershire, and garlic in a medium bowl. Season with salt and pepper.

5  Spoon the pimiento mixture into the center of the dip. Serve hot, with crackers alongside.

# CHEDDAR & CHUTNEY PUFF PASTRY

½ cup **orange juice**

⅓ cup **granulated sugar**

⅓ cup packed **dark brown sugar**

⅓ cup **cider vinegar**

⅓ cup **golden raisins**

1 tablespoon fresh **lemon juice**

1 teaspoon **kosher salt**

¾ teaspoon **chili powder**

½ teaspoon **freshly ground black pepper**

¼ teaspoon **ground cloves**

¼ teaspoon **ground cinnamon**

2 **shallots**, finely chopped

1 (2-inch) piece fresh **ginger**, peeled and minced

2 **mangoes** (about 2 pounds), peeled and finely chopped (about 3½ cups)

1 **garlic clove**, minced

2 (9-inch) square sheets **puff pastry**, thawed if frozen (see box, page 288)

3 cups shredded **extra-sharp Cheddar cheese** (8 ounces)

1 large **egg**

1 teaspoon **dried thyme**

Sweet, savory, a little spicy, rich and irresistible—this one has it all! Starting with puff pastry and cutting it into a pretty shape yields a slice-and-serve specialty few are likely to have seen before. Here's the puff pastry lowdown: Use it right and you'll look like a pastry genius. When you go to cut the puff pastry, make sure to use an extra-sharp knife or pizza wheel—and don't be shy about breaking out a ruler to ensure nice even lines.

---

1   In a medium saucepan, combine the orange juice, granulated sugar, brown sugar, vinegar, raisins, lemon juice, salt, chili powder, pepper, cloves, cinnamon, shallots, ginger, mangos, and garlic and bring to a simmer over medium heat. Cook, stirring, until the chutney is thickened and soft, 25 to 30 minutes. Scrape the chutney into a small bowl (you should have about 2½ cups) and let cool for 1 hour.

2   Preheat the oven to 375°F. Line a baking sheet with parchment paper.

3   Cut each sheet of puff pastry crosswise into 4 equal rectangles, then cut each rectangle diagonally to make 2 long triangles; you should have 16 triangles total.

4   Place a 5-inch-diameter bowl right-side up in the center of the prepared baking sheet. Arrange the puff pastry triangles around the bowl so they resemble a starburst pattern, spacing them evenly and overlapping them slightly.

5   Arrange half the Cheddar on the dough in a ring around the bowl, then top with the chutney. Sprinkle the remaining Cheddar over the chutney, then remove the bowl. Fold the point of one pastry triangle over the cheese and chutney, tucking it underneath its bottom layer. Repeat with the remaining triangles until the filling is enclosed.

6   Beat the egg with 1 tablespoon water in a small bowl, then brush the puff pastry with the egg wash. Sprinkle with the thyme and bake until golden brown and the cheese has melted, about 30 minutes. Let the ring cool for 5 minutes before slicing and serving.

# SLOW COOKER QUESO DE CERVEZA

We think the description "slow cooker" is misleading here . . . this is a lazy cooker at its best! *Queso* means "cheese" in Spanish, but it also refers to this rich, swirly dip that has never met a crowd who didn't love it. After all, who could resist velvety cheese swirled through with beer and fire-roasted diced tomatoes—in a vessel that practically makes the dish itself?

3 pounds **Velveeta cheese**, cut into 1-inch cubes

2¾ cups drained canned diced **green chiles** (24 ounces)

2 tablespoons **chili powder**

2 tablespoons **ground cumin**

1 tablespoon **ground coriander**

4 **garlic cloves**, minced

1 (28-ounce) can **fire-roasted diced tomatoes**, drained

1 (12-ounce) bottle or can **Mexican beer**, such as Corona or Modelo

1 cup drained prepared **pico de gallo**

1 cup finely chopped **fresh cilantro**

1 cup thinly sliced **scallions**

1 cup shredded **Monterey Jack cheese**

**Tortilla chips**, for serving

1 Combine the Velveeta cheese, green chiles, chili powder, cumin, coriander, garlic, tomatoes, and beer in a 6-quart slow cooker and stir to evenly incorporate. Cover and cook on High for 2 hours.

2 Uncover and stir in the pico de gallo, cilantro, and scallions. Sprinkle the Monterey Jack over the top. Cover and cook on High for 30 minutes more.

3 Switch the slow cooker setting to Warm, and serve the queso dip with the tortilla chips alongside.

# BAKED HAM & CHEESE RING

Entertaining? Give this crafty party dish a ring. It all starts with your favorite crescent-style dinner rolls, which you unfurl to create the base for a layered, luscious slice of heaven. Since your main ingredients come from the meat and cheese cases at your local store, this deli is definitely going to be your jelly. Mozzarella cheese comes in part-skim or full-fat versions—either works fine here.

2 (8-ounce) cans **crescent roll dough**

1 cup shredded low-moisture **mozzarella cheese** (4 ounces)

½ cup sliced **pepperoncini**

¼ cup packed **fresh basil leaves**

6 ounces deli-style sliced **salami**, each slice folded in half

6 ounces deli-style sliced **ham**, each slice folded in half

4 ounces sliced **prosciutto**

8 slices deli-style **Provolone cheese**, cut in half

**Kosher salt** and **freshly ground black pepper**

**Olive oil** and **balsamic vinegar**, for serving (optional)

1. Preheat the oven to 375°F.

2. Open each can of dough and unroll the dough, separating it along the perforated lines into triangles.

3. Line a baking sheet with parchment paper. Place a 5-inch-diameter bowl right-side up in the center of the baking sheet. Arrange the dough triangles around the bowl so they resemble a starburst pattern, spacing them evenly and overlapping them slightly **A**.

4. Layer, in this order, the mozzarella, pepperoncini, basil **B**, salami, ham, prosciutto **C**, and Provolone on top of one another in a ring around the bowl **D**. Remove the bowl and season the filling with salt and pepper.

5. Fold the tip of 1 dough triangle over the filling and tuck it underneath itself. Repeat with remaining triangles until the filling is enclosed **E**.

6. Bake until the dough is golden brown and the cheese is melted and bubbling, about 30 minutes. Transfer to a wire rack and let cool for 5 to 10 minutes.

7. Transfer to a serving plate and cut into slices. Serve with a small bowl of olive oil and balsamic vinegar in the center of the ring for dipping, if you like.

# CLEAN-OUT-THE-FRIDGE CHEESE & HERB DIP

This cheese and herb dip is where orphan bits of deliciousness come together to create something whose sum is greater than its parts.

8 ounces any leftover **soft** or **semi-firm cheeses**, without rinds, coarsely chopped (about 2 cups)

2 tablespoons finely chopped **mixed fresh herbs**

2 **garlic cloves**, smashed

½ cup **dry white wine**, such as pinot grigio

**Olive oil**, for drizzling

**Freshly ground black pepper**

**Crudités** and **crackers**, for serving

1   Combine the cheeses, herbs, and garlic in a food processor and pulse until very finely chopped. Add the wine and pulse until smooth, 30 to 45 seconds.

2   Scrape the cheese mixture into a serving bowl, drizzle with olive oil, and sprinkle with pepper. Serve at room temperature with crudités and crackers.

## combos we heart:

Brie, Emmentaler, and **goat cheese** with **rosé**, **thyme**, and **tarragon**

Smoked Gouda, pecorino, and **feta cheese** with **chives** and **parsley**

Blue cheese, white Cheddar, and **Camembert** with **ruby port**, **rosemary**, and **marjoram**

# CHORIZO FUNDIDO BREAD DIP

SERVES
**6**

I dip, you dip, we all dip for this dip. We took inspiration from the classic Mexican melty cheese appetizer but threw in some cream cheese to stabilize it and make it creamier. It gets topped with a bright, refreshing pico de gallo to balance the cheese, officially ensuring the "fun" in "fundido."

**Vegetable oil**, for brushing

1½ pounds **prepared pizza dough**

8 ounces fresh **Mexican chorizo**

2 **garlic cloves**, minced

1 small **yellow onion**, finely chopped

1 **poblano chile**, finely chopped

½ teaspoon **ground cumin**

½ teaspoon **chili powder**

¼ teaspoon **ground coriander**

**Kosher salt** and **freshly ground black pepper**

4 cups shredded **Monterey Jack cheese** (12 ounces)

1 (8-ounce) package **cream cheese**, at room temperature

2 **vine-ripe tomatoes**, cored, seeded, and finely chopped

1 **jalapeño**, seeded and finely chopped (see box, page 165)

2 tablespoons finely chopped **fresh cilantro**

1 tablespoon fresh **lime juice**

1  Coat a 10-inch cast-iron skillet with vegetable oil. Cut the dough into 12 equal pieces and roll each into a ball. Arrange the dough balls in a ring around the outer edge of the skillet, leaving the center uncovered. Cover with a kitchen towel or plastic wrap and let stand until the dough has puffed, about 30 minutes.

2  Meanwhile, heat a large nonstick skillet over medium-high heat. Crumble the chorizo into the skillet and cook stirring, until no longer pink, about 5 minutes. Add the garlic, onion, and poblano and cook, stirring, until the vegetables have softened, 6 to 8 minutes. Stir in the cumin, chili powder, and coriander, cook for 1 minute, then remove the skillet from the heat and season the mixture with salt and pepper. Let cool completely, about 30 minutes.

3  Preheat the oven to 375°F.

4  Stir the Monterey Jack and cream cheese into the chorizo mixture. Scrape the cheese mixture into the space in the center of the dough balls and smooth the top. Transfer the skillet to the oven and bake until the cheese is melted and bubbling and the bread is golden brown and cooked through, 25 to 30 minutes. Transfer the skillet to a wire rack and let cool for 5 minutes.

5  Meanwhile, combine the tomatoes, jalapeño, cilantro, and lime juice in a medium bowl. Season with salt and pepper. Using a slotted spoon, transfer the salsa onto the warm cheese in the center of the bread. Serve warm.

faux pho for one vs.
traditional vietnamese beef pho 50
crackling-crust roast pork with mojo 53
slow cooker honey & spice
lamb shanks 54
sweet & sour sunday brisket 55
provençal slow-roasted leg of lamb 56

# MEAT

italian herbed pork belly roast 59
skirt steak with charred
chimichurri sauce 63
roast pork four ways 64
cheesy mushroom-stuffed
meat loaf 68

# FAUX PHO FOR ONE

4 cups **chicken stock**

4 sprigs **cilantro**, stems and leaves separated

2 (⅛-inch-thick) slices fresh **ginger**, peeled

1 **scallion**, cut into 3-inch pieces

1 **star anise pod**

1 **cinnamon stick**

6 to 8 ounces **pork tenderloin** (see box, page 55)

2 ounces **flat rice noodles**

**Kosher salt**

**Fish sauce, hoisin sauce,** and **Vietnamese hot sauce**, such as Sriracha, for serving

If you've ever eaten at a Vietnamese restaurant, the star soup is always pho—a steaming bowl of broth filled with noodles, meat, and herbs. With 10 pounds of beef bones and steps that include charring aromatics like ginger and onions, the traditional version takes some work, but is really pho-nomenal. Still, when you need a steaming bowl of goodness for a solo supper, the Faux Pho—which starts with a base of boxed broth—is a worthy substitute that packs an authentic Vietnamese flavor wallop thanks to authentic condiments like fish sauce (fermented from anchovies and salt) and Sriracha.

1 In a medium saucepan, combine the stock, cilantro stems, ginger, scallion, star anise, and cinnamon stick and bring to a simmer over medium heat, 6 to 8 minutes.

2 Lower the pork tenderloin into the broth and poach until cooked through and an instant-read thermometer inserted into the center registers 160°F, 10 to 12 minutes. Using tongs, transfer the tenderloin to a cutting board and let rest for 5 minutes.

3 Remove the pan from the heat; remove and discard the whole spices from the broth. Add the noodles and let stand until softened, about 2 minutes. Taste the broth and season with salt.

4 Transfer the noodles and broth to a serving bowl. Thinly slice the pork and add it to the soup.

5 Top with the cilantro leaves and serve hot, with fish sauce, hoisin, and hot sauce on the side.

# TRADITIONAL VIETNAMESE BEEF PHO

8 to 10

Position a rack in the upper third of the oven and preheat the broiler.

Place the beef bones in a large stockpot and add enough cold water to cover by 2 inches. Bring the water to a boil over high heat and cook for 10 minutes to blanch the bones and remove any impurities.

Drain the bones in a colander and rinse with cold running water. Rinse out the stockpot, and return the bones to the stockpot.

Put the onions, ginger, and garlic cut-side up on a rimmed baking sheet and broil until charred in spots, 4 to 8 minutes (see box, page 57). Remove from the oven and add to the stockpot with the bones.

In a medium skillet, combine the peppercorns, cinnamon sticks, and star anise and toast over medium-high heat, shaking the pan occasionally, until the spices are darkened in spots and extremely fragrant, about 5 minutes. Add the toasted spices to the stockpot.

Season the brisket liberally with salt and add it to the stockpot.

Fill the pot with enough cold water to cover everything by 1 inch. Bring to a boil over high heat, then reduce the heat to medium to maintain a gentle simmer, and cook, skimming off and discarding any scum from the top as needed, until the brisket is fork-tender, 2 to 3 hours.

Using tongs, transfer the brisket to a plate and let cool for 1 hour. Refrigerate the cooled brisket until ready to serve.

Simmer the broth for 3 to 4 hours more to get as much flavor out of the bones as possible.

Shortly before serving, cook the rice noodles according to the package instructions. Drain the noodles and divide them among six to eight large bowls. Thinly slice the brisket and very thinly slice the raw sirloin against the grain (see box, page 63). Top the noodles in each bowl with the brisket and raw sirloin.

Using tongs, remove and discard the solids from the broth. Slowly strain the broth through a fine-mesh strainer set over a large pot. Skim off and discard the fat from the broth, then stir in the fish sauce. Taste and add more as desired.

Ladle the hot broth into the bowls over the noodles and meat and serve immediately, with the bean sprouts, Thai basil, jalapeños, lime wedges, onion, hoisin, and hot sauce on the side for guests to customize their pho as they wish.

10 pounds **mixed beef bones**, such as shin, knuckle, and marrow bones

4 **yellow onions** (about 2 pounds), halved lengthwise

12 ounces **fresh ginger** (about 2 large roots), halved lengthwise

1 large **head garlic**, halved crosswise

¼ cup **whole black peppercorns**

8 **cinnamon sticks**

6 **star anise pods**

1 (1-pound) piece **beef brisket** (see box, page 55)

**Kosher salt**

1 pound **boneless sirloin steak** (see box, page 55)

## TO SERVE

1 pound **flat rice noodles**

¼ cup **fish sauce**, plus more to taste

2 to 4 cups fresh **mung bean sprouts**

1 large bunch **Thai basil**

1 or 2 **jalapeños**, sliced into thin rounds

1 or 2 **limes**, cut into wedges

1 small **yellow onion**, halved and very thinly sliced lengthwise

**Hoisin sauce** and **Vietnamese hot sauce**, such as Sriracha

# CRACKLING-CRUST ROAST PORK WITH MOJO

SERVES
8

Get your mojo back with this magnificent pork shoulder marinated in a garlicky bitter-orange sauce that's a staple of the Cuban kitchen (and, as of this moment, yours). If you like, cook the pork shoulder in a slow cooker set to Low for seven to eight hours. Transfer to a baking sheet to broil as directed.

1 (8- to 8 ½-pound) bone-in, skin-on **pork shoulder** (see box, page 55)

24 **garlic cloves**

2 tablespoons **kosher salt**

½ cup **olive oil**

¼ cup lightly packed fresh **oregano leaves**, plus 1 tablespoon finely chopped

1 tablespoon **ground cumin**

Finely grated zest of 2 **limes** (see box, page 203)

Finely grated zest of 2 **oranges** (see box, page 203)

2 cups fresh **lime juice** (from about 16 limes)

1½ cups fresh **orange juice** (from 6 to 8 oranges)

1 Preheat the oven to 350°F.

2 Using a sharp knife or cleaver, score the pork skin and fat in a diamond pattern (see box, page 100), taking care not to cut down to the meat and spacing the slashes ½ inch apart **A** . Transfer the pork shoulder to a large baking dish or roasting pan.

3 Combine the garlic and salt in a food processor and pulse until the garlic is finely chopped. Add the olive oil, whole oregano leaves, cumin, and lime and orange zests; process into a smooth paste **B** .

4 Scrape the paste onto the pork shoulder and rub it all over, making sure it gets into the slashes in the skin and fat **C** . Pour the lime and orange juices around the pork.

5 Cover the baking dish completely with foil and bake until an instant-read thermometer inserted into the center of the pork registers between 180°F and 190°F, 6 to 7 hours. Remove the pork from the oven and turn on the broiler (see box, page 57).

6 Uncover the pork, return it to the oven, and broil until the skin puffs and is golden brown and crisp, 10 to 15 minutes **D** . Transfer the pork to a cutting board and let rest for 20 minutes.

7 Meanwhile, pour the pan juices into a medium saucepan and bring to a boil over high heat. Cook until reduced slightly, about 10 minutes. Remove the sauce from the heat and pour it through a fine-mesh strainer into a small bowl. Skim off the fat, if you like. Stir the finely chopped oregano into the sauce.

8 Serve the pork shoulder with the sauce alongside.

# SLOW COOKER HONEY & SPICE LAMB SHANKS

1 tablespoon **ground allspice**

1 tablespoon **ground coriander**

1 tablespoon **ground cumin**

1 tablespoon **freshly ground black pepper**, plus more as needed

2¼ teaspoons **ground ginger**

1¾ teaspoons **ground cinnamon**

1½ teaspoons **ground cloves**

1½ teaspoons **cayenne**

1 teaspoon crushed **saffron threads**

6 **lamb shanks** (about 5 pounds; see box, opposite)

**Kosher salt**

1 large **white onion**, coarsely chopped

2 cups blanched **whole almonds** (8 ounces)

1½ cups **golden raisins** (6½ ounces)

1½ cups **beef stock**

1 cup **honey**

**Cooked rice** or **couscous**, for serving

Finely chopped **fresh flat-leaf parsley**, for garnish

Honey, spice, and *everything* nice go into these lamb shanks. We aren't kidding about the everything—half your spice drawer will go into this dish! Saffron has a very unique flavor and aroma that's tough to replicate, but if you don't want to spring for the pricey spice (by weight it's more expensive than gold), you can substitute an equal amount of turmeric to mimic the color. Lamb not your thing? Use pork shanks in their place.

1   Combine the allspice, coriander, cumin, black pepper, ginger, cinnamon, cloves, cayenne, and saffron in a small bowl.

2   Season the lamb shanks with salt and black pepper, then rub them all over with the spice mixture.

3   Transfer the shanks to a 6-quart slow cooker and scatter the onion, almonds, and raisins over the top. Pour over the stock and honey. Cover and cook on Low for 7 to 8 hours, until the lamb shanks are very tender. Uncover and let the shanks cool for 20 minutes.

4   Use two forks to pull large chunks of lamb from the bones.

5   To serve, spoon the warm meat and sauce over rice and sprinkle with parsley, if you like.

# SWEET & SOUR SUNDAY BRISKET

SERVES
8

For creating sweet family memories that last, you can't beat this brisket. After eight hours of cooking, it will be hard to resist a taste, but give the meat a generous fifteen-minute rest before carving it into slices. And yeah, we named it *Sunday* brisket, but it tastes equally good any day of the week. Briskets labeled "first-cut" generally are more expensive and, since they have less fat, yield leaner results. But if you like yours falling-apart rich and fatty, seek out a second-cut specimen.

1 (3- to 4-pound) **whole brisket** (see box, below)

1 large **yellow onion**, thinly sliced

2 cups **ketchup**

1 (14-ounce) can **cranberry sauce**

2 tablespoons **onion powder**

1 tablespoon **kosher salt**

2 teaspoons **freshly ground black pepper**

2 teaspoons **ground turmeric**

2 teaspoons **celery seed**

½ cup finely chopped **fresh flat-leaf parsley**

1  Place the brisket in a 6-quart slow cooker and scatter over the onion.

2  Combine the ketchup, cranberry sauce, onion powder, salt, pepper, turmeric, and celery seed in a large bowl and whisk until smooth.

3  Pour the sauce over the brisket and onion and stir to combine. Cover the slow cooker and cook on Low for 7 to 8 hours, until the brisket is very tender.

4  Using tongs, transfer the brisket to a cutting board, leaving the sauce and onion in the slow cooker. Stir the parsley into the sauce.

5  Let the brisket rest for 15 minutes, then slice and serve hot (see box, below), with the onions and sauce spooned over top.

## 101

## Working with Meat

With so many options and price points, cooking meat can be confusing! Whether you are buying the cheapest or most expensive steak on the market, it's how you treat it that will make the biggest difference. No matter what you choose, here are the important rules to follow: Always allow meat to come to room temperature before cooking; doing so will ensure that the whole piece of meat cooks at an even rate. If you're new to cooking meat, invest in an instant-read thermometer to ensure perfectly cooked results every time. Whether broiling, searing, or anything else, always allow the meat to rest on the counter for 5 to 10 minutes after cooking; it lets the juices inside redistribute. If you slice it right away, all that yummy stuff will end up on your cutting board instead of in your mouth.

# PROVENÇAL SLOW-ROASTED LEG OF LAMB

1 (10- to 12-pound) **whole leg of lamb** (see box, page 55)

**Kosher salt** and **freshly ground black pepper**

½ cup **olive oil**

20 **garlic cloves**, smashed

15 sprigs **thyme**

15 sprigs **flat-leaf parsley**

10 sprigs **sage**

10 sprigs **rosemary**

6 dried **bay leaves**

2 cups **dry white wine**, such as sauvignon blanc

The fragrance of thyme, parsley, sage, and rosemary used to season a roasted leg of lamb is the closest you can get to teleporting yourself to the sunny fields of Southern France. Yes, you read it right—that's five to seven hours in the oven, but it's sooo worth it when you discover the fun of pulling crazy tender pieces of lamb straight off the bone. With a serving size of 12, you can bring your friends along on the taste vacation too.

1 Preheat the oven to 250°F.

2 Generously season the lamb leg all over with salt and pepper, then rub with the olive oil. Arrange the lamb leg diagonally on a rimmed baking sheet so it fits, then scatter over the garlic cloves, thyme, parsley, sage, rosemary, and bay leaves, letting them fall over and around the lamb. Cover the baking sheet tightly with foil and bake until an instant-read thermometer inserted into the thickest part of lamb leg registers 190°F, 5 to 7 hours.

3 Remove the lamb from the oven and uncover the baking sheet; carefully pick off the garlic cloves and herbs and transfer them to a small saucepan. Add the wine and any pan juices and bring to a boil. Cook until reduced by half, about 10 minutes. Pour the sauce through a fine-mesh strainer into a small bowl and season with salt and pepper.

4 If you want crispy lamb pieces, turn on the broiler (see box, opposite).

5 After the lamb has rested for 20 minutes, using two spoons, pull the meat from the bone in large pieces, leaving them on the baking sheet. Discard the leg bone once all the meat has been picked off. Transfer the baking sheet to the oven and broil the lamb, turning the pieces once, until golden brown and crisp on the outside, 5 to 10 minutes.

6 Serve hot, with the sauce on the side.

# Broiling

Using high heat to finish a dish is a great way to develop flavor and color. Most ovens have a broiler setting, which sends high heat from the top of the oven down onto your food. Some ovens have both low and high settings—either way, watch your food closely when it's under the broiler, as it can go from golden to gone (as in burnt) in a snap! In the summer, if you want to make a recipe that calls for grilling but you don't have one, broil your proteins or veggies to get that slightly charred, smoky flavor you're after.

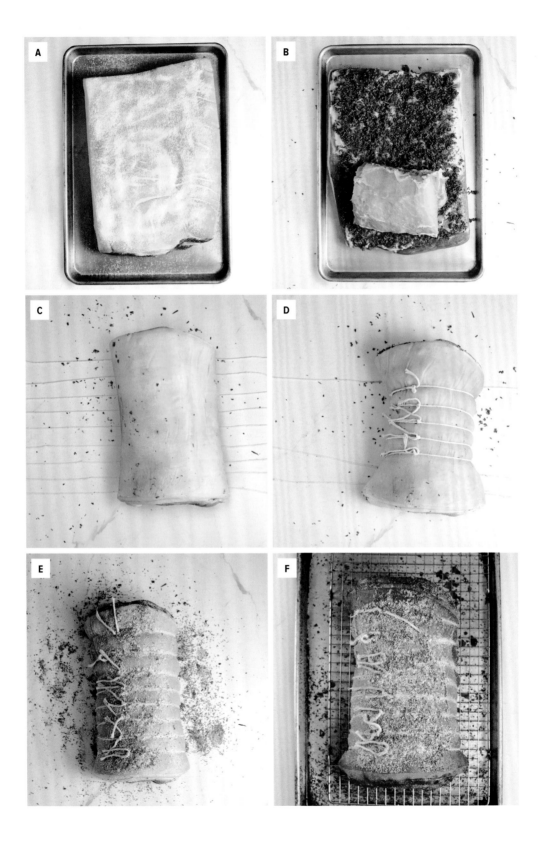

# ITALIAN HERBED PORK BELLY ROAST (PORCHETTA)

SERVES
12

You likely are acquainted with pork belly in one of its most delicious forms—bacon. Introduce pork belly into other areas of your life by taking a spin with this classic Italian preparation, which can be the centerpiece of a holiday meal or provide the center for a week's worth of awesome sandwiches. A salt-and-sugar rub helps tenderize and infuse the meat with flavor before it gets lavished with herbs and spends a few hours in the oven. When you go to tie the pork belly, enlist a friend to assist you. Like tying ribbon on a gift box, it helps to have someone hold one knot down with a finger while you tie the second knot to secure it.

1 (8- to 10-pound) piece skin-on **pork belly** (see box, page 55)

1 cup plus 2 teaspoons **kosher salt**

½ cup **sugar**

½ cup packed fresh **rosemary leaves**

⅓ cup packed fresh **thyme leaves**

1 teaspoon **coarsely ground black pepper**

8 **garlic cloves**

Finely grated zest of 4 **lemons** (about ¼ cup) (see box, page 203)

1 (2½-pound) **boneless pork loin** (not tenderloin), trimmed of excess fat

2 tablespoons **fennel seeds**

1 Rub the pork belly all over with ½ cup of the salt and the sugar **A** . Wrap it tightly in plastic wrap and refrigerate for 24 hours.

2 When ready to cook the pork, preheat the oven to 250°F.

3 Unwrap the pork belly and rinse it with cold water. Pat dry with paper towels, then place it skin-side down on a large cutting board.

4 Combine 2 teaspoons of the salt, the rosemary, **thyme**, pepper, garlic, and lemon zest in a food processor and pulse until finely chopped and evenly combined. Spread the garlic-herb paste evenly over the meat side of the pork belly.

5 Arrange the trimmed pork loin parallel to and on top of one short side of the pork belly **B** . Roll up the belly to enclose the loin and position the roll seam-side down on the cutting board.

6 On a separate cutting board or clean work surface, arrange eight 30-inch-long pieces of kitchen twine (see box, page 61) parallel to one another and spaced 1½ inches apart. Transfer the pork roll, seam-side down, so it lies across the center of the twine pieces **C** .

7 Starting with the centermost piece, tie the twine as tightly as you can around the pork roll using two double knots. Working your way from the center toward either end, continue tying the twine around the pork roll **D** .

*recipe continues*

8   Place the fennel seeds in a spice grinder and process until finely ground. Stir together the remaining ½ cup salt and the ground fennel seeds in a small bowl. Sprinkle the salt-fennel mixture over the pork roll and rub it all over the outside and ends **E** .

9   Place the pork roll on a wire rack set on a rimmed baking sheet and roast until an instant-read thermometer inserted into the center of the roll registers 145°F, about 3 hours **F** . Transfer the pork roll, still on the wire rack, to a cutting board. Pour any pan juices into a small bowl and skim off any fat. Increase the oven temperature to 450°F.

10  Return the pork roll on the wire rack to the baking sheet, return it to the oven, and roast until the skin is bubbling, crisp, and golden, about 30 minutes more.

11  Transfer the pork roll to a cutting board and let rest for 20 minutes. Remove the twine and cut the pork roll into ½-inch-thick slices. Serve hot, with the pan juices spooned over each slice.

# Kitchen Twine

Tie it up! That perfect pork roll or leg of lamb comes with the help of kitchen twine, string made of food-safe cotton that you can use to create pieces of meat with even thickness, ensuring even cooking. Kitchen twine also keeps a large chicken or turkey from losing its stuffing; tie its legs together to hold all the goodness inside. You can also use twine to bundle herbs: just leave the long ends on the bundle so you can easily fish it out and discard it when the food is cooked. Don't ever use string made of plastic; it can impart its flavor or chemicals into long-simmering dishes.

# SKIRT STEAK WITH CHARRED CHIMICHURRI SAUCE

SERVES
4

A well-cooked steak hardly needs any improvement, but a good chimichurri—with its blend of fresh herbs and tangy red wine vinegar—is a match made in steak heaven. Once you chimi once, you'll never stop, especially once you realize it's as good spread on a sandwich or topping scrambled eggs as it is in this recipe. Consider doubling the chimichurri portion of the recipe and you'll have enough to squirrel away in the fridge.

1½ pounds **skirt steak**, trimmed of excess fat and cut into 3 pieces (see box, page 55)

1 tablespoon **vegetable oil**

**Kosher salt** and **freshly ground black pepper**

8 **garlic cloves**

2 small **shallots**, halved lengthwise

1 **jalapeño**, stemmed

1 cup packed **fresh flat-leaf parsley leaves**

¾ cup packed **fresh cilantro leaves**

½ cup **olive oil**

¼ cup packed **fresh oregano leaves**

¼ cup **red wine vinegar**

1  Heat a large cast-iron skillet over high heat until it begins to smoke.

2  Brush the steaks with the vegetable oil and season them liberally with salt and pepper, then place them in the skillet, working in batches as needed (see box, page 272). Cook, flipping once halfway through, until charred on the outside and medium-rare inside, 4 to 8 minutes, depending on the thickness of the steak. (If working in batches, wipe out the skillet in between batches.)

3  Transfer the steaks to a cutting board and let rest for 10 minutes.

4  Reduce the heat under the skillet to medium-high. Add the garlic, shallots, and jalapeño and cook, turning as needed, until blackened in spots and softened, about 8 minutes.

5  Transfer the vegetables to a blender or food processor. Add the parsley, cilantro, olive oil, oregano, and vinegar and puree until smooth. Season the chimichurri with salt and pepper. (You should have about 1 cup.)

6  To serve, cut the steaks against the grain into ¼-inch-thick slices (see box, right). Divide the steak among four plates and spoon the charred chimichurri over the top.

## 101
## Against the Grain

In order to get the perfect slice of meat, cut it against the grain, the fibers of meat that appear as a series of lines on top of a steak or some other cuts of meat. Identify the direction of the lines, then using your knife, cut the opposite direction—which produces super-short fibers and, therefore, perfect bites of meat. Cutting *with* the grain can turn even the most perfectly cut roast or steak into strings that are tough to chew.

# ROAST PORK FOUR WAYS

1 (3½-pound) boneless **pork loin roast**, untrimmed (see box, page 55)

**Kosher salt** and **freshly ground black pepper**

Here, roast pork serves as a blank canvas for four different types of deliciousness. One simple recipe and you're off on a choose-your-own-dinner adventure. Which variation will become your time-honored favorite? We hope you enjoy trying them all to figure it out.

1 Preheat the oven to 350°F.

2 Season the pork all over with salt and pepper. Place it in a large baking dish or roasting pan, fat-side up. Roast until golden brown on top and an instant-read thermometer inserted into the center registers 145°F, about 1 hour.

3 Transfer the pork to a cutting board and let rest for 30 minutes. Thinly slice the pork roast (see box, page 63). If not using immediately, store the pork in an airtight container in the refrigerator for up to 5 days.

## ROAST PORK TACOS

3 slices **roast pork** (4 to 5 ounces)

3 **corn tortillas**

¼ cup plus 2 tablespoons prepared **salsa verde**

3 tablespoons crumbled **queso fresco**

2 tablespoons minced **white onion**

2 tablespoons coarsely chopped **fresh cilantro leaves**

1 small **radish**, thinly sliced

3 **lime wedges**

1 Chop up the pork and divide it among the tortillas.

2 Divide the salsa verde among the tacos, followed by the queso fresco, onion, and cilantro.

3 Top each taco with some sliced radishes, and serve each with a lime wedge.

## ROAST PORK
## TEX-MEX BURRITO

3 slices **roast pork** (4 to 5 ounces)

⅓ cup shredded **Monterey Jack cheese** (1 ounce)

1 tablespoon fresh **lime juice**

1 tablespoon finely chopped **fresh cilantro leaves**

1 teaspoon chopped canned **chipotle chiles in adobo**, with sauce

1 medium **vine-ripe tomato**, cored, seeded, and finely chopped (about ½ cup)

1 **scallion**, thinly sliced

**Kosher salt** and **freshly ground black pepper**

1 large (10-inch) **flour tortilla**, warmed

¼ **avocado**, thinly sliced

**Salsa** and **sour cream**, for serving (optional)

1  Thinly slice the pork crosswise, then place it in a medium bowl and add the cheese, lime juice, cilantro, chipotle, tomato, and scallion, and season with salt and pepper. Toss to combine, then pile it all in the center of the warmed tortilla.

2  Top with the avocado slices, then roll up into a burrito. Serve with salsa and sour cream, if you like.

## ROAST PORK
## MARKET BOWL

1 cup **cooked rice**

2 slices **roast pork** (3 ounces)

½ cup roasted or steamed **broccoli florets**

½ cup roasted cubed **potatoes**

⅓ cup diced skin-on **apples**

3 tablespoons crumbled **blue** or **goat cheese**

2 tablespoons chopped **almonds**

**Kosher salt** and **freshly ground black pepper**

2 tablespoons **red wine vinegar**

1 tablespoon **olive oil**

1 tablespoon finely chopped **fresh flat-leaf parsley**

1  Place the rice in the center of a wide, shallow bowl. Chop the pork, then arrange the pork, broccoli, potatoes, and apples side-by-side around the bowl.

2  Place the cheese and almonds in the bowl. Season the whole bowl with salt and pepper.

3  Just before serving, drizzle the vinegar and olive oil over the whole bowl and season again with salt and pepper. Sprinkle with the parsley and toss to combine, then serve.

## CUBAN
## SANDWICH

1 (8-inch) **Cuban** or **hoagie roll**

2 slices **roast pork** (3 ounces)

1 tablespoon **yellow mustard**

3 slices **deli-style ham**

6 **dill pickle chips**

3 slices **Swiss** or **Provolone cheese**

2 tablespoons **mayonnaise**

1  Preheat the broiler.

2  Split the roll, place it cut-side up on a baking sheet, and broil until lightly toasted, 2 to 3 minutes.

3  Arrange the pork on the bottom bun and top with the mustard, followed by the ham, pickle chips, and cheese. Remove the top bun from the baking sheet and broil the sandwich until the cheese is melted and bubbling, about 2 minutes.

4  Spread the mayonnaise over the top bun, then close the sandwich and serve warm.

ROAST PORK TACOS

ROAST PORK
TEX-MEX BURRITO

ROAST PORK
MARKET BOWL

CUBAN SANDWICH

# CHEESY MUSHROOM-STUFFED MEAT LOAF

## CHEESY MUSHROOM FILLING

2 tablespoons **unsalted butter**

8 ounces **cremini mushrooms**, thinly sliced (3 cups)

**Kosher salt** and **freshly ground black pepper**

1 tablespoon **all-purpose flour**

½ teaspoon **dry mustard**

4 ounces low-moisture **mozzarella cheese**, cut into ½-inch cubes (¾ cup)

4 ounces **sharp Cheddar cheese**, cut into ½-inch cubes (¾ cup)

## MEAT LOAF

1 tablespoon **olive oil**, plus more for greasing

1 small **yellow onion**, finely chopped

1 tablespoon **fresh thyme leaves**, finely chopped

1 teaspoon **tomato paste**

1 tablespoon **Worcestershire sauce**

12 ounces **ground beef**

6 ounces **ground pork**

¼ cup plus 2 tablespoons **plain dried bread crumbs**

3 tablespoons **beef stock**

1 teaspoon **kosher salt**

½ teaspoon **freshly ground black pepper**

1 large **egg**, lightly beaten

½ cup shredded low-moisture **mozzarella cheese** (1½ ounces)

½ cup shredded **sharp Cheddar cheese** (1½ ounces)

This is not your mother's meatloaf. Sure, all the meatloaf-musts like ground beef, pork, tomato paste, and Worcestershire sauce are present, but it's the addition of the blissful mozzarella, Cheddar, and 'shroom filling that sends this recipe into new territory. Try it and you'll be anointed as the master of a *new* classic.

1  Make the cheesy mushroom filling: In a large skillet, melt the butter over medium-high heat. Add the mushrooms, season with salt and pepper, and cook, stirring, until browned and lightly caramelized, about 10 minutes.

2  Stir in the flour and dry mustard and cook for 1 minute. Remove the skillet from the heat, stir in the mozzarella and Cheddar cheeses (they will melt a bit), and let cool while you make the meat loaf.

3  Make the meat loaf: In a large nonstick skillet, heat the olive oil over medium-high heat. Add the onion and cook, stirring, until browned and soft, about 6 minutes. Stir in the thyme and tomato paste and cook for 1 minute. Add the Worcestershire and cook, stirring, until it has evaporated, about 1 minute  A .

4  Scrape the onion mixture into a large bowl and let cool for 10 minutes.

5  Add the beef, pork, bread crumbs, stock, salt, pepper, and egg to the bowl with the onion mixture and mix to combine evenly  B .

6  Preheat the oven to 350°F. Grease a 9 by 5-inch loaf pan with oil.

7  Place two-thirds of the meat mixture in the bottom of the prepared loaf pan and spread the mixture up the sides of the pan by 1 inch, making a "bowl" for the filling  C .

8  Spoon the cheesy mushroom filling into the "bowl" and smooth the top with a spatula  D . Top the filling with the remaining meat mixture, covering it completely, and smooth the top again  E .

9  Bake the meat loaf until golden brown on top and an instant-read thermometer inserted into the center registers 160°F, 45 to 50 minutes. Set the pan on a wire rack. Leave the oven on.

10  Sprinkle the top of the meat loaf with the shredded mozzarella and Cheddar. Bake until the cheese is melted and golden brown in spots, about 5 minutes **F** . Let cool in the pan on a wire rack for 10 minutes.

11  Slice and serve from the pan **G** .

korean fried chicken wings vs.
baked buffalo chicken wings 72
adobo chicken drumsticks 74
cheesy french onion chicken 75
nashville hot turkey tenders 76
the best crispy chicken parmesan 79
ultimate buttermilk fried chicken 80
easy orange chicken 84
slow cooker honey-garlic chicken 85

# POULTRY

40 garlic clove chicken 87
one pan teriyaki chicken 88
turkey burrito bowls 89
herbed chicken thighs 90
classic lemon roast chicken 91
greek spatchcocked chicken 92
indian yogurt chicken curry 97
baked bbq chicken drumsticks 98
classic orange duck breasts 99

# KOREAN FRIED CHICKEN WINGS

¼ cup plus 2 tablespoons
**gochujang**

¼ cup plus 2 tablespoons
**low-sodium soy sauce**

3 tablespoons **rice vinegar**

3 tablespoons **honey**

2 tablespoons **toasted
sesame oil**

8 **garlic cloves**, finely chopped
(about 3 tablespoons)

1 (4-inch) piece **ginger**, peeled
and finely chopped (about ⅓ cup)

**Vegetable oil**, for frying

2 cups **all-purpose flour**

3 tablespoons **cornstarch**

4 pounds **whole chicken wings**

**Kosher salt** and **freshly ground
black pepper**

We're all about winging it, and two wing recipes are better than one! There's a reason KFC (no, not that one—we're talking about Korean Fried Chicken) has become so popular. Its light, crispy coating—courtesy of a pancake-y batter made with cornstarch—and seasoning with a spicy Korean chili paste called gochujang make these irresistible. The buffalo wings, on the other hand, get their spice from vinegary hot sauce, and they're baked for ease; the final toss in the sauce means they're as delicious as their finely fried friends.

1 Combine the gochujang, soy sauce, vinegar, honey, sesame oil, garlic, and ginger in a food processor and process until smooth. Transfer the sauce to a large bowl and set aside.

2 Pour vegetable oil into a large Dutch oven to a depth of 2 inches and attach a deep-fry thermometer to the side of the pot (see box, page 81). Heat the oil over medium-high heat to 350°F.

3 Meanwhile, in a large bowl, whisk together the flour, cornstarch, and 2 cups water to make a smooth slurry; it will look like pancake batter (see box, page 289). Season the chicken with salt and pepper, then add to the slurry and toss with a large spoon to coat evenly.

4 Using tongs, lift 6 to 8 chicken pieces from the slurry and drop them directly into the hot oil. Fry the chicken until golden brown and crispy and an instant-read thermometer inserted into each piece registers 165°F, about 15 minutes. Use the tongs to transfer the fried chicken to a wire rack placed over paper towels to drain. Repeat with the remaining chicken, letting the oil return to 350°F after each batch.

5 Add the fried chicken to the prepared sauce and toss to coat completely. Transfer to a serving platter and serve hot.

# BAKED BUFFALO CHICKEN WINGS

SERVES
4 to 6

1. Arrange the chicken pieces in a single layer on a rimmed baking sheet. Using a fine-mesh strainer, dust half the baking powder evenly over the chicken. Flip the pieces over and dust with the remaining baking powder. Use your hands to rub the baking powder into the wings, then transfer them to a wire rack set over another rimmed baking sheet. Liberally season both sides of the chicken with salt and pepper. Cover with plastic wrap and refrigerate for at least 1 hour or preferably overnight.

2. Preheat the oven to 450°F.

3. Remove the chicken pieces from the refrigerator, uncover, and immediately transfer them to the oven. Bake, turning once halfway through, until the chicken is golden brown all over and cooked through, 50 to 55 minutes..

4. Meanwhile, make the blue cheese dressing: Whisk together the blue cheese, sour cream, mayonnaise, buttermilk, and lemon juice in a medium bowl until smooth. Season the dressing with salt and pepper.

5. Pour the melted butter and hot sauce into a large bowl and stir to combine. Add the baked chicken pieces to the bowl and toss to coat evenly in the sauce.

6. Transfer the chicken to a serving platter and serve with the blue cheese dressing for dipping and celery and carrot sticks alongside.

4 pounds **chicken wings**, split into flats and drumettes

1 tablespoon **baking powder**

**Kosher salt** and **freshly ground black pepper**

½ cup crumbled **blue cheese** (about 2½ ounces)

½ cup **sour cream**

¼ cup **mayonnaise**

1 tablespoon **buttermilk**

1 tablespoon fresh **lemon juice**

½ cup (1 stick) **unsalted butter**, melted

½ cup **mild hot sauce**, such as Frank's

**Celery** and **carrot sticks**, for serving

# ADOBO CHICKEN DRUMSTICKS

2 cups **distilled white vinegar**

2 cups **low-sodium soy sauce**

2 tablespoons **freshly ground black pepper**

16 **garlic cloves**, smashed

12 **bay leaves**

4 **shallots**, thinly sliced

4 pounds small **chicken drumsticks**

No siree, that's not a typo in the recipe. We really *do* want you to use two cups of vinegar and two cups of soy in this classic Filipino dish with all of its salty, tangy, garlicky, glazed goodness. Usually it's made with beef or pork, but we swapped in chicken drumsticks, which makes it both party *and* wallet friendly. Adobo for life!

1  Combine the vinegar, soy sauce, pepper, garlic, bay leaves, and shallots in a large resealable plastic bag. Add the drumsticks, seal the bag, and turn to coat. Marinate in the refrigerator for at least 2 hours (see box, below). Don't marinate the chicken for more than 3 hours, though, or the soy sauce and vinegar will start to pickle the meat.

2  Using tongs, transfer the drumsticks to a deep 12-inch nonstick skillet, then pour over the marinade from the bag. Place the skillet over high heat and bring the marinade to a boil. Cook the drumsticks, gently flipping occasionally, until cooked through, about 25 minutes.

3  Use tongs to transfer the drumsticks to a serving platter, allowing any marinade to drip back into the pan, and set aside.

4  Continue cooking the marinade over high heat, stirring occasionally, until reduced by half and thickened to the consistency of a glaze, 10 to 15 minutes. Remove and discard the bay leaves. Pour the glaze evenly over the drumsticks and serve hot.

**101**

## Marinating

Letting protein sit in a flavorful mix that usually contains oil, acid, aromatics, and herbs will make it sing. You can do this in a bowl, a baking dish, or even in a resealable plastic bag. Mix together your ingredients, make sure your food is fully coated—maybe even submerged—and let it soak. Usually the longer a protein marinates, the more flavorful it becomes; a recipe will always give instructions, but a good rule is at least one hour and up to overnight. (The exception is fish, which should be marinated only briefly, since the acid can start to "cook" it.) When you're ready to cook the meat, scrape off any solid bits from the marinade— they can burn while cooking—and make sure you dry the meat off as much as possible since the excess moisture will make it more difficult to get a golden brown color on the outside.

# CHEESY FRENCH ONION CHICKEN

SERVES
**6**

Take all that is delicious and holy about French onion soup—then ditch the bowl and add chicken thighs. Whaaaaat? Truly caramelized onions take time and patience, so give them the full hour called for so they can do their thing. The broiler action at the end of the recipe is crucial for the melted cheese topping, so don't skip it.

6 boneless, skinless **chicken thighs** (about 2 pounds)

**Kosher salt** and **freshly ground black pepper**

1 tablespoon **minced garlic**

1 tablespoon **dried parsley**

1 tablespoon **olive oil**

1 tablespoon **unsalted butter**

6 large **yellow onions**, thinly sliced

1 cup **beef stock**

1 tablespoon **fresh thyme leaves**

2 cups shredded **Gruyère cheese** (6 ounces)

6 (½-inch-thick) slices **french bread** or **baguette**, toasted

1 Place the chicken thighs in a large bowl and season with salt and pepper. Add the garlic, dried parsley, and olive oil and toss to coat evenly.

2 Heat a large ovenproof saucepan or Dutch oven over medium-high heat. Add the chicken and cook, flipping once halfway through, until golden brown on both sides and cooked through, about 10 minutes total (see box, page 272). Transfer the chicken to a plate.

3 Melt the butter in the same saucepan, then add the onions and season with salt and pepper. Reduce the heat to medium-low and cook, stirring occasionally, until the onions are deeply caramelized, about 1 hour.

4 Preheat the broiler (see box, page 57).

5 Add the stock and thyme to the pot with the onions and bring the mixture to a simmer over medium heat.

6 Return the chicken to the pot, nestling it on top of the onions, and sprinkle with the Gruyère. Transfer the pan to the oven and broil until the cheese is melted and golden brown, about 5 minutes.

7 Divide the chicken thighs among six plates. Top with the onions and sauce and serve warm, with a slice of toast alongside.

# NASHVILLE HOT TURKEY TENDERS

½ cup plus 1 tablespoon **cayenne**

¼ cup **hot paprika**

¼ cup **garlic powder**

3 tablespoons **onion powder**

2 tablespoons **sugar**

2 cups **buttermilk**

2 pounds boneless, skinless **turkey breast**, cut lengthwise into ½-inch-thick strips

3 cups **all-purpose flour**

2 tablespoons **baking powder**

1 tablespoon **kosher salt**, plus more as needed

1 teaspoon **baking soda**

**Vegetable oil**, for frying

4 tablespoons (½ stick) **unsalted butter**, melted

1 tablespoon **honey**

**Blue cheese dressing** and **dill pickle chips**, for serving

Your childhood favorite will never be the same after a turkey takes the leading role and has a run-in with cayenne and hot paprika. To get in on these delicious turkey tenders, note that they need to marinate for at least 4 hours or overnight, so plan a little bit ahead—then love me tender.

1 Whisk together ½ cup of the cayenne, the paprika, garlic powder, onion powder, and sugar in a large bowl until evenly combined. Transfer half the spice mixture to a separate large bowl, stir in the buttermilk, then add the turkey, tossing to coat the strips completely. Cover the bowl with plastic wrap and marinate in the refrigerator for at least 4 hours or up to overnight (see box, page 74).

2 To the remaining spice mixture, add the flour, baking powder, salt, and baking soda. Whisk to combine and set aside.

3 When ready to fry the turkey strips, fill a large pot with vegetable oil to a depth of 2 inches (see box, page 81). Attach a deep-fry thermometer to the side and heat the oil over medium-high heat to 375°F.

4 While the oil heats up, working one at a time, use tongs to remove each turkey strip from the buttermilk marinade, allowing the excess to drip off, and dredge in the flour mixture, dusting off any excess (see box, page 247). Place the strip on a wire rack to dry and repeat with the remaining turkey.

5 Once the oil is heated, fry the turkey strips four at a time until golden brown and cooked through, 3 to 5 minutes. Using tongs, transfer the fried turkey strips to a wire rack set over paper towels to drain. Repeat with the remaining turkey strips, letting the oil come back to temperature between batches.

6 Once all the turkey tenders are fried, whisk together the remaining 1 tablespoon cayenne, the butter, and the honey in a large bowl until smooth. Add the tenders and toss to coat completely.

7 Transfer the tenders to a large serving platter and season with salt. Serve hot, with blue cheese dressing for dipping and dill pickle chips alongside.

# THE BEST CRISPY CHICKEN PARMESAN

You can forget the rest, because this is the best. Trends are all well and good, but this crispy chicken Parmesan—which basically means "lavished with cheese" in Italian—is forever. If you can't find seasoned bread crumbs in the store, spruce up some plain ones with dried Italian seasoning, salt, paprika, and pepper. For the marinara sauce, feel free to go with either store-bought or your own treasured recipe.

2 boneless, skinless **chicken breasts** (about 1½ pounds)

½ teaspoon **onion powder**

**Kosher salt** and **freshly ground black pepper**

1 cup **all-purpose flour**

2 large **eggs**

1 cup seasoned **bread crumbs**

**Vegetable oil**, for frying

2 cups (16 ounces) prepared **marinara sauce**

8 ounces fresh **mozzarella cheese**, cut into 8 slices

½ cup grated **Parmesan cheese** (2 ounces)

Thinly sliced **fresh basil leaves**, for serving

1  Preheat the oven to 450°F.

2  Slice the chicken breasts in half horizontally to create 4 thin pieces total. Season on both sides with the onion powder, salt, and pepper.

3  Place the flour, eggs, and bread crumbs in three separate shallow bowls. Season each with salt and pepper. Dip the chicken in the flour, shaking off any excess, then in the egg, allowing any excess to drip off, and finally in the bread crumbs to coat completely (see box, page 247).

4  Fill a large cast-iron skillet with vegetable oil to a depth of ¼ inch. Heat the oil over medium-high heat until it just begins to smoke (see box, page 81).

5  Working in batches as needed, add the chicken cutlets and fry, flipping once halfway through, until golden brown on both sides, about 10 minutes total. Using tongs, transfer the cutlets to a paper towel–lined plate to drain. Repeat with the remaining cutlets.

6  Arrange the fried chicken cutlets in a small rectangular baking dish, overlapping them slightly. Pour the marinara over the chicken, then top with the mozzarella slices and Parmesan.

7  Bake the chicken Parmesan until the cheese is browned and bubbling, 15 to 20 minutes. Sprinkle with basil, and serve warm.

# ULTIMATE BUTTERMILK FRIED CHICKEN

8 mixed bone-in, skin-on **chicken thighs** and **drumsticks**
(about 2½ pounds)

3 tablespoons **freshly ground black pepper**

2 tablespoons **kosher salt**

3 cups **buttermilk**

3 cups **all-purpose flour**

**Vegetable oil**, for frying

A long bath in tangy buttermilk helps tenderize the chicken before a back-and-forth double-dip in seasoned flour. Once fried to perfection, the chicken can be served hot, at room temperature, or—if you're lucky—cold out of the fridge the next day as leftovers. Extra credit alert: Try any of our suggested hacks for taking your bird in smoky, spicy, or herby directions.

1 Place the chicken in a large bowl. Stir together the pepper and salt in a small bowl and sprinkle half of this spice blend over the chicken (set aside the other half). Toss to coat all the pieces evenly.

2 Pour the buttermilk over the chicken and turn the chicken to coat completely. Cover the bowl with plastic wrap and marinate the chicken in the refrigerator for at least 2 hours and up to 8 hours (see box, page 74).

3 When ready to fry the chicken, fill a large Dutch oven with vegetable oil to a depth of 2 inches (see box, opposite). Attach a deep-fry thermometer to the side of the pot and heat the oil over medium-high heat to 325°F.

4 While the oil heats, in a large bowl, whisk to combine the flour with the remaining spice blend. Remove the chicken from the buttermilk marinade and set the pieces on a large plate, leaving the marinade in the bowl. Working with one piece at a time, coat the chicken in the seasoned flour, shaking off any excess (see box, page 247). Dip the chicken into the buttermilk marinade, letting any excess drip back into the bowl, then coat with the seasoned flour once again, shaking off any excess. Set the coated chicken piece on a wire rack and repeat with the remaining chicken.

5 Fry the chicken 4 pieces at a time, turning them occasionally, until golden brown and crispy and an instant-read thermometer inserted into each piece registers 165°F, about 15 minutes. Using tongs, transfer the fried chicken to a wire rack placed over paper towels to drain. Repeat with the remaining chicken, letting the oil return to temperature between each batch.

6 Arrange the hot chicken on a serving platter and serve immediately.

**FOR SPICY FRIED CHICKEN:** Mix 2 tablespoons cayenne pepper into the black pepper and salt mixture.

**FOR HERBY FRIED CHICKEN:** Mix 2 tablespoons each dried parsley and dried basil and 1 tablespoon each dried tarragon and dried chives into the black pepper and salt mixture.

**FOR SMOKEY FRIED CHICKEN:** Mix 3 tablespoons smoked paprika into the black pepper and salt mixture.

**FOR LEMONY FRIED CHICKEN:** Mix the finely grated zest of 4 lemons (about ⅓ cup; see box, page 203) into the black pepper and salt mixture. Serve the chicken with lemon wedges on the side.

## 101

# Frying

Is there anything better than freshly fried food? You can be your home kitchen's official fry master if you follow just a few simple rules.

For starters, having everything prepped ahead of time is a huge help. Lay out your thermometer, tongs, and a cooling rack lined with paper towels.

The most important thing during frying is keeping your oil temperature consistent—always give it time to return to the optimal temp between batches and don't overcrowd your frying vessel with food; this leads to drastic drops in oil temperature.

After you feast on your food, carefully dispose of the oil. Make sure it cools down completely and never, ever chuck it down your sink drain . . . unless you're prepared to incur the wrath of your plumber.

If you've only used the oil once and used it to fry relatively neutral-flavored foods, oil can be strained through a fine-mesh strainer, through a funnel back into its original bottle for use another time or two; once the oil begins to darken or seems thin, it's time to get rid of it.

To dispose of oil, make sure it's completely cool, funnel it into a bottle, seal it tightly, and leave it next to your wet garbage visible to the garbage man; some sanitation companies dispose of large amounts of oil separately. For small amounts of oil, pour it directly over several layers of paper towels directly into the trash.

# EASY ORANGE CHICKEN

¾ cup plus 2 tablespoons
**orange juice**

¼ cup plus 1 tablespoon
**low-sodium soy sauce**

2 tablespoons **cornstarch**

2 pounds boneless, skinless
**chicken breasts**, cut into
¾-inch pieces

2 tablespoons **vegetable oil**

1 tablespoon **rice vinegar**

2 tablespoons **light brown sugar**

1 tablespoon **hoisin sauce**

**Cooked white rice**, for serving

**Toasted sesame seeds**,
for garnish

You know and love it from your favorite Chinese takeout spot. Now, you can make it at home in less time than it calls to find the number, place the order and wait hungrily by the door. A little bit of cornstarch goes a long way in this recipe, helping the sauce thicken in the skillet. Don't skip a pot of fluffy white (or brown) rice on the side; it's ideal for soaking up all that wonderful sauce.

1   Whisk together 2 tablespoons of the orange juice, ¼ cup of the soy sauce, and 1 tablespoon of the cornstarch in a large bowl. Add the chicken and toss to coat evenly. Cover the bowl with plastic wrap and marinate in the refrigerator for at least 1 hour and up to 4 hours (see box, page 74).

2   In a large skillet, heat the vegetable oil over medium-high heat. Using tongs, remove the chicken from the marinade, allowing the excess to drip back into the bowl, and dry briefly and gently on paper towels. Arrange the chicken in a single layer in the skillet and sear, turning occasionally, until golden brown all over, 10 to 12 minutes (see box, page 272).

3   Stir together the remaining 1 tablespoon soy sauce, 1 tablespoon cornstarch, and the vinegar in a small bowl until smooth. Pour the soy sauce mixture into the skillet along with the remaining ¾ cup orange juice, the brown sugar, and the hoisin. Bring to a boil and cook, stirring continuously, until the sauce thickens, about 2 minutes.

4   Spoon the chicken and sauce over rice and sprinkle with sesame seeds before serving.

# SLOW COOKER HONEY-GARLIC CHICKEN

SERVES
6 to 8

Think of this recipe as a challenge to cram as much flavor as you can into one slow-cooked chicken recipe. Honey, garlic, soy—the gang's all here! Carrots, bell peppers, and broccoli are all included, making this a complete one-pot meal—no other side dishes needed. If you don't have baby carrots on hand, just cut regular carrots into smaller pieces.

⅓ cup **honey**

¼ cup **low-sodium soy sauce**

1 tablespoon minced fresh **ginger**

½ teaspoon **crushed red pepper flakes**

½ teaspoon **freshly ground black pepper**

4 **garlic cloves**, minced

4 bone-in, skin-on **chicken breasts** (about 3½ pounds), halved crosswise

**Kosher salt**

2 cups **baby carrots**

2 cups **broccoli florets**

1 **red bell pepper**, thinly sliced

1  Whisk together the honey, soy sauce, ginger, red pepper flakes, black pepper, and garlic in a small bowl.

2  Place the chicken breasts, bone-side down, in a 6-quart slow cooker, season with salt, and pour the honey sauce over top. Cover and cook on High for 1½ hours.

3  Add the carrots, broccoli, and bell pepper to the slow cooker. Stir to combine with the chicken and honey sauce. Cover and cook on High for 1½ hours more.

4  Just before the chicken has finished cooking, preheat the broiler (see box, page 57). Line a rimmed baking sheet with parchment paper.

5  Using tongs, remove the chicken from the slow cooker and place it skin-side up on the prepared baking sheet. Broil the chicken until the skin is golden and crispy, 2 to 3 minutes.

6  Serve the chicken warm, with the vegetables alongside and the honey sauce spooned over the top.

# 40 GARLIC CLOVE CHICKEN

We won't tell if you end up with 39 (or 41) cloves of garlic in your version—the important thing is that there is a whole lotta delicious garlic flavor going on in here. This is the perfect dish for both feeding friends and scaring away vampires. Plus, the recipe requires only half a cup of white wine, leaving you with plenty of vino to enjoy while you prepare dinner. Score!

4 bone-in, skin-on **chicken thighs** (about 1½ pounds)

2 teaspoons **dried poultry seasoning**

**Kosher salt** and **freshly ground black pepper**

2 tablespoons **vegetable oil**

3 **shallots**, finely chopped

40 **garlic cloves** (from 3 to 4 heads), unpeeled

½ cup **white wine** or **dry vermouth**

1 teaspoon **dried tarragon**

3 sprigs **fresh flat-leaf parsley**

¾ cup **chicken stock**

**Crusty bread**, for serving

1  Preheat the oven to 350°F.

2  Sprinkle the chicken thighs all over with the poultry seasoning, then season with salt and pepper.

3  In a large ovenproof skillet, heat the vegetable oil over medium-high heat. Add the chicken, skin-side down, and sear, flipping once halfway through, until golden brown on both sides, 10 to 15 minutes total (see box, page 272). Transfer the chicken to a plate.

4  Add the shallots to the skillet, reduce the heat to medium, and cook, stirring, until soft, about 5 minutes. Add the garlic and cook, stirring, until beginning to take on some color, about 2 minutes more. Pour in the wine and cook, scraping up the browned bits from the bottom of the skillet, until the liquid reduces slightly, about 2 minutes (see box, page 33).

5  Return the chicken to the skillet, scatter the tarragon and parsley sprigs over the top, and pour in the stock.

6  Transfer the skillet to the oven and roast until the chicken is cooked through and the sauce has thickened, 20 to 25 minutes.

7  Serve the chicken and garlic cloves with crusty bread alongside to soak up all the sauce.

# ONE PAN TERIYAKI CHICKEN

½ cup **low-sodium soy sauce**

¼ cup **honey**

1 tablespoon **cornstarch**

1½ teaspoons **minced garlic**

3 boneless, skinless **chicken breasts** (about 2 pounds)

1 cup **broccoli florets**

1 cup **baby carrots**

1 cup **green beans**

½ **red bell pepper**, thinly sliced

**Kosher salt** and **freshly ground black pepper**

**Toasted sesame seeds** and thinly sliced **scallions**, for serving

**Cooked rice**, for serving

Do yourself a lunch solid and make this dish. This easy one-pan recipe promises a perfectly proportioned meal of teriyaki-glazed chicken and a beautiful rainbow of vegetables all week long. Make this a meal prep by distributing the chicken and veggies over cooked brown rice among four plastic containers. Refrigerate the containers for up to four days.

1 Preheat the oven to 400°F. Line a baking sheet with parchment paper.

2 In a medium saucepan, whisk together the soy sauce, honey, cornstarch, garlic, and 3 tablespoons water. Heat over medium heat, stirring occasionally, until the sauce begins to bubble, then stir continuously until the sauce thickens, about 2 minutes. Remove the pan from the heat.

3 Spoon a little bit of the teriyaki onto the center of the prepared baking sheet, creating a strip of sauce. Arrange the chicken breasts on top of the sauce. Arrange the broccoli, carrots, green beans, and bell pepper strips in separate piles on either side of the chicken.

4 Season the chicken and vegetables with salt and black pepper, then spoon over as much of the teriyaki sauce as necessary to coat them (you should have some sauce left over).

5 Roast the chicken and vegetables until the chicken is cooked through and the juices run clear, and the vegetables are tender, about 20 minutes.

6 Transfer the baking sheet to a wire rack and let cool for 5 minutes. Drizzle the remaining teriyaki sauce over the chicken and sprinkle with sesame seeds and scallions. Cut the chicken into thick slices.

7 Serve the chicken and vegetables warm, over rice.

# TURKEY BURRITO BOWLS

SERVES
**4**

We can't be the only ones out there who could eat a burrito every damn day of the week. If you are raising your hand, let this be the recipe to make your burrito habit Tasty approved. Don't skip the foil on the baking sheet; you'll be thanking us come cleanup time. Make this a meal prep by distributing the turkey and veggies over cooked brown rice among four plastic containers. Refrigerate the containers for up to four days.

1 (2-pound) boneless, skinless **turkey breast**, cut crosswise into 3 equal pieces

3 **bell peppers** (mixed red, orange, and yellow), thinly sliced

1 large **red onion**, halved and cut into ½-inch-thick slices

2 tablespoons **vegetable oil**

1 tablespoon **taco seasoning**

**Kosher salt** and **freshly ground black pepper**

1 (16-ounce) jar **chunky-style salsa**, plus more for serving

3 cups **cooked brown rice**

1 (15-ounce) can **black beans**, drained and rinsed

1 (15.25-ounce) can **whole-kernel corn,** drained and rinsed

1 cup shredded **Cheddar cheese** (3 ounces)

**Fresh cilantro leaves**, for serving

1 **lime**, cut into 4 wedges

1 Preheat the oven to 400°F. Line a baking sheet with foil.

2 Arrange the turkey breast pieces in a strip in the center of the prepared baking sheet. In even layers, arrange the bell peppers along one side of the turkey and the onion on the other side.

3 Drizzle the turkey and vegetables evenly with the vegetable oil, then sprinkle the taco seasoning evenly over both sides of the turkey. Season the turkey and vegetables with salt and black pepper, tossing the vegetables to coat. Top each turkey breast piece with about one-third of the salsa.

4 Roast the turkey and vegetables until the turkey is cooked through and the vegetables are lightly browned, about 25 minutes.

5 Transfer the pan to a wire rack and let cool for 5 minutes. Cut the turkey into ½-inch-thick slices.

6 Divide the rice among four plates. Top each with black beans, corn, more salsa, the Cheddar cheese, the cooked bell peppers and onions, and the sliced turkey. Garnish with cilantro leaves and serve warm, with a lime wedge for squeezing.

# HERBED CHICKEN THIGHS

2 bone-in, skin-on **chicken thighs**
(about 1 pound)

**Kosher salt** and **freshly ground black pepper**

1 teaspoon coarsely chopped **thyme leaves**

1 teaspoon coarsely chopped **rosemary leaves**

2 tablespoons **vegetable oil**

1 **yellow onion**, finely chopped

5 round **lemon slices**, seeds removed

When in doubt, go with chicken thighs. Chicken breasts get most of the airtime, but thighs, with their dark meat and moist layer of skin, is where all the flavor is at.

1  Preheat the oven to 375°F.

2  Heat a cast-iron skillet over medium heat. Season the chicken thighs all over with salt and pepper, then sprinkle with the thyme and rosemary.

3  Pour the vegetable oil into the skillet, then add the chicken thighs, skin-side down, and sear until the skin is golden brown and crisp, 6 to 8 minutes (see box, page 272). Flip and cook until the chicken is browned on the bottom, about 4 minutes more (see box, below). Transfer the chicken to a plate.

4  Add the onion to the skillet and cook, stirring, until soft, about 5 minutes. Remove the skillet from the heat and arrange the lemon slices evenly on top of the onion.

5  Return the chicken to the skillet, skin-side up, placing it on top of the lemons. Transfer to the oven and roast until cooked through, about 20 minutes.

6  Divide the chicken, lemon slices, and onion between two plates and serve hot.

## 101

## Rendering Fat

Ever watched the stripes of fat disappear from a slice of bacon, leaving a crisp piece of meat? It would make an excellent fast motion video. But more important, that's rendering—cooking meat to drain it of its fat. You can render the fat from chicken skin, duck, or even the side of a juicy steak. The fat will melt off the meat and collect in the pan. If the recipe calls for discarding it, save it and use it in place of the cooking fat in a different recipe.

# CLASSIC LEMON ROAST CHICKEN

SERVES
4

You'll never go wrong with a whole roast chicken; keeping the bird in one piece helps it stay moist and juicy—and, once done, feeds a small army. This version is simplicity at its finest; the olive oil, lemon, and garlic are so harmonious together, they practically sing a concerto. Don't be scared off by the size of a whole chicken; leftovers can be tucked into salads, made into sandwiches— and the carcass can be revamped into the base of a soup stock.

2 **garlic cloves**, minced

**Kosher salt**

¼ cup **extra-virgin olive oil**

1 tablespoon fresh **thyme leaves**

2 **lemons**: 1 whole,
1 cut into wedges

1 (3½- to 4-pound) **whole chicken**,
at room temperature

**Freshly ground black pepper**

1  Preheat the oven to 400°F.

2  On a cutting board, sprinkle the minced garlic with a liberal pinch of salt (see box, page 257). Using the side of your knife, scrape and mash the garlic and salt together until they form a paste.

3  Scrape the paste into a small bowl and stir in the olive oil and thyme. Finely grate the zest of the whole lemon into the bowl (see box, page 203) and stir to combine; quarter the zested lemon and set aside.

4  Using your fingers, gently separate the skin from the flesh over the chicken breasts and thighs and spoon some of the garlic-oil mixture between the meat and skin. Pour any remaining garlic-oil mixture over the skin and rub it evenly all over the chicken. Season the chicken all over with salt and pepper. Stuff the lemon quarters into the cavity of the chicken.

5  Transfer the chicken to a rectangular baking dish or roasting pan. Roast until the skin is browned, an instant-read thermometer inserted into the thigh registers 165°F, and the juices run clear, about 1 hour.

6  Transfer the baking dish to a wire rack and let the chicken cool for 20 minutes.

7  Cut the chicken into serving pieces and serve warm, with the lemon wedges for squeezing.

# GREEK SPATCHCOCKED CHICKEN

1 (3½- to 4-pound) **whole chicken**

½ cup plus 2 tablespoons **extra-virgin olive oil**

½ cup plus 1 tablespoon **white wine**

¼ cup plus 1 tablespoon fresh **lemon juice** (from 2 or 3 lemons)

2 tablespoons **dried mint**

2 tablespoons **dried oregano**

1 tablespoon **kosher salt**, plus more as needed

12 **garlic cloves**

2 dried **bay leaves**

4 **russet potatoes** (2 pounds), peeled and cut lengthwise into 6 wedges each

**Freshly ground black pepper**

2 tablespoons finely chopped **fresh flat-leaf parsley**

**Flaky sea salt**

Yeah, we know the name is hilarious, but once you learn this technique, you are going to be spatchcocking every chicken you see. The vibrant green marinade is made in the blender (read: easy). Leave time to marinate the chicken—at least 4 hours—but it's simplest to do it before going to bed. You will sleep tight knowing dinner is almost ready for the next day.

1   Working on a large cutting board, use kitchen shears to spatchcock the chicken (see box, page 94). Place the flattened chicken skin-side up in a wide baking dish large enough to accommodate it with a little room on all sides.

2   Combine ½ cup of the olive oil, ½ cup of the wine, ¼ cup of the lemon juice, the mint, oregano, salt, garlic, and bay leaves in a blender and purée until smooth. Pour the sauce over the chicken, turning to coat. Cover the dish with plastic wrap and refrigerate for at least 4 hours or up to overnight (see box, page 74).

3   When ready to cook the chicken, preheat the oven to 425°F.

4   Place the potato wedges on a rimmed baking sheet and drizzle with the remaining 2 tablespoons olive oil. Season with salt and pepper, toss to coat, then arrange them in an even layer, clustered together in the center of the baking sheet.

5   Uncover the chicken and remove it from the marinade, letting the excess drip back into the baking dish; reserve the marinade. Lay the chicken skin-side up on top of the potatoes. Roast until golden brown and crisp and an instant-read thermometer inserted into the breast meat registers 160°F, 55 minutes to 1 hour.

6   Meanwhile, pour the marinade into a small saucepan and bring to a boil over high heat. Cook, stirring, until slightly thickened, 6 to 8 minutes. Remove the pan from the heat and pour the sauce through a fine-mesh strainer into a medium bowl.

recipe continues

7 Transfer the chicken to a cutting board and let rest for 15 minutes.

8 Scrape the hot potatoes into a serving bowl and pour over the sauce and the remaining 1 tablespoon wine and lemon juice. Toss to coat and let stand to soak in the sauce.

9 Cut the chicken into quarters, transfer to a serving platter, and sprinkle with the parsley and sea salt. Serve hot, with the roasted potatoes alongside.

# Spatchcocking

Spatchcocking is the act of flattening a whole chicken, which makes it perfect for the grill or for roasting in half the normal time. It also exposes more of that marinade-soaked skin, which will crisp up nicely when roasted.

1 To spatchcock, turn your chicken breast-side down.

2 Cut along one side of the backbone with sharp kitchen shears **A** .

3 Cut along the opposite side to free the backbone **B** .

4 Remove the backbone and discard or save for stock **C** .

5 Flip the chicken back over and flatten the breastbone with the heel of your hand (yep, you'll hear it crack) **D** .

6 After that it's ready, steady, go **E** !

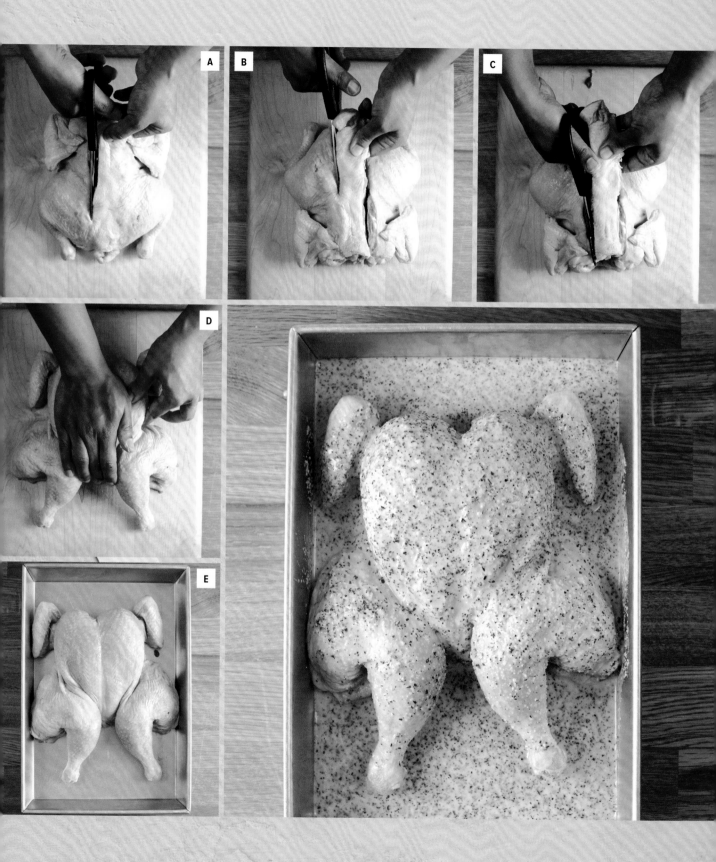

# INDIAN YOGURT CHICKEN CURRY

SERVES
6

With the addition of creamy, cooling yogurt, even your spice-averse friends should be able to handle this dish. If you want an even milder dish, remove the seeds from the serrano chiles. For best results, use a plain, creamy, full-fat yogurt—not Greek-style.

¾ cup **vegetable oil**

1 tablespoon **whole black peppercorns**

2 teaspoons **fennel seeds**

4 whole **green cardamom pods**, crushed

4 whole **cloves**

1 **bay leaf**

1 small **cinnamon stick**, crushed into pieces

3 large **yellow onions**, halved and thinly sliced

4 **garlic cloves**, thinly sliced

1 (2-inch) piece fresh **ginger**, peeled and thinly sliced

6 bone-in, skin-on **chicken thighs** (about 2½ pounds)

**Kosher salt** and **freshly ground black pepper**

2 teaspoons **ground turmeric**

2 teaspoons **sweet paprika**

2 **green serrano chiles**, minced

1½ cups **full-fat plain yogurt** (not Greek yogurt)

**Cooked white rice**, for serving

Chopped **fresh cilantro leaves**, for garnish

1 In a large pot, heat ½ cup of the vegetable oil over medium-high heat. Add the peppercorns, fennel seeds, cardamom, cloves, bay leaf, and cinnamon stick and cook, stirring, until toasted and fragrant, about 2 minutes.

2 Add the onions, garlic, and ginger, reduce the heat to medium, and cook, stirring often, until the onions are deeply caramelized, 45 minutes to 1 hour.

3 Scrape the onions and spices into a blender or food processor, add ½ cup water, and purée until smooth.

4 Wipe out the pot, pour in the remaining ¼ cup oil, and heat it over medium-high heat.

5 Season the chicken thighs with salt and pepper. Add the chicken to the pot, skin-side down, and sear, flipping once halfway through, until golden brown all over, about 12 minutes total (see box, page 272). Transfer the chicken to a plate.

6 Return the puréed onion paste to the pot and reduce the heat to medium. Cook, stirring often, until the oil separates from the paste and the paste darkens in color, about 6 minutes. Add the turmeric, paprika, and chiles and cook, stirring, until fragrant, about 1 minute.

7 Stir in 1 cup water, return the chicken to the pot, and reduce the heat to medium to maintain a steady simmer. Cover the pot and simmer until the chicken is just cooked through, 20 to 25 minutes.

8 Remove the lid and use tongs to transfer the chicken to a plate, leaving the sauce behind in the pot. Stir the yogurt into the sauce and cook until the sauce is warmed through, about 3 minutes.

9 Serve the chicken hot, with rice. Spoon over the sauce and sprinkle with cilantro.

SERVES
4

# BAKED BBQ
# CHICKEN DRUMSTICKS

½ cup packed **light brown sugar**

¼ cup **low-sodium soy sauce**

2 teaspoons **molasses**

8 **chicken drumsticks**
(about 2½ pounds)

¼ cup plus 2 tablespoons
**ketchup**

¼ cup plus 2 tablespoons
**chili sauce**, such as Heinz

1 tablespoon
**Worcestershire sauce**

2 tablespoons **dry mustard**

**Kosher salt** and **freshly ground
black pepper**

Chopped **fresh flat-leaf parsley**,
for garnish

Bang the drum for these killer drummies!
Even the simplest of recipes can elicit oohs and
ahhs all around when it's as spot-on as this one.
You'll find most of the ingredients for the BBQ
sauce in your pantry; mix them together
for a better-than-bottled experience.

1  In a large resealable plastic bag, combine 2 tablespoons of the brown sugar, the soy sauce, molasses, and ¼ cup water. Add the drumsticks, seal the bag, and turn to coat. Marinate the chicken in the refrigerator for at least 2 hours and up to 4 hours (see box, page 74).

2  When ready to cook the chicken, preheat the oven to 375°F.

3  Whisk together the remaining brown sugar, the ketchup, chili sauce, Worcestershire, dry mustard, and 2 tablespoons water in a medium bowl.

4  Remove the chicken from the marinade, letting any excess drip back into the bag; reserve the marinade. Arrange the chicken in a 9 by 13-inch baking dish and season with salt and pepper.

5  Add the marinade to the ketchup sauce and whisk until smooth.

6  Pour the sauce over the chicken and bake, turning the drumsticks and basting with the sauce every 10 minutes, until they are cooked through and the sauce has thickened, 50 minutes to 1 hour (see box, page 282).

7  Sprinkle the drumsticks with parsley and serve with any extra sauce on the side.

# CLASSIC ORANGE DUCK BREASTS
## (DUCK À L'ORANGE)

SERVES
2

This restaurant-worthy recipe is a classic for a reason: The bright acid and tartness of the citrus sauce does the tango with the deep flavor of the meat. While juicy duck breasts are as lean as white meat chicken or turkey, the skin is inherently fatty. Scoring the skin in a diamond pattern ensures that the fat will render off during the cooking process, meaning that you end up with a golden crispy finish.

2 (8- to 10-ounce) boneless, skin-on **duck breasts**

**Kosher salt** and **freshly ground black pepper**

1 **yellow onion**, finely chopped

1 **carrot**, finely chopped

1½ cups **chicken stock**

½ cup **orange juice**

2 sprigs **thyme**

1 **bay leaf**

¼ cup **orange marmalade**

1 tablespoon **sherry vinegar**

2 tablespoons **unsalted butter**, cut into ½-inch cubes and chilled

1   Place the duck breasts fat-side up on a cutting board and use a sharp knife to score the skin and fat in a diamond pattern all over (see box, page 100), taking care not to cut into the meat and spacing the cuts ¼ inch apart. Season the meat side of the breasts with salt and pepper.

2   Place the duck breasts fat-side down in a large skillet (see box, page 272). Place the skillet over medium-low heat and cook the duck breasts, undisturbed, until they render about 2 tablespoons of their fat, 6 to 8 minutes (see box, page 90) **A** . Pour the fat into a small bowl and set it aside **B** . Return the skillet to medium-low heat and repeat this process until almost all the fat has rendered and the duck breasts are golden brown and crisp on their fat side, 8 to 10 minutes more.

recipe continues

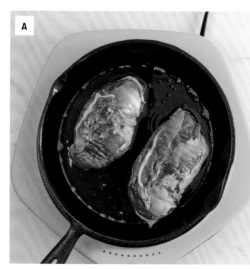

3 Once the fat side of the duck breasts is golden brown, flip them and cook on the second side until the duck is medium-rare inside, about 6 minutes more.

4 Meanwhile, in a medium saucepan, heat the reserved duck fat over medium-high heat. Add the onion and carrot, season with salt and pepper, and cook, stirring, until the onion is soft and golden brown, about 6 minutes.

5 Pour in the stock and orange juice and add the thyme and bay leaf. Bring the liquid to a boil and cook until reduced by half, 15 to 20 minutes.

6 Discard the thyme stems and bay leaf, then pour the sauce into a blender or food processor and purée until smooth.

7 Return the sauce to the pan and stir in the marmalade and vinegar. Add the butter and swirl the pan until the butter has melted completely and the sauce is smooth and thick.

8 Transfer the duck breasts to a cutting board and let rest for 5 minutes. Cut into ¼-inch-thick slices.

9 Serve the sliced duck breast hot, with the sauce spooned over the top.

## 101

## Scoring

Cutting slits on the surface of a piece of food accomplishes several things: It can tenderize a tougher cut of meat, prevent the skin on a piece of fish from curling away from its fillet, open up the layer of fat on a duck breast to help it render more easily, or allow heat to penetrate a halved eggplant or zucchini more quickly for short, high-heat cooking. Just make sure to remember that in this case, shallow is better. Score!

# FISH & SEAFOOD

# MANHATTAN CLAM CHOWDER

4 (6.5 ounce) cans chopped **clams in clam juice** (1¼ cups meat and 2 cups juice)

¾ cup coarsely chopped thick-cut **bacon** (4 slices)

6 **celery stalks**, finely chopped (about 3 cups)

2 medium **white onions**, finely chopped (about 3 cups)

1 **garlic clove**, smashed

2 teaspoons **dried thyme**

1 teaspoon **dried marjoram**

2 **bay leaves**

1 (28-ounce) can **whole peeled tomatoes in juice**, crushed by hand

2 medium **russet potatoes**, peeled and cut into ½-inch cubes

**Kosher salt** and **freshly ground black pepper**

**Oyster crackers**, for serving

As usual, New England and New York have some things to work out between them. Exhibit A: chowder. New England, which is home to some of our country's best seafood, cloaks its clams in a creamy white sauce for a comfort-food soup that eats like a meal. Always the upstart, Manhattan throws caution to the wind and adds tomatoes to the mix. One thing's for sure: No matter the chowder, get ready to chow down.

1 Place a fine-mesh strainer over a medium bowl and strain the clams, letting the juices collect in the bowl. Transfer the drained clams to a separate medium bowl and refrigerate until ready to use (the strained juice can remain at room temperature).

2 In a large pot, cook the bacon over medium-high heat, stirring occasionally, until the fat has rendered and the bacon is crispy, about 8 minutes (see box, page 90). Add the celery, onion, and garlic and cook, stirring, until slightly softened, 3 to 5 minutes.

3 Stir in the thyme, marjoram, and bay leaves, then the reserved clam juice, tomatoes, and potatoes. Increase the heat to high and bring the soup to a boil, stirring occasionally. Reduce the heat to medium-low and simmer, stirring occasionally, until the potatoes are tender, 15 to 20 minutes.

4 Stir in the reserved clams and cook just to warm through, 2 to 4 minutes.

5 Remove the soup from the heat and season with salt and pepper. Serve hot with oyster crackers alongside.

# NEW ENGLAND CLAM CHOWDER

1 Place a fine-mesh strainer over a medium bowl and strain the clams, letting the juices collect in the bowl. Transfer the drained clams to a separate medium bowl and refrigerate until ready to use (the strained juice can remain at room temperature).

2 In a large pot, cook the bacon over medium-high heat, stirring occasionally, until the fat has rendered and the bacon is crispy, about 8 minutes (see box, page 90). Add the onion, celery, and carrots and cook, stirring, until slightly softened, 3 to 5 minutes. Reduce the heat to low and add the flour. Cook, stirring continuously, until the raw taste is removed from the flour, 1 to 2 minutes.

3 Stir in the reserved clam juice, 1 teaspoon black pepper, the thyme, bay leaf, chicken stock, and potatoes. Increase the heat to high and bring the soup to a boil, stirring occasionally, to prevent the flour from scorching on the bottom of the pot.

4 Reduce the heat to medium-low and simmer, stirring occasionally, until the potatoes are tender, 15 to 20 minutes.

5 Stir in the cream and continue simmering until the soup is thickened, about 10 minutes. Stir in the reserved clams and cook just to warm through, 2 to 4 minutes more.

6 Remove the soup from the heat and season with salt and pepper. Serve hot with oyster crackers alongside.

4 (6.5 ounce) cans chopped **clams in clam juice** (1¼ cups meat and 2 cups juice)

½ cup coarsely chopped **cooked bacon** (4 slices)

1 large **yellow onion**, roughly chopped (about 2 cups)

2 large stalks **celery**, roughly chopped (about 1 cup)

2 medium **carrots,** roughly chopped (about 1 cup)

⅓ cup **all-purpose flour**

**Kosher salt** and **freshly ground black pepper**

1 teaspoon **dried thyme**

1 **bay leaf**

1½ cups **chicken stock**

2 medium **russet potatoes** (about 1¼ pounds), peeled and cut into ½-inch cubes

2 cups **heavy cream**

**Oyster crackers**, for serving

# CLAMS CARBONARA

This pasta dish is a beautiful marriage of two dishes: the cheesy rich touch of spaghetti carbonara (read: bacon and eggs) and the briny goodness of spaghetti with clams (read: heaven). May the couple share many happy years together.

Kosher salt

¼ cup **extra-virgin olive oil**

4 ounces **pancetta**, minced

2½ pounds **littleneck clams**, cleaned (see box, below)

⅓ cup **dry white wine**, such as sauvignon blanc

2 teaspoons **freshly ground black pepper**, plus more as needed

1 pound **linguine**

1¾ cups grated **Parmesan cheese** (7 ounces)

1 large **egg**

3 **egg yolks** (see box, page 149)

Chopped **fresh flat-leaf parsley**, for garnish

1   Bring a large pot of salted water to a boil over high heat.

2   Meanwhile, in a large skillet, heat the olive oil over medium heat. Add the pancetta and cook, stirring occasionally, until lightly browned, about 3 minutes.

3   Add the clams, wine, and pepper, and increase the heat to high. Cover and cook, shaking the pan occasionally, until the clams open, 6 to 10 minutes. Discard any clams that have not opened after 10 minutes.

4   Add the pasta to the boiling water and cook according to package instructions until al dente (see box, page 158).

5   Use tongs to transfer the clams to a medium bowl and set aside. Scrape the contents of the pan into a large bowl. Whisk in 1½ cups of the Parmesan, the egg, and the egg yolks until smooth.

6   Drain the pasta in a colander and add it to the Parmesan-egg mixture. Quickly toss to coat evenly. Season with salt and pepper. Stir the clams into the pasta.

7   Transfer the clams and pasta to a large serving dish. Sprinkle with the remaining ¼ cup Parmesan and the parsley. Serve hot.

## 101

## Cleaning Clams

Put the clams in a large bowl and cover them with 2 inches of very cold water. Let them sit for 1 hour to make sure they are grit and sand free. (Most clams have already been cleaned, so this is just insurance.)

# SCALLOPS WITH CAPER PAN SAUCE

4 tablespoons **unsalted butter**

1 tablespoon **olive oil**

12 large **sea scallops** (about 1 pound)

**Kosher salt** and **freshly ground black pepper**

2 **shallots**, minced

1 **garlic clove**, minced

¼ cup drained **capers**, rinsed

½ cup **white wine**, such as sauvignon blanc

Briny and fresh, these scallops are divine. When preparing this dish, make sure to pick a white wine that is as good for sipping as it is for drinking— no so-called cooking wine, please! As for the scallops, look for plump, snowy specimens; if there's a ton of water swimming around in the package, there's a chance they've been injected with water—if in doubt, ask your fish guy.

1　In a large skillet, heat 1 tablespoon of the butter with the olive oil over high heat. Season the scallops with salt and pepper. When the butter has melted, add the scallops to the pan and sear, flipping once halfway through, until golden brown on both sides and nearly opaque all the way through, 3 to 4 minutes total (see box, page 272). Divide the scallops between two plates and return the skillet to medium-high heat.

2　Melt 2 tablespoons butter in the skillet. Add the shallots and garlic. Cook, stirring, until soft and lightly browned, about 2 minutes.

3　Stir in the capers and cook until fragrant, about 1 minute. Pour in the wine and cook, stirring, until slightly reduced, about 3 minutes.

4　Remove the skillet from the heat and add the remaining 1 tablespoon butter, swirling the pan until it melts into the sauce. Season the sauce with salt and pepper and spoon it over the scallops. Serve hot.

# SEARED TUNA WITH RÉMOULADE SAUCE

SERVES
2

We're going to let you in on a little secret: Rémoulade is really just the adult version of tartar sauce. Upgrade your childhood memories with this snappy accompaniment to a beautiful tuna steak. Get your cast-iron grill pan raring to go with a five-minute preheat over a high flame, then prepare yourself for some serious sizzle when the tuna goes in.

### RÉMOULADE SAUCE

1 cup **mayonnaise**

¼ cup **dill pickle relish**

1 teaspoon **garlic powder**

1 teaspoon **onion powder**

½ teaspoon **cayenne**

Juice of ½ **lemon**

**Kosher salt** and **freshly ground black pepper**

### TUNA

1 (12-ounce) **tuna belly steak,** at room temperature

1 tablespoon **olive oil**

**Kosher salt** and **freshly ground black pepper**

1 Whisk together the mayonnaise, relish, garlic powder, onion powder, cayenne, and lemon juice in a small bowl. Season with salt and black pepper and refrigerate until ready to use, up to 3 days.

2 Make the tuna: Heat a cast-iron grill pan over high heat until it begins to smoke, about 5 minutes. Brush the tuna steak all over with the olive oil, then season liberally with salt and pepper.

3 Place the tuna steak on the grill pan and sear, flipping once halfway through, until lightly charred with grill marks outside and medium-rare inside, about 5 minutes total (see box, page 272). Transfer to a cutting board and let rest for 5 to 10 minutes.

4 Cut the tuna steak against the grain into ¼-inch-thick slices (see box, page 63), and serve with a dollop of the rémoulade sauce on the side.

# LEEK & DILL POACHED SALMON

1 large **leek**, white and light green parts only

¼ cup fresh **lemon juice** (from 2 lemons)

¼ cup **kosher salt**, plus more as needed

4 large **dill sprigs**, plus more for garnish

1 (1¼-pound) skin-on **salmon fillet**, at room temperature

1 tablespoon **unsalted butter**

**Freshly ground black pepper**

Poaching sounds difficult, but you'll find that it's one of the easiest ways to gently cook fish. Leeks, a mild cousin in the onion family, are grown in sandy soil, so it is important to clean them well, as dirt can hide between the many leaves and layers; just follow the recipe instructions and you'll be guaranteed a grit-free experience. Consider serving seasoned roasted carrots (page 283) on the side.

1   Halve the leek lengthwise through the root and rinse each half under cold running water to get rid of any dirt or grit stuck between its layers. Drain well, then cut crosswise into ¼-inch-thick slices. You should have about 1 cup.

2   Place the leeks, lemon juice, salt, and dill sprigs in a large pot and add 10 cups water. Bring the water to just below a boil over high heat. Reduce the heat to medium-low to maintain a bare simmer; there shouldn't be any bubbles breaking the surface of the water (see box, page 112).

3   Gently lower the salmon fillet into the water A B , and cover the pot. Poach until the salmon is light pink and opaque outside, easily flakes when prodded with a fork, and is medium inside, 12 to 14 minutes. An instant-read thermometer inserted into the center of the fillet should register between 140°F and 180°F, depending on how you like your salmon cooked C .

4   Using two large metal spatulas, gently lift the salmon fillet out of the poaching liquid and transfer it to a cutting board.

5   Drain the poaching liquid through a fine-mesh strainer set in the sink. Discard the dill sprigs and reserve the leeks.

6   In a small skillet, melt the butter over medium heat. Add the reserved leeks and cook, stirring occasionally, until golden, 1 to 2 minutes D . Season with salt and pepper.

7   Cut the salmon into 4 pieces, discarding the skin. Serve warm, with the leek sauce spooned over top and garnish with more dill.

recipe continues

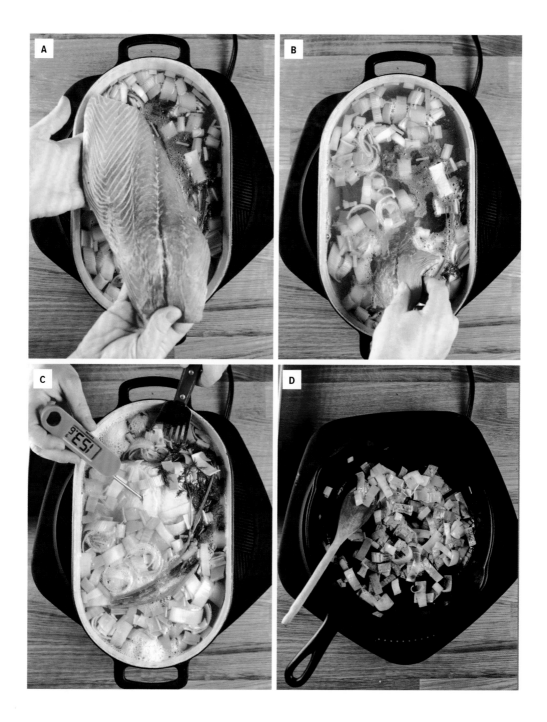

# Poaching Fish and Chicken

Poaching is a pretty straightforward way to cook fish or chicken, but it doesn't have to be a snooze.

By adding acid (think lemon or vinegar), salt, and aromatics (herbs, onions, shallots, garlic), you infuse the poaching liquid with flavor that gets imparted into your protein as it cooks at a gentle simmer.

Make sure you keep the water temperature low—too high a heat will cause the protein to tighten, resulting in tough meat.

The goal is to never bring the water to a boil; keep it low and steady the whole time. Standard poaching temperature is 160°F.

# FRIED COD FISH TACOS WITH CABBAGE SLAW

MAKES
**16**
TACOS

We love a good DIY to really get a party going, and nothing gets people in a great mood like pitching in. Appoint yourself captain of the frying station and have your friends gather round and help assemble their tacos complete with a tangy cabbage slaw, pico de gallo, and lime wedges. Flour tortillas are traditional for fish tacos, but feel free to switch it up with corn tortillas if the mood strikes you.

3 tablespoons **vegetable oil**, plus more for frying

1¾ cups **all-purpose flour**

2 teaspoons **Old Bay seasoning**

1 teaspoon **chili powder**

1 teaspoon **garlic powder**

1 teaspoon **kosher salt**, plus more to taste

¼ teaspoon **freshly ground black pepper**, plus more to taste

1 (12-ounce) bottle **lager-style beer**, such as Corona or Modelo

1 large **egg**

1 (2-pound) **cod fillet**, cut into 2 by 1-inch pieces (about 16 pieces total)

3 tablespoons fresh **lime juice**

5 cups thinly shredded **green** or **purple cabbage** (14 ounces)

16 small **flour** or **corn tortillas**, warmed

**Pico de gallo**, for serving

2 **limes**, cut into wedges, for serving

1. Fill a large pot with vegetable oil to a depth of 2 inches. Attach a deep-fry thermometer to the side and heat the oil over medium-high heat to 350°F (see box, page 81).

2. Meanwhile, whisk together the flour, Old Bay, chili powder, garlic powder, salt, and pepper in a large bowl. Pour in the beer, add the egg, and whisk until a smooth batter forms.

3. Working with 4 pieces of fish at a time, dip them in the batter to coat completely, letting any excess drip off, then drop them into the hot oil. Fry until golden brown on the outside and cooked through inside, 2 to 3 minutes. Using a slotted spoon, transfer the fried fish pieces to paper towels to drain and immediately season with salt while hot. Batter and fry the remaining fish in three additional batches, letting the oil return to temperature after each batch.

4. Whisk together the remaining 3 tablespoons oil and the lime juice in a large bowl. Add the cabbage, season liberally with salt and pepper, and toss to combine. Let stand for 5 minutes to soften slightly.

5. To assemble the tacos, place 1 piece of fish in each tortilla and top with some of the cabbage slaw. Serve with pico de gallo for spooning on top and lime wedges on the side.

Vegetable oil, for frying

1 cup **all-purpose flour**

5 large **eggs**, lightly beaten

2 cups **panko bread crumbs**

**Kosher salt** and **freshly ground black pepper**

1 pound large (16/20-count) peeled (tail-on) and deveined **raw shrimp** (see box, below)

**Sweet chili sauce**, such as Thai Kitchen, for dipping

# PERFECT FRIED SHRIMP

Oh yes, we went there, and these shrimp are indeed perfect. How could tender, sweet shrimp enveloped in the crunchiest coating you ever did see (or taste, for that matter) be anything but? This recipe is a great opportunity to put your dredging skills to work. A deep-fry thermometer is crucial to ensure spot-on oil temperature.

1   Fill a large pot with vegetable oil to a depth of 2 inches. Attach a deep-fry thermometer to the side and heat the oil over medium-high heat to 350°F (see box, page 81).

2   Meanwhile, place the flour, eggs, and bread crumbs in three separate shallow dishes. Season each with salt and pepper.

3   Season the shrimp all over with salt and pepper. Holding a shrimp by its tail, coat it completely in the flour, shaking off the excess, then dip it into the beaten egg, letting any excess drip back into the bowl (see box, page 247). Dredge the shrimp in the bread crumbs to coat fully, then transfer to a wire rack to dry. Repeat to coat the remaining shrimp **A** .

4   Working in batches of five or six, fry the shrimp, turning occasionally with a slotted spoon **B** , until golden brown and cooked through, about 2 minutes. Using a slotted spoon **C** , transfer the shrimp to paper towels to drain and season with salt while hot. Repeat with the remaining shrimp, letting the oil return to temperature after each batch.

5   Arrange the shrimp on a plate and serve immediately, with a bowl of sweet chili sauce alongside for dipping.

**101**

## Shrimp Size

You may see shrimp described by their "ct" or "count"—this refers to the number of shrimp per pound. Though these guidelines vary, jumbo shrimp are usually 16-count; extra large 26/30 count; and large 36/40. Though shrimp come smaller than that, you want to stick with larger shrimp for the Tasty recipes.

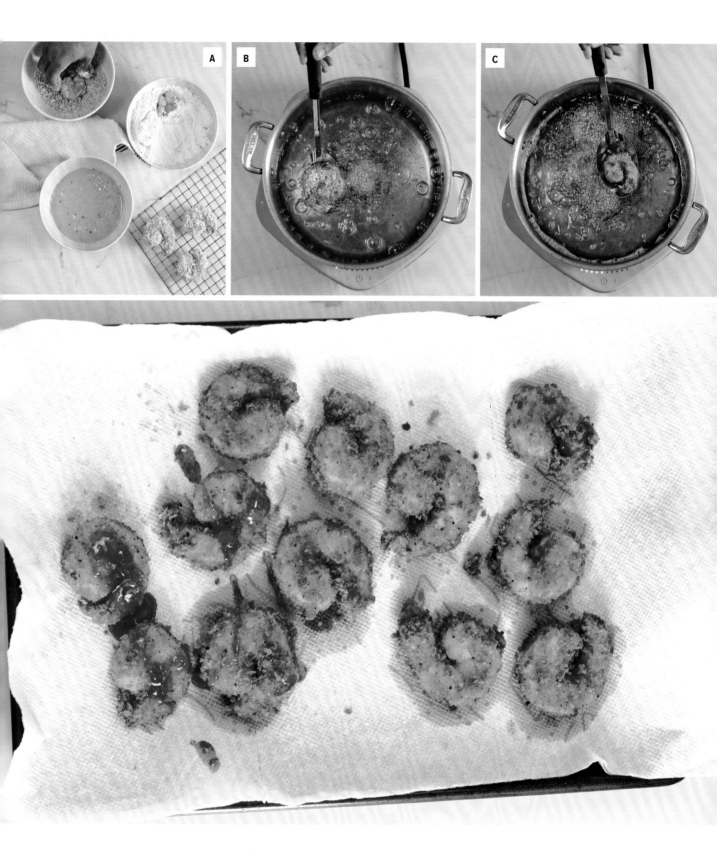

# Boiling Eggs

Place eggs in a saucepan, cover them with an inch of cold water, and bring to a boil over medium-high heat. Once the water is at a rolling boil (the entire surface of the water is violently bubbling), remove the pan from the heat, cover, and set your timer. Let the eggs sit 5 to 6 minutes for soft-boiled, 8 to 9 minutes for medium-boiled, and 13 to 14 for hard-boiled. Once your timer goes off, immediately plunge the eggs into an ice bath to stop the cooking. Let the eggs sit in the water for five minutes, then tap the hollow bottom of the egg against the counter (the natural air pocket will collapse the shell). Peel under cold running water. Pro tip: The older your eggs, the easier they will be able to peel, as the protein that holds the whites to the shell is weaker, so buy them 5 to 7 days before you need to boil them.

# WARM NIÇOISE SALAD

SERVES
2 to 4

We've put our own twist on this salad, named Niçoise after its birthplace in Nice, France. The potatoes, green beans, and tomatoes all get roasted using the oil from the drained jar of tuna (yes, tuna comes in oil and, yes, it's delish). Smart *and* Tasty, our favorite combination. *Merci, salad.*

2 (6.7-ounce) jars high-quality **tuna packed in olive oil**

4 **plum tomatoes**, halved lengthwise and cored

1 pound **fingerling potatoes**, halved

8 ounces **green beans**

### VINAIGRETTE

1 **garlic clove**, finely chopped

**Kosher salt**

⅓ cup **extra-virgin olive oil**

2 tablespoons fresh **lemon juice**

1 tablespoon **Dijon mustard**

2 teaspoons finely chopped fresh **tarragon leaves**

1 **shallot**, minced

**Freshly ground black pepper**

### TO ASSEMBLE

½ cup pitted small **kalamata** or black niçoise **olives**

8 small **radishes**, quartered

4 **soft-boiled eggs**, halved lengthwise (see box, opposite)

1 small **cucumber**, thinly sliced

**Flaky sea salt** and **coarsely ground black pepper**

½ cup loosely packed **fresh basil leaves**, torn

1  Preheat the oven to 400°F.

2  Drain the tuna, reserving the olive oil from the jars and keeping the tuna as intact as possible.

3  Arrange the tomato halves, cut-sides up, over one-third of a rimmed baking sheet and drizzle with 1 tablespoon of the reserved olive oil, tossing to coat. Roast the tomatoes for 10 minutes.

4  Remove the baking sheet from the oven and pile the potatoes in the center. Drizzle with 1 tablespoon of the reserved olive oil and toss to coat. Return the baking sheet to the oven and roast for 10 minutes.

5  Remove the baking sheet from the oven and arrange the green beans on the empty portion. Drizzle with 1 tablespoon of the reserved olive oil and toss to coat. Return the baking sheet to the oven once more and roast until all the vegetables are golden brown and tender, about 40 minutes more.

6  Meanwhile, make the vinaigrette: On a cutting board, sprinkle the chopped garlic heavily with salt. Using a knife, scrape and mash the garlic and salt together repeatedly to form a paste (see box, page 257). Scrape the paste into a small lidded container and add the olive oil, lemon juice, mustard, tarragon, and shallot. Season with salt and pepper. Close the container and shake until the vinaigrette is emulsified.

7  To assemble the salad, pile the tuna chunks in the center of a large serving plate. Arrange the warm potatoes, green beans, and tomato halves in separate piles around the tuna, then do the same with the olives, radishes, egg halves, and cucumber. Drizzle each pile, including the tuna, with about 1½ teaspoons of the vinaigrette, then season each pile with sea salt and coarse pepper. Scatter the basil over the salad and serve with the remaining dressing on the side.

# PAN-FRIED SOLE WITH CARAMELIZED LEMONS

2 (4-ounce) skinless **sole fillets**

**Kosher salt** and **freshly ground black pepper**

1 cup **all-purpose flour**

6 tablespoons (¾ stick) **unsalted butter**

6 (⅛-inch-thick) **lemon slices**

Once upon a time, lemon met fish and they became BFFs forever. Learn this classic preparation, and then you can even use it with other delicate, mild-tasting white fish, like cod, red snapper, or tilapia. Just don't deprive these besties of each other!

1   Season the sole fillets all over with salt and pepper.

2   Place the flour on a plate or in a shallow bowl. Dip 1 fillet in the flour, turning to coat it completely, then shaking off any excess (see box, page 247).

3   In a large skillet, melt 3 tablespoons of the butter over high heat. Add the flour-coated fillet and cook until golden brown on the bottom, 1½ to 2 minutes. Flip the fillet and add 3 lemon slices to the skillet around the sole. Cook until the fillet is golden brown on the second side, cooked through, and the lemon slices are lightly caramelized on the bottom, 1½ to 2 minutes more.

4   Transfer the fillet and lemons to a plate, wipe out the skillet, and repeat the dredging and cooking process with the remaining fillet. Serve hot.

# GRILLED MEXICAN-STYLE SPICED SNAPPER

This recipe is fabulous when prepared on the grill, but if you don't own one (or the weather isn't cooperating), it is equally tasty done in the oven. Bright red achiote paste is made with annatto seeds, cumin, coriander, oregano, cloves, and garlic and is available in Latin grocery stores (or online). Blessedly, it's not a one-trick pony that will not hang around unused in your cabinet; it works as well with poultry or pork as it does with fish.

3 tablespoons **olive oil**

1 tablespoon **achiote paste**

2 teaspoons **dried oregano**, preferably Mexican

2 teaspoons **ground coriander**

2 teaspoons **sweet paprika**

½ teaspoon **cayenne**

2 **garlic cloves**, minced

4 (8-ounce) skin-on **red snapper fillets**

**Kosher salt** and **freshly ground black pepper**

**Lime wedges**, for serving

1   Heat a charcoal or gas grill to medium-high using direct heat. Alternatively, preheat the oven to 425°F and line a baking sheet with foil.

2   Whisk together the olive oil, achiote paste, oregano, coriander, paprika, cayenne, and garlic in a small bowl.

3   Season the snapper fillets with salt and black pepper. Place on the grill skin-side down and brush each liberally with the spice mixture. Close the grill and cook until the fish flakes easily with a fork and is cooked through, about 8 minutes. (Alternatively, put the fillets on the prepared baking sheet, brush with the spice mixture, and bake for 8 to 12 minutes.)

4   Transfer each fillet to a plate and serve warm, with lime wedges for squeezing.

# EASY LOBSTER BISQUE

½ cup (1 stick) **unsalted butter**

1 large **yellow onion**, finely chopped

1 **carrot**, finely chopped

1 **celery stalk**, finely chopped

4 fresh or frozen, thawed raw **lobster tails** (1 to 1½ pounds total)

2 tablespoons **tomato paste**

½ cup **brandy** or **Cognac**

6 cups **seafood stock** or **water**

¼ cup lightly packed **fresh flat-leaf parsley leaves**, plus more for garnish

2 teaspoons fresh **thyme leaves**

1 dried **bay leaf**

½ cup **heavy cream**

1 tablespoon fresh **lemon juice**

½ teaspoon **cayenne**

**Kosher salt** and **freshly ground black pepper**

**Crème fraîche**, for serving

We guarantee that this version of bisque (French for "creamy soup") is as easy as making a simple chicken soup. Start by sautéing onion, carrot, and celery (which, if you've read this book carefully, you know as mirepoix) and you'll be off to the (delicious) races. Pro tip: Heat your bowls ahead of time to hold the heat of the soup longer; place oven-safe bowls in the oven set to its lowest setting for 10 to 15 minutes before serving.

1  In a large pot, melt 4 tablespoons of the butter over medium-high heat. Add the onion, carrot, and celery and cook, stirring, until soft and beginning to brown, about 6 minutes.

2  Add the lobster tails and cook, covered, until the shells are bright red and the meat is cooked through, about 10 minutes. Using tongs, transfer the lobster tails from the pot to a cutting board to cool.

3  Add the tomato paste to the pot and cook, stirring, until lightly caramelized, about 2 minutes. Pour in the brandy and cook, stirring, until almost completely evaporated, about 1 minute. Add the stock, parsley, thyme, and bay leaf and bring to a simmer.

4  Meanwhile, use kitchen shears to cut away the lobster shells, leaving the tail meat intact. Place the meat on a plate and cover with foil to keep warm. Add the lobster shells to the pot with the soup and cook, stirring occasionally, until reduced slightly, 30 to 35 minutes.

5  Remove the pot from the heat, remove and discard the lobster shells and bay leaf, then purée the soup directly in the pot with an immersion blender until very smooth. (Alternatively, working in batches, carefully transfer the soup to a standing blender and purée until very smooth, then return it to the pot.)

6  Stir the remaining 4 tablespoons (½ stick) butter, the cream, lemon juice, and cayenne into the soup. Season with salt and black pepper, then ladle the soup into four soup bowls.

7  Slice each lobster tail crosswise into about five ¾-inch-thick medallions, then arrange the lobster meat on the surface of the soup in the center of each bowl.

8  Drizzle some crème fraîche in the soup around the lobster meat and sprinkle with more parsley leaves before serving.

# SWEET & SPICY MARINATED TILAPIA

3 tablespoons **agave syrup**

3 tablespoons **low-sodium soy sauce**

2 tablespoons **ketchup**

2 teaspoons minced **garlic**

2 teaspoons minced fresh **ginger**

½ teaspoon **toasted sesame oil**

½ teaspoon **crushed red pepper flakes**

4 (4-ounce) **tilapia fillets**

1 teaspoon toasted **sesame seeds**

This recipe works best when the fish has had time to marinate, so leave time for the sweet and spicy sauce to work its magic. The "work" here is just in the waiting, since the fish cooks in 12 minutes. Bam, and that's dinner served.

1 Combine the agave syrup, soy sauce, ketchup, garlic, ginger, sesame oil, and red pepper flakes in a large resealable plastic bag. Add the tilapia fillets, seal the bag, and turn to coat. Marinate the tilapia in the refrigerator for at least 1 hour and up to 4 hours (see box, page 74).

2 Preheat the oven to 400°F. Line a baking sheet with foil.

3 Remove the tilapia fillets from the marinade, letting the excess drip back into the bag, and arrange them on the prepared baking sheet; reserve the marinade. Bake until the tilapia is cooked through and lightly caramelized at the edges, 10 to 12 minutes.

4 Meanwhile, pour the marinade into a small microwave-safe bowl and microwave until bubbling and thickened, about 1 minute.

5 As soon as the fillets come out of the oven, brush the marinade over them and sprinkle evenly with the sesame seeds. Transfer each fillet to a plate and serve warm.

# BROWN BUTTER TROUT WITH ALMONDS & THYME

SERVES
**4**

Butter lovers everywhere, meet brown butter. This fragrant, nutty, toasty upgrade of butter, which you make by taking it just a little further on heat in the skillet, enhances pretty much anything (sweet or savory) that it touches—just watch the butter closely when browning, because it can go from brown to burnt before you know it.

6 tablespoons (¾ stick) **unsalted butter**

4 (8-ounce) skin-on **trout fillets**

**Kosher salt** and **freshly ground black pepper**

1 cup **all-purpose flour**

½ cup **whole almonds** (about 3 ounces), coarsely chopped

2 teaspoons **fresh thyme leaves**

1 tablespoon fresh **lemon juice**

1  In a large nonstick skillet, melt 3 tablespoons of the butter over medium-high heat.

2  Season the trout fillets with salt and pepper. Place the flour on a shallow plate. Dredge 2 fillets in the flour, coating them completely and shaking off any excess (see box, page 247). Add the coated fillets to the skillet and cook, flipping once halfway through, until golden brown and just cooked through, about 3 minutes total. Transfer each fillet to a plate and set aside. Wipe the skillet clean and return it to the heat.

3  Melt the remaining 3 tablespoons butter in the skillet. Dredge and cook the remaining 2 fillets as above, but do not wipe out the skillet.

4  To the browned butter left in the skillet, add the almonds and thyme and cook, stirring, until the almonds are lightly browned, about 5 minutes. Remove the skillet from the heat and stir in the lemon juice.

5  Spoon the sauce and almonds over the fillets, dividing them evenly. Serve hot.

# SALMON POKĒ BOWL

One of the freshest, tastiest, healthiest new food trends around is ready to make its debut in your kitchen. It's essential to get the freshest salmon possible; this is where having friends behind the fish counter can really come in handy. Our version combines salmon, cucumbers, edamame, and avocado. Serve it over brown rice for a heartier meal.

1 cup **cooked white rice**

6 ounces skinless **salmon fillet**, cut into ½-inch cubes

½ cup ½-inch cubed **cucumber**

½ cup steamed **edamame**, cooled

½ cup ½-inch cubed **avocado**

¼ cup prepared **seaweed salad**, such as wakame

1 teaspoon **toasted sesame seeds**

1 **scallion**, thinly sliced

1 small sheet **dried nori seaweed**

3 tablespoons **low-sodium soy sauce**

1 tablespoon **rice vinegar**

¾ teaspoon **toasted sesame oil**

¼ teaspoon **crushed red pepper flakes**

1  Pile the rice in the middle of a large serving bowl. Working around the edge of the bowl, arrange the salmon, cucumber, edamame, avocado, and seaweed salad in separate piles. Sprinkle the sesame seeds and scallions over the whole bowl.

2  Heat a small skillet over high heat. Using tongs, add the dried nori sheet and cook, turning once, until lightly toasted and fragrant, 1 to 2 minutes. Transfer to a cutting board and let cool slightly. Slice the nori into thin threads, then pile them in the middle of the bowl.

3  Stir together the soy sauce, vinegar, sesame oil, and red pepper flakes in a small bowl. Drizzle the sauce over the pokē bowl and toss to combine. Serve immediately.

# EGGS

# CLASSIC FRENCH OMELET

**SERVES
1**

3 large **eggs**

**Kosher salt**

1 tablespoon **unsalted butter**

Finely chopped **fresh chives**,
for serving

Let us eggsplain: A French omelet is the *ne plus ultra* of classic cooking techniques. Master it and you'll know it (and use it) for life. A good nonstick pan and a rubber spatula are crucial to success, as is realizing that you actually scramble the eggs a bit in the pan before letting them come together as an omelet. Japanese omelets are a little sweeter. Fish stock works great here, but this recipe is traditionally made with dashi broth. To make your own, combine 3 cups boiling water, ½ ounce dried kelp, and ½ cup bonito flakes, let steep for 10 minutes, then strain out the solids. The broth keeps for 5 days; after you make the omelet, you can use it for miso or udon soup, or whatever you like! If you don't own a tamagoyaki pan, available online, a nonstick will do just fine.

1  Whisk the eggs in a small bowl until the whites and the yolks are completely combined, with no spots of egg white remaining. Season with salt.

2  In a medium skillet, melt the butter over medium-low heat. Continue to heat the butter until it foams and then subsides.

3  Add the eggs and, using a small rubber spatula, continuously scrape the bottom of the pan while moving the pan in a circular motion to ensure the eggs cook slowly, forming small curds, 3 to 4 minutes.

4  Once you start to see the bottom of the pan for more than a second after scraping, push the eggs into an even layer that completely covers the bottom of the skillet. Cook until the edges solidify, 4 to 6 minutes more.

5  Tilt the handle side of the skillet up and carefully roll the omelet downward onto itself and then out onto a plate. Sprinkle with chives and serve immediately.

# JAPANESE "TAMAGOYAKI" OMELET

⅓ cup **fish stock** or **dashi**

2 teaspoons **sugar**

1 teaspoon **sake**

1 teaspoon **mirin**

4 large **eggs**

**Kosher salt**

**Vegetable oil**

**Shiso leaf**, grated **Japanese radish**, and **soy sauce**, for serving

1　Whisk together the stock, sugar, sake, mirin, and eggs in a large bowl until smooth. Season with salt.

2　Heat a 5 by 7-inch tamagoyaki pan over medium heat. Brush a thin layer of vegetable oil over the bottom of the pan.

3　Add ⅓ cup of the egg mixture to the pan and quickly swirl the pan so the egg covers the bottom. When the egg is set, about 1 minute, use a spatula to gently loosen it from the side of the pan and roll it away from you into a log. Leave it in the pan.

4　Brush the skillet with more oil, then add another ⅓ cup of the egg mixture to the pan. Lift up the rolled egg log and let the raw mixture run under it, coating the pan. When the new layer of egg is set, roll it toward you, with the first log, into another log.

5　Repeat this process four more times, brushing with oil between batches, until you have used all the egg and there is one large log in the pan; this is the tamagoyaki.

6　Transfer the tamagoyaki to a cutting board and cut it in half lengthwise. Pierce each half on its short end with a skewer.

7　To serve, place a shiso leaf on a plate and place the tamagoyaki on top. Top with a small spoonful of grated radish and serve with soy sauce for dipping.

# 3-MINUTE MUG OMELET

¼ cup packed **baby spinach leaves**

¼ cup finely chopped **red bell pepper**

¼ cup finely chopped **green bell pepper**

2 slices **deli-style ham**, finely chopped

2 large **eggs**, lightly beaten

**Kosher salt** and **freshly ground black pepper**

If you've got a microwave, a mug, and three minutes, you have exactly zero excuses for not making this balanced breakfast. Since everything is mixed and cooked in the same mug, you can concentrate on tucking into your meal (or take it to go!) and not be weighed down with thoughts of an arduous clean-up.

1. Combine the spinach, bell peppers, ham, and eggs in a microwave-safe mug and stir to combine evenly. Season with salt and pepper.

2. Microwave the mug on full power for 2 to 3 minutes, stopping halfway through to stir, until the eggs are puffed and set. Serve hot.

# POTATO-CRUSTED QUICHE

In this version of quiche, there's no rolling out of finicky dough; thinly sliced potatoes act as your "crust," giving support to the cast of ingredients. Genius! No need to tell anyone how easily it all came together. You can take a bow as the culinary superstar that you are, and now you *parlez-vous* delicious.

1 pound **russet potatoes**, peeled

3 tablespoons **olive oil**

1 tablespoon grated **Parmesan cheese**

2 teaspoons **kosher salt**

½ teaspoon **freshly ground black pepper**

1 cup **whole milk**

1 teaspoon **garlic powder**

5 large **eggs**

½ cup coarsely chopped cooked **bacon** (4 slices)

½ cup shredded **Cheddar cheese** (2 ounces)

¼ cup thinly sliced **scallions**

1 **vine-ripe tomato**, cored and finely chopped

1 Preheat the oven to 400°F.

2 Using a knife or mandoline, cut the potatoes crosswise into ⅛-inch-thick slices.

3 Place the sliced potatoes in a large bowl and drizzle with the olive oil. Sprinkle with the Parmesan, 1 teaspoon of the salt, and ¼ teaspoon of the pepper and gently toss to coat.

4 Arrange the potato slices over the bottom of a 9-inch pie plate, overlapping them in a spiral pattern starting from the center and working your way out toward the sides of the dish and going up the edges. Fill in any gaps with leftover potato slices.

5 Bake until the potatoes are just cooked through and not yet brown, about 15 minutes. Set the pie plate on a wire rack. Leave the oven on.

6 Whisk together the milk, garlic powder, and eggs in a large bowl. Stir in the bacon, Cheddar, scallions, and tomatoes.

7 Slowly pour the egg mixture over the potatoes. If the potatoes begin to lift up, stop and press them down with a spoon.

8 Bake the quiche until the eggs are set in the middle and the potatoes are golden brown, about 30 minutes. Transfer the quiche to a wire rack and let cool for 10 minutes.

9 Cut into wedges and serve warm.

# BOWL-POACHED EGG BREAKFAST SALAD

2 cups torn **frisée lettuce** or your favorite mixed salad greens

1 tablespoon **olive oil**

1 tablespoon **red wine vinegar**

**Kosher salt** and **freshly ground black pepper**

2 large **eggs**

2 thick-cut **bacon slices**, cooked and coarsely chopped

1 (1-inch-thick) slice **sourdough bread**, toasted

We'd tumble out of bed with joy if we knew something this fresh and lively was waiting for us. If you've shied away from poaching eggs, this is the recipe to get started on. The trick of using small glass bowls submerged in simmering water guarantees a perfect poached egg every time.

1  Combine the lettuce, olive oil, and vinegar in a large bowl and toss to coat the lettuce. Season with salt and pepper and transfer to a plate.

2  Place two 3- to 4-ounce small glass prep bowls in a Dutch oven. Add enough water to cover the rims of the bowls by ½ to 1 inch and bring the water to a bare simmer over medium-low heat. There should be no bubbles breaking the surface of the water.

3  Crack 1 egg into a separate small glass bowl **A**, then slide it into one of the submerged bowls **B**. Repeat with the second egg **C**. Poach the eggs until the whites are set but the yolks are still runny, 3 to 5 minutes. The bowls will help the eggs maintain their rounded shape.

4  Using tongs, carefully lift the submerged bowls out of the water, tilting them slightly to drain off any water that might have seeped in **D** **E**.

5  Invert the bowls onto the salad, letting the eggs fall out. Season the eggs with salt and pepper.

6  Sprinkle the bacon over the salad and serve with the toast.

## Poaching Eggs

A perfect poached egg doesn't have to scare the shell off you! The water should be at a "hard simmer"—more than a simmer but less than a full rolling boil. This is the old-school traditional way to poach an egg, but to learn our new favorite method for poaching eggs for a crowd, see the recipe instructions.

1  Crack your eggs into small individual bowls (ramekins are great for this task).

2  Create a whirlpool by swirling the water with a spoon, then drop the one egg into the center of the whirlpool and let it cook for about 3 mintues for a large egg.

3  To gauge doneness, lift the eggs out of the water with a slotted spoon; they will look totally opaque and fluffy; dab them on paper towels to dry before serving.

# BAKED AVOCADO EGGS

SERVES
4

Who needs special equipment (or even a bowl)
when an avocado is its own perfectly proportioned
receptacle? It's nature's ideal bowl, taking our
favorite breakfast treat beyond the toast.
If you don't fancy basil and chives, try swapping
them out for cilantro and parsley.

2 ripe large **avocados,**
halved and pitted

4 large **eggs**

**Kosher salt** and **freshly ground
black pepper**

2 tablespoons finely crumbled
cooked **bacon**

4 **cherry tomatoes**, quartered

¼ cup shredded **Cheddar cheese**
(1 ounce)

2 tablespoons finely chopped
**fresh basil**

2 teaspoons minced **fresh chives**

1   Preheat the oven to 400°F. Line a baking sheet with parchment paper.

2   Place the avocado halves skin-side down on the prepared baking
sheet, pressing them gently to stabilize them. Using a large spoon,
scoop out some of the flesh from around the pit impression to make
a hole that will fit an egg.

3   Crack 1 egg into each avocado half and season with salt and pepper.

4   On the avocado flesh around each egg, layer, in this order,
one-quarter of the bacon, 4 quarters of cherry tomato, and
1 tablespoon Cheddar.

5   Bake the avocados until the egg whites are set but the yolks are still
runny, and the cheese has melted, about 15 minutes. Transfer the
avocados to individual plates and sprinkle evenly with the basil and
chives before serving.

# BAKED EGG BREAKFAST SANDWICHES

Nonstick cooking spray

¾ cup **whole milk**

½ teaspoon **kosher salt**

½ teaspoon **freshly ground black pepper**

½ teaspoon **garlic powder**

10 large **eggs**

2 cups small **broccoli florets**, coarsely chopped

1 small **red bell pepper**, finely chopped

½ medium **red onion**, finely chopped

6 slices deli-style **Cheddar cheese**

6 whole-grain **English muffins**, split and toasted

Prep these breakfast sammies for safe storage in your freezer, and you'll always be a mere two minutes away from piping-hot breakfast goodness. (Or eat them for a late-night snack; we won't tell.) Just add bacon, turkey bacon, cooked sausage patties, or deli-sliced ham to each sandwich to customize, and wrap them in a damp paper towel then parchment paper, making sure to label and date the paper with a marker for quick-and-easy identification later. Store in an airtight plastic bag or container in the freezer for up to 1 month. When ready to eat, remove the parchment paper and microwave on high for 2 to 3 minutes.

1   Preheat the oven to 375°F. Coat a 9 by 13-inch baking dish with cooking spray.

2   Whisk together the milk, salt, black pepper, garlic powder, and eggs in a large bowl until smooth.

3   Pour the eggs into the prepared baking dish. Sprinkle the broccoli, bell pepper, and onion evenly over the eggs. Bake until the eggs are set and golden brown on top, 20 to 25 minutes.

4   Transfer the baking dish to a wire rack and cut the eggs into 6 large squares. Place a slice of cheese on each egg square, then sandwich the eggs with toasted English muffins. Serve hot.

# CHEESE-STUFFED MUSHROOM & HERB FRITTATA

The first thing you need to know about this frittata is that it has a cheese disk center. Think of the eggs in the frittata like the bread layers in a sandwich and the duo cheese center as the melty heart of the whole thing. (P.S. If your mouth is watering after reading that description and looking at the photos on the following pages, you're not alone.)

2 cups shredded **Monterey Jack cheese** (8 ounces)

1 (8-ounce) package **cream cheese**, at room temperature

2 **scallions**, thinly sliced

18 large **eggs**, lightly beaten

½ cup grated **Parmesan cheese** (2½ ounces)

¼ cup finely chopped **fresh chives**

¼ cup finely chopped **fresh flat-leaf parsley**

2 teaspoons **kosher salt**

1 teaspoon **freshly ground black pepper**

4 tablespoons (½ stick) **unsalted butter**

1 cup thinly sliced **cremini** or **button mushrooms**

1 large **yellow onion**, halved and thinly sliced

6 **fresh basil leaves**, torn into pieces

1   Preheat the oven to 425°F. Line an 8-inch round metal pan with plastic wrap, letting the excess hang over the edge.

2   Stir together the Monterey Jack, cream cheese, and scallions in a large bowl until evenly incorporated. Transfer the mixture to the prepared pan. Press it down and smooth out the top to make an even disc **A** . Transfer the pan to the freezer and chill until the cheese disc is stiff, at least 1 hour and up to 24 hours.

3   Whisk together the eggs, Parmesan, chives, parsley, salt, and pepper in a large bowl.

4   In a 12-inch nonstick ovenproof skillet, melt the butter over medium-high heat. Add the mushrooms and onion and cook, stirring occasionally, until soft and lightly browned, about 8 minutes **B** . Scrape them into the egg mixture and stir to combine.

5   Return the skillet to medium heat, and pour in 1½ cups of the egg mixture. Cook, without stirring, until the eggs are partly but not completely set on the bottom, about 6 minutes.

6   Using the plastic wrap overhang as a handle, lift the cheese disc out of the pan. Discard the plastic. Center the cheese disc on top of the eggs. Pour the remaining egg mixture over the top **C** . Transfer to the oven and bake until the frittata is lightly browned on top, the center is set, and the cheese has melted, 20 to 25 minutes.

7   Run a rubber spatula around the edges of the skillet to loosen the frittata, then slide it onto a serving plate and cut it into 8 wedges. Sprinkle with the basil and serve.

recipe continues

TASTY ULTIMATE

# BIRD'S NESTS WITH HAWAIIAN HASH

6 tablespoons **coconut oil**

1 pound **purple potatoes**, cut into
½-inch cubes

1 **yellow onion**, finely chopped

**Kosher salt** and **freshly ground
black pepper**

2 cups finely diced fresh
**pineapple** (12 ounces)

3 **scallions**, thinly sliced

5 ounces **cooked ham**, cut into
¼-inch cubes (about 1 cup)

4 **Hawaiian sweet rolls**,
such as King's

4 large **eggs**

Say aloha: The classic egg-in-a-hole just took a jet plane to Hawaii. If you can't find purple potatoes, you can substitute a regular white variety.

1   In a large cast-iron skillet, melt 4 tablespoons of the coconut oil over medium-high heat. Add the potatoes and onion, season with salt and pepper, and cook, stirring occasionally, until tender and well browned, about 10 minutes.

2   Add the pineapple and scallions and cook, stirring, until lightly browned, about 10 minutes.

3   Stir in the ham and cook until it is browned at the edges, about 6 minutes. Season the hash with more salt and black pepper and divide it among four plates.

4   Meanwhile, cut out the centers of the rolls, leaving a ½-inch-thick wall around the edges.

5   Wipe the skillet clean and return it to medium heat. Melt the remaining 2 tablespoons coconut oil. Place the rolls in the skillet, hollowed-side up, and crack an egg into each one. Cover the skillet and cook until the egg whites are set but the yolks are still runny, and the bottoms of the rolls are golden brown, 15 to 20 minutes.

6   Transfer a bird's nest to each plate and serve hot with the hash.

# SAUSAGE, EGG & CHEESE PIE

Nonstick cooking spray

1 cup **ketchup**

⅓ cup **mild hot sauce**, such as Cholula

¼ cup **Worcestershire sauce**

**All-purpose flour**, for dusting

2 (9-inch) square sheets frozen **puff pastry**, thawed and chilled (see box, page 288)

20 large **eggs**

2 cups crumbled cooked **breakfast sausage** (1 pound)

**Kosher salt** and **freshly ground black pepper**

2 cups shredded **American cheese** (9 ounces)

We emphatically answer "yes" when asked if pie is a legitimate breakfast food—especially when layered with eggs, sausage, and cheese. Frozen puff pastry is a gift from on high to lazy flaky pastry lovers everywhere. It's all of the decadent butter layers, none of the work. Defrost the frozen puff pastry sheets either overnight in the refrigerator or for forty-five minutes to one hour at room temperature before using.

1  Preheat the oven to 400°F. Coat a 9 by 13-inch metal baking pan with cooking spray. Line the bottom and the two long sides with a piece of parchment paper cut to fit.

2  Whisk together the ketchup, hot sauce, and Worcestershire in a small bowl.

3  On a lightly floured surface, roll out 1 sheet of puff pastry into an 11 by 15-inch rectangle. Transfer the pastry sheet to the prepared baking pan, pressing it lightly into the bottom and up the sides and letting the excess hang over the edges.

4  Gently crack all but one of the eggs over the pastry, being sure not to break the yolks, then gently sprinkle the eggs with the sausage, again trying to avoid breaking any of the yolks. Drizzle half the ketchup sauce evenly over the eggs and sausage, season with salt and pepper, then top evenly with the cheese. Fold the overhanging puff pastry to partially enclose the filling.

5  In a small bowl, lightly beat the remaining egg with 1 tablespoon water. Brush the egg wash over the exposed puff pastry.

6  Roll the second pastry sheet into a 10 by 14-inch rectangle and place it over the exposed filling, tucking the edges between the sides of the pan and the first sheet of pastry. Cut four 3-inch-long slits in the top sheet of pastry, then brush the pastry all over with egg wash. Season the top with pepper. Bake until the pie is golden brown on top and the eggs are cooked through, 40 to 45 minutes.

7  Transfer the pie to a wire rack for 5 minutes. Cut into large squares and serve hot, with the remaining ketchup sauce for dipping.

# BREAKFAST TOSTADAS

SERVES
**8**

Swap your regular breakfast toast for tostadas piled high with scrambled eggs. The sour cream and guacamole are optional, but we highly recommend them for maximum breakfast impact.

¼ cup **vegetable oil**

2 **plum tomatoes**, cored, seeded, and finely chopped

2 **jalapeños**, finely chopped

1 **white onion**, finely chopped

**Kosher salt** and **freshly ground black pepper**

12 large **eggs**, lightly beaten

¼ cup finely chopped **fresh cilantro leaves**, plus more for serving

8 **tostadas**

1½ cups canned **refried black** or **pinto beans**

½ cup shredded **Pepper Jack cheese** (2 ounces)

**Sour cream** and **guacamole**, for serving (optional)

1  Preheat the broiler (see box, page 57).

2  In a large nonstick skillet, heat the vegetable oil over medium-high heat. Add the tomatoes, jalapeños, and onion, season with salt and pepper, and cook, stirring, until soft and beginning to brown, about 8 minutes.

3  Add the eggs, reduce the heat to medium, and cook, stirring occasionally, until cooked through, 12 to 15 minutes. Remove the skillet from the heat and stir in the cilantro.

4  Arrange the tostadas on a baking sheet and broil, flipping once halfway through, until lightly golden and fragrant, about 1 minute total.

5  Spread 3 tablespoons of the beans evenly over each tostada. Divide the scrambled eggs among the tostadas, piling them in the center of the beans, then sprinkle evenly with the cheese. Broil until the cheese is just melted, 1 to 2 minutes.

6  Transfer the tostadas to plates and garnish with more cilantro. Serve hot, with sour cream and guacamole on the side, if you like.

8 large **eggs**

1 cup shredded **Colby Jack cheese** (4 ounces)

½ cup coarsely chopped cooked **bacon** (4 slices)

⅓ cup **heavy cream**

2 **scallions**, thinly sliced

**Kosher salt** and **freshly ground black pepper**

1 **baguette**, 20 to 22 inches long and 2½ to 3 inches wide

# B.E.C. BOAT

Need to feed a hungry crowd in the a.m.? Pack your bags and grab your coat, because you and your besties are about to sail away on a mouthwatering breakfast boat full of bacon, eggs, and cheese. No Colby Jack? No worries, just substitute sharp shredded Cheddar or Pepper Jack for an equally luscious take on the recipe. Lining a rimmed baking sheet with foil before you get started will ensure that cleanup is a snap . . . you won't even need to wash the pan afterward!

1  Preheat the oven to 350°F. Line a baking sheet with foil.

2  Crack the eggs into a large bowl and whisk until smooth. Stir in the cheese, bacon, cream, and scallions. Season with salt and pepper.

3  Using a paring knife, cut a long rectangle (1¼ to 1½ inches wide and 18 to 19 inches long) into the top of the baguette and partially hollow out the baguette, taking care not to tear any holes in the bottom or sides of the bread.

4  Place the baguette on the prepared baking sheet and spoon the egg mixture into the hollowed-out center. Bake until the eggs puff up and are cooked through in the middle, 20 to 25 minutes.

5  Transfer the baguette to a cutting board, cut into 1-inch-thick slices, and serve.

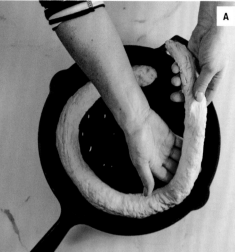

# FRIED EGG "PIZZA"

You already knew that pizza makes the best breakfast, so let us help you embrace your beliefs with this recipe. We also approve of its use for dinner.

SERVES
4

12 ounces **prepared pizza dough**

2 tablespoons **olive oil**

8 large **eggs**

½ cup prepared **pizza sauce**

1 (10-ounce) package **frozen spinach**, thawed and squeezed dry

**Kosher salt** and **freshly ground black pepper**

½ cup shredded **whole-milk mozzarella cheese** (2 ounces)

½ teaspoon **dried oregano**

¼ teaspoon **crushed red pepper flakes**

2 tablespoons grated **Parmesan cheese**

1  Preheat the oven to 375°F.

2  Roll the pizza dough into a rope 36 inches long and ½ inch thick. Arrange the rope around the outer edge of a 12-inch nonstick ovenproof skillet **A** and pinch together the ends to form a ring. Cover with a kitchen towel or plastic wrap and let stand until the dough is slightly puffed, about 30 minutes.

3  Drizzle 1 tablespoon of the olive oil into the center of the skillet.

4  Separate the eggs (see box, right), placing the egg whites in one medium bowl and the yolks in another (do not break the yolks and keep them covered with plastic wrap). Lightly beat the egg whites to loosen them. Pour them into the center of the skillet. Spoon the pizza sauce evenly on top, then sprinkle with the chopped spinach **B** . Season with salt and black pepper. Sprinkle the mozzarella evenly over the spinach **C** . Sprinkle the oregano and red pepper flakes over the whole skillet.

5  Brush some of the remaining 1 tablespoon olive oil over the dough ring, then drizzle any remaining olive oil over the cheese.

6  Bake the pizza until the dough is golden brown, the cheese has melted, and the egg whites are cooked through, about 25 minutes **D** . Remove the skillet from the oven and arrange the egg yolks on top of the pizza **E** . Return it to the oven and bake until the yolks are warmed through but still soft, about 5 minutes more (a thin film will develop on top of the yolks).

7  Transfer the skillet to a wire rack. Sprinkle evenly with the Parmesan and let cool for 1 minute. Run a spatula around the edges of the skillet to loosen the pizza, then carefully slide it onto a serving plate and cut it into 4 large wedges. Serve hot.

101

## Separating Eggs

Always crack eggs against a flat surface (like a counter), rather than against the edge of a bowl; doing so cuts down on the amount of errant shell that could make its way into your dish. To separate the white and yolk, set up two small bowls on your counter and crack the egg into the bowl. Using your clean hand, pull the yolk up out of the whites, letting the whites run down through your fingers back into the bowl.

# VEGETARIAN

# QUICK SNACK NACHOS

SERVES
1 or 2

5 cups large **corn tortilla chips**
(7 to 8 ounces)

8 ounces shredded **sharp
Cheddar cheese**

**Kosher salt** and **freshly ground
black pepper**

½ cup **pickled jalapeños**, drained

**Hot sauce, sour cream**, and
**guacamole**, for serving

As far as we are concerned, nachos are always a party, even if it's just a party for one. Our quick version, with one kind of cheese and minimal fuss, is ready in two minutes. (Thank you, microwave gods, for providing us with our secret couch dinner.) The party nachos, with multiple cheeses and spices, are for those times when you want to get down, hard, with every nacho topping known to humankind—and for when you want to share the wealth with a crowd.

1  Spread out the chips on a plate in an even layer. Sprinkle the cheese evenly over the top.

2  Season the nachos with salt and pepper, then microwave the nachos until the chips are slightly crisp and the cheese has melted completely, about 2 minutes.

3  Remove the plate from the microwave and sprinkle the jalapeños on top. Serve immediately, with hot sauce, sour cream, and guacamole on the side.

# FANCY PARTY NACHOS

1  Preheat the oven to 425°F. Line a rimmed baking sheet with foil.

2  In a large skillet, heat the vegetable oil over medium-high heat. Add the onion and cook, stirring, until soft and beginning to brown, about 3 minutes. Stir in the chili powder, coriander, cumin, and garlic and cook until fragrant, about 1 minute.

3  Add the beans and tomatoes (with their juices) and cook, stirring occasionally, until thickened and warmed through, about 10 minutes. Mash the beans and tomatoes to your desired consistency and season with salt and pepper.

4  Spread the tortilla chips out on the prepared baking sheet in an even layer. Pour the bean mixture over the chips. Sprinkle both cheeses evenly over the top, then sprinkle with the poblanos. Bake the nachos until the cheese has melted completely and the edges of the chips are lightly browned, about 10 minutes.

Dollop the nachos with the guacamole and sour cream, then sprinkle with the jalapeño, lime zest, and lettuce. Serve immediately, with the lime wedges alongside.

2 tablespoons **vegetable oil**

1 **yellow onion**, finely chopped

2 tablespoons **chili powder**

1 tablespoon **ground coriander**

1½ teaspoons **ground cumin**

4 **garlic cloves**, minced

1 (15-ounce) can **pinto or black beans**, undrained

1 (15-ounce) can **diced tomatoes**, preferably fire-roasted

**Kosher salt** and **freshly ground black pepper**

1 (12- to 16-ounce) bag large **corn tortilla chips**

2 cups shredded **Monterey Jack cheese** (8 ounces)

2 cups shredded **Gouda cheese** (8 ounces)

2 **poblano chiles,** seeded and diced (see box, page 165)

1½ cups **guacamole**

1 cup **sour cream**

1 **jalapeño**, finely chopped

1 **lime**, zested and cut into wedges (see box, page 203)

½ small head **iceberg lettuce**, cored and shredded

# EASY CHICKPEA CURRY
## (CHANA MASALA)

1 tablespoon **vegetable oil**

1 large **yellow onion**, finely chopped

2 **garlic cloves**, minced

1 (1-inch) piece fresh **ginger**, peeled and grated

1 **jalapeño**, seeded and thinly sliced (see box, page 165)

2 tablespoons **garam masala**

1 teaspoon **ground turmeric**

1 teaspoon **kosher salt**, plus more to taste

1 teaspoon **freshly ground black pepper**, plus more to taste

2 cups finely chopped **vine-ripe tomatoes**

2 (15-ounce) cans **chickpeas**, drained and rinsed

¼ cup finely chopped **fresh cilantro**

Juice of ½ **lemon**

**Cooked basmati rice** or warmed **naan bread**, for serving

Put down the phone—we've got all the Indian takeout you need right here. The secret to dialing up the supercharged flavors in the dish lies on a superhero team of garlic, ginger, fresh chile, and a dried spice mix called garam masala that contains many spices, including cumin, coriander, cardamom, pepper, cinnamon, and cloves. Prep and arrange as much as you can before you begin, and the dish will come together even quicker. Pro tip for peeling the fresh gingerroot: Scrape the thin skin off with the edge of a spoon.

1 In a large pot or Dutch oven, heat the vegetable oil over medium-high heat. Add the onion and cook, stirring, until soft and beginning to brown, 3 to 5 minutes.

2 Add the garlic, ginger, and jalapeño and cook, stirring, until the garlic is fragrant and the jalapeño is tender, 2 to 4 minutes.

3 Stir in the garam masala, turmeric, salt, and pepper and cook, stirring, for 1 minute more.

4 Add the tomatoes, chickpeas, and ½ cup water and stir to combine, scraping up any brown bits from the bottom and sides of the pot. Bring to a simmer, then cover and cook, stirring once halfway through, until thickened, about 15 minutes.

5 Uncover, reduce the heat to low, and stir in the cilantro and lemon juice. Cook, uncovered, until the cilantro wilts and turns bright green, 1 to 2 minutes. Season with salt and pepper.

6 Spoon the chickpea stew over rice or serve with a side of naan. Serve hot.

# ROASTED RATATOUILLE

You've seen the movie; now make the namesake dish. The genius upgrade here is that the eggplant, zucchini, yellow squash, and tomatoes are toasted on a single sheet pan, meaning you just have to make the tomato sauce and crunchy bread crumb topping while the vegetables get their roast on. Maybe you'll be starring in the sequel.

1 small **eggplant** (about 8 ounces)

2 small **zucchini** (about 6 ounces each)

2 small **yellow squash** (about 6 ounces each)

6 tablespoons **olive oil**

1 pint **cherry tomatoes**, preferably multicolored

**Kosher salt** and **freshly ground black pepper**

1 small **yellow onion**, finely chopped

3 **garlic cloves**, finely chopped

1 (15-ounce) can **crushed tomatoes**

1 cup **panko bread crumbs**

¼ cup lightly packed **fresh basil leaves**, roughly chopped

¼ cup lightly packed **fresh flat-leaf parsley leaves**, roughly chopped

Finely grated zest of ½ **lemon** (see box, page 203)

1 Preheat the oven to 425°F.

2 Arrange the eggplant, zucchini, and squash on a rimmed baking sheet and drizzle with 1 tablespoon of the olive oil. Toss to coat evenly. Roast the vegetables, until lightly charred and tender inside, flipping once halfway through, about 30 minutes total. (The eggplant will be softer inside than the other vegetables.)

3 Remove the baking sheet from the oven and move the roasted vegetables to one side of the baking sheet. Arrange the cherry tomatoes on the other side and drizzle with 1 tablespoon of the olive oil, tossing to coat. Season the roasted vegetables and cherry tomatoes liberally with salt and pepper and return the baking sheet to the oven. Bake until the cherry tomatoes burst and are lightly caramelized, 10 to 12 minutes.

4 Meanwhile, make the tomato sauce: In a large skillet, heat 2 tablespoons of the olive oil over medium-high heat. Add the onion and garlic and cook, stirring, until soft and beginning to brown, 6 to 8 minutes. Add the crushed tomatoes, season with salt and pepper, and cook, stirring, until the sauce is thickened, 8 to 10 minutes. Remove the skillet from the heat and spread the tomato sauce on the bottom of a serving platter. Wipe the skillet clean and set aside.

5 Transfer the roasted zucchini and squash to a cutting board and cut into bite-size pieces, then arrange them over the tomato sauce. Split the eggplant open, scoop out the flesh, keeping it in large pieces, and arrange around the squash and zucchini. Sprinkle the roasted cherry tomatoes over everything.

6 Heat the remaining 2 tablespoons olive oil in the reserved skillet over medium-high heat. Add the bread crumbs and cook, stirring, until golden brown and toasted, about 8 to 10 minutes. Transfer them to a small bowl and stir in the basil, parsley, and lemon zest. Season with salt and pepper.

7 Sprinkle the bread crumb mixture over the vegetables and serve.

# EASY KOREAN RICE BOWL
## (BIBIMBAP)

2 teaspoons **toasted sesame oil**

2 ounces **firm tofu**, drained
and cut into ½-inch-thick cubes
(see box, below)

2 tablespoons **vegetable oil**

½ cup thinly sliced **cremini
mushrooms**

1 small **garlic clove**, minced

2 ounces **baby spinach leaves**
(about 3 cups packed)

1 cup cooked **rice**, preferably
sushi rice

1 large **egg**, fried

3 tablespoons **fresh mung
bean sprouts**

2 **radishes**, grated

3 tablespoons grated **carrot**
(about ½ small carrot)

½ teaspoon **toasted
sesame seeds**

**Gochujang**, for serving

Bibim—what? This Korean word means "mixed rice," but to us the true translation of this dish—with its tofu slices, mushrooms, spinach, bean sprouts, radishes, and carrots—should be something like "the ultimate rice bowl packed full of flavor, colors, textures, and toppings."

1  In a medium skillet, heat the sesame oil over medium-high heat. Add the tofu slices and cook until golden brown on both sides, 1½ to 2 minutes per side. Transfer the tofu to a plate and return the skillet to medium-high heat.

2  Heat 1 tablespoon of the vegetable in the skillet. Add the mushroom caps and cook, stirring, until golden brown, 4 to 5 minutes. Transfer the mushrooms to the plate with the tofu and return the skillet to the heat.

3  If the skillet is dry, add another tablespoon of vegetable oil. Add the garlic and cook, stirring, until fragrant, 10 to 15 seconds. Stir in the spinach and cook until wilted and tender, 1½ to 2 minutes. Remove the skillet from the heat.

4  Mound the rice in the middle of a shallow serving bowl and top with the fried egg. Arrange the tofu slices, mushrooms, spinach, mung bean sprouts, radishes, and carrots in separate piles around the perimeter of the rice. Sprinkle the sesame seeds over the egg.

5  Serve the bibimbap warm with the gochujang alongside.

## 101

### Draining Tofu

Tofu is usually packaged in liquid, which is great for keeping it moist—but it won't sear or absorb flavors well unless you drain it. Place the block of tofu on a double-thick layer of paper towels on a plate, cover with more paper towels and another plate, then weigh down the whole setup with a heavy skillet (a cast-iron one works great for this) or a couple of large cans of tomatoes or whatever you have on hand. Let sit for 15 minutes, drain off the excess water, and repeat the process one more time.

## 101

### Al Dente

Make like the Italians do and cook your pasta al dente. Literally this translates to "to the tooth"; figuratively, it means it still has some bite, or is slightly firm. For regular pasta, cook according to the package directions for al dente. To test, remove a single piece of pasta from the pot and taste it; if it's firm and *just* cooked through, but not raw in the center, you're there. It's particularly useful if you're going to continue cooking your pasta for a minute or two in a sauce—if you start with fully-cooked pasta, then it will be *over*cooked by the time your dish is done.

# WHOLE-WHEAT PASTA WITH CARAMELIZED LEMON, MUSHROOMS & THYME

If you've been skittish about trying whole-wheat pasta, this recipe will convert you. The zinginess of both lemon zest *and* flesh—that's right, you chop up the lemon flesh and cook it until it's gorgeously caramelized—transforms this dish. Covering the zest with plastic while you finish the recipe is a pro move: It prevents it from drying out and keeps that punchy lemon flavor *in* your dish.

1 **lemon**

5 tablespoons **extra-virgin olive oil**

**Kosher salt** and **freshly ground black pepper**

1 pound **cremini mushrooms,** thinly sliced

1 tablespoon **fresh thyme leaves**

2 **garlic cloves,** thinly sliced

1 pound **whole-wheat spaghetti**

¼ teaspoon **crushed red pepper flakes**

Grated **Parmesan cheese,** for serving

1  Using a microplane, grate the zest of the lemon, leaving no patchy parts, into a small bowl (see box, page 203). Cover with plastic wrap. Trim and discard the ends from the zested lemon, then chop the lemon into ½-inch square pieces, discarding any seeds. Set aside.

2  In a large skillet, heat 2 tablespoons of the olive oil over medium-high heat. Add the chopped lemon, season with salt and pepper, and cook, stirring occasionally, until the lemon is caramelized in spots and the white pith is tender, 6 to 8 minutes. Transfer the lemon pieces to a bowl.

3  Wipe out the skillet with a paper towel, add the remaining 3 tablespoons olive oil, and heat it over medium-high heat. Add the mushrooms, thyme, and garlic and cook, stirring occasionally, until the mushrooms are browned and caramelized, 16 to 20 minutes.

4  Meanwhile, bring a large pot of salted water to a boil over high heat. Add the pasta and cook according to package instructions until al dente (usually 7 to 10 minutes; see box, opposite). Drain the pasta in a colander, reserving 1 cup of the pasta cooking water.

5  Add the cooked pasta and ½ cup reserved pasta cooking water, the lemon zest, caramelized lemons, and red pepper flakes to the skillet with the mushrooms. Cook, tossing, until everything is combined and warmed through, adding up to 4 tablespoons more pasta cooking water (one at a time) as needed to keep everything well-moistened.

6  Transfer the pasta to a serving dish and season with salt and pepper. Sprinkle with Parmesan and serve hot.

# FRESH CORN CHOWDER

1 tablespoon **olive oil**

3 **garlic cloves**, minced

1 **yellow onion**, finely chopped

**Kosher salt** and **freshly ground black pepper**

2 teaspoons **sweet paprika**

1 teaspoon **fresh thyme leaves**

1 **bay leaf**

1 **red bell pepper**, finely chopped

1 **russet potato**, peeled and cut into ½-inch cubes

Kernels from 1 ear **corn** (about 1 cup)

8 cups **vegetable stock**

1 cup **almond** or **cashew milk**

Chowder doesn't need to mean "clams"—it can refer to any thick soup, like this one with fresh corn, potatoes, and bell peppers. And since we love finding new uses for old kitchen equipment, lend us your ear: Stand an ear of corn upright, fitting the bottom into the center hole of a Bundt pan. This will help to keep the ear stable as you scrape down with a knife to remove the kernels and capture them at the same time. Boom.

1 In a large pot, heat the olive oil over medium heat. Add the garlic and onion and cook, stirring, until soft and beginning to brown, about 5 minutes. Season with salt and black pepper.

2 Add the paprika, thyme, bay leaf, bell pepper, potato, and corn and cook, stirring, until the bell pepper is slightly softened, about 5 minutes.

3 Pour in the stock and stir to combine. Bring the soup to a simmer, cover the pot with the lid slightly ajar, and cook until the soup reduces slightly and the vegetables are very tender, 20 to 25 minutes.

4 Remove the pot from the heat and stir in the milk. Remove and discard the bay leaf and season the soup with salt and black pepper. Ladle the soup into bowls and serve hot.

# EASY GREEN PEA SOUP

If it's cloudy with a chance of sucky weather, it means it is time to get this soup going on the stove. With a base made from frozen peas and only one potato needed, it's highly likely you already have everything you need in the house. If you are not vegetarian, feel free to swap the vegetable stock for chicken.

2 tablespoons **olive oil**

4 **garlic cloves**, coarsely chopped

1 **yellow onion**, coarsely chopped

1 **carrot**, coarsely chopped

**Kosher salt** and **freshly ground black pepper**

2½ pounds **frozen peas**

1 large **russet potato**, peeled and cut into 1-inch cubes

6 cups **vegetable stock**

8 **thyme sprigs**

2 **bay leaves**

½ cup finely chopped **fresh flat-leaf parsley**

1  In a large pot, heat the olive oil over medium-high heat. Add the garlic, onion, and carrot and cook, stirring, until soft and beginning to brown, 8 to 10 minutes. Season the vegetables with salt and pepper.

2  Stir in the peas and potato, then pour in the broth. Add the thyme and bay leaves and bring the soup to a boil. Reduce the heat to medium to maintain a simmer and cook, stirring occasionally, until the peas and vegetables are very tender, 20 to 25 minutes.

3  Remove the pot from the heat. Discard the thyme and bay leaves. Purée directly in the pot with an immersion blender until very smooth. (Alternatively, working in batches, carefully transfer the soup to a standing blender and purée until smooth.)

4  Ladle the soup into bowls and sprinkle with parsley before serving.

# CHOPPED MEDITERRANEAN SALAD WITH AVOCADO & CHICKPEAS

¼ cup packed **fresh parsley leaves**, coarsely chopped

4 **plum tomatoes**, quartered lengthwise and cut into ½-inch-thick slices

3 ripe **avocados,** cut into ½-inch-thick slices

1 English **cucumber**, halved lengthwise and cut into ½-inch-thick half-moons

½ medium **red onion**, halved and cut into ¼-inch-thick slices

1 (15-ounce) can **chickpeas**, drained and rinsed

⅓ cup fresh **lemon juice** (from 2 or 3 lemons)

3 tablespoons **extra-virgin olive oil**

**Kosher salt** and **freshly ground black pepper**

2 cups **full-fat plain Greek yogurt**

**Pita chips**, for serving

You'll find salads like this all over the Middle East, where crispy, crunchy vegetable- and herb-filled salads are a staple. We like to dice our vegetables into larger pieces for a chunky texture—an added bonus is it makes the chopping go by even faster—and we include avocado because that's *never* a bad idea. Chop chop!

1   In a large salad bowl, combine half the parsley, the tomatoes, avocados, cucumber, red onion, and chickpeas.

2   Drizzle over the lemon juice and olive oil and season with salt and pepper. Toss the salad to evenly coat the vegetables with the dressing.

3   Spread the yogurt over the bottom of a large platter, then pile the salad on top. Sprinkle with the remaining parsley and serve the salad with pita chips on the side.

# BAKED FALAFEL IN PITA SANDWICHES

**SERVES 8**

## FALAFEL

2 cups **dried chickpeas** (13 ounces)

1 cup packed **fresh flat-leaf parsley leaves**

½ cup packed **fresh cilantro leaves**

1 tablespoon **ground coriander**

1 tablespoon **ground cumin**

1 tablespoon **kosher salt**

1½ teaspoons **baking soda**

1 teaspoon **cayenne**

½ teaspoon **ground allspice**

3 large **shallots**, coarsely chopped

2 **garlic cloves**

½ cup **olive oil**

## HUMMUS SAUCE

1 cup prepared **hummus**

1 cup fresh **lemon juice** (from 6 to 8 lemons)

2 tablespoons **sesame seeds**

2 teaspoons **garlic powder**

**Kosher salt** and **freshly ground black pepper**

## TO SERVE

8 **pita breads**, lightly toasted

Shredded **iceberg lettuce**

Chopped **tomatoes**

Chopped **cucumbers**

**Tahini**

**Fresh cilantro leaves**

Goodness gracious, great balls of (baked) falafel. Give yourself a head start with this one—chickpeas cook best when soaked overnight. If you're cutting down on the carbs, skip the pita and layer the falafel on a crunchy bed of shredded lettuce, tomatoes, and cucumbers instead. Store any leftover hummus sauce in an airtight container in the refrigerator for up to one week.

1  Make the falafel: Place the chickpeas in a large bowl and add cold water to cover by at least 3 inches. Cover the bowl with plastic wrap and let stand at room temperature for at least 12 hours or up to overnight.

2  Drain the chickpeas and transfer to a food processor. Add the parsley, cilantro, coriander, cumin, salt, baking soda, cayenne, allspice, shallots, and garlic and process until smooth, about 3 minutes. Transfer the falafel dough to a large bowl and place in the freezer to chill for 30 minutes, until firm.

3  Meanwhile, preheat the oven to 350°F. Line a baking sheet with parchment paper.

4  Using a 1-ounce ice cream scoop or 2 tablespoons, shape the falafel dough into about thirty-six 1½-inch balls. Arrange the balls on the prepared baking sheet and drizzle with the olive oil, turning them gently to coat completely. Bake the falafel until golden brown and crisp on the outside, 20 to 25 minutes. Transfer the baking sheet to a wire rack and let cool completely, about 20 minutes.

5  Meanwhile, make the hummus sauce: Whisk together the hummus, lemon juice, sesame seeds, garlic powder, and ½ cup water in a small bowl until smooth. Season with salt and pepper.

6  To serve, stuff each pita bread with shredded lettuce, tomatoes, and cucumbers, then add 4 to 6 falafel balls. Drizzle each with some of the hummus sauce, followed by some tahini. Top with cilantro leaves and serve hot.

# ITALIAN STEWED PEPPERS (PEPERONATA)

Make like an Italian *nonna* and keep a jar of this flavor-packed mixture, made with a rainbow of bell peppers, handy for a week's worth of cooking. Try pureeing it with veggie stock for an instant soup, spoon it onto rice in a hearty grain bowl, or spread it on toast with cheese for appetizers. Store in an airtight container in the refrigerator for up to 5 days—but with so many uses, we doubt it will last that long.

2 tablespoons **olive oil**

3 large **bell peppers** (mixed red, orange, and yellow; about 2 pounds), seeded and chopped into 1-inch pieces (see box, below)

1 large **yellow onion**, finely chopped

**Kosher salt** and **freshly ground black pepper**

1 tablespoon **tomato paste**

2 **garlic cloves**, minced

3 vine-ripe **tomatoes** (1 pound), cored, peeled, and coarsely chopped (about 3 cups)

2 tablespoons finely chopped **fresh flat-leaf parsley** plus more for serving

1 tablespoon finely chopped **fresh thyme leaves**

1 **bay leaf**

1  In a large skillet, heat the olive oil over medium-high heat. Add the bell peppers and onion and cook, stirring, until soft and beginning to brown, about 15 minutes. Season the vegetables with salt and black pepper.

2  Stir in the tomato paste and garlic and cook, stirring, until soft, about 2 minutes.

3  Reduce the heat to medium, add the tomatoes, parsley, thyme, and bay leaf, and cook, stirring occasionally, until the tomatoes break down and the pepper stew is thick, about 15 minutes more.

4  Remove the skillet from the heat, discard the bay leaf, and season with salt and black pepper. Let cool slightly before serving.

## 101

## Seeding Peppers

When it comes to spicy peppers like jalapeños, serranos, and habaneros, seeds equal spice, so make sure to remove them if you want milder heat. Just slice the pepper lengthwise with a paring knife, then remove the ribs (those raised white strips between the chile flesh and its seeds) and seeds (where the majority of the heat lives). Pro tip: When it comes to fiery peppers, we like to take precaution and wear single-use gloves to prevent the essential oils from adhering to our fingers. This is especially important if you have any plans to touch your eyes, nose, or any other sensitive body parts in the near future, as the oils can linger for hours and burn you, especially if you have sensitive skin.

To seed bell peppers, slice off the bumpy top and bottom of the pepper, stand the pepper up, and make a single cut from top to bottom to open up the pepper into one long strip. Then use your knife to remove the seeds and ribs.

# CLASSIC TOMATO SOUP

**SERVES 6**

Tomato soup is a classic for all the right reasons, and since it comes together in a snap, you don't even need a snow day as an excuse for making it. You'll notice we use canned tomatoes, not fresh, since for most of the year, they're a better bet for intense tomato flavor.

1 In a large pot, heat the butter with the olive oil over medium-high heat. When the butter has melted, add the garlic, carrots, and onion and cook, stirring, until softened, 8 to 10 minutes. Season with salt and pepper.

2 Add the tomato paste and cook, stirring, until lightly caramelized, about 3 minutes. Stir in the flour, cook for 1 minute, then stir in the broth, thyme, bay leaf, and tomatoes. Bring to a boil, then reduce the heat to medium to maintain a simmer and cook, stirring occasionally, until reduced and thickened, about 30 minutes.

3 Remove the pot from the heat. Purée the soup directly in the pot with an immersion blender until smooth. (Alternatively, working in batches, carefully transfer the soup to a standing blender and purée until smooth.) Season with salt and pepper.

4 Ladle the soup into bowls, sprinkle with the parsley, and serve hot.

4 tablespoons (½ stick) **unsalted butter**

2 tablespoons **olive oil**

6 **garlic cloves,** finely chopped

2 **carrots,** finely chopped

1 large **yellow onion,** finely chopped

**Kosher salt** and **freshly ground black pepper**

¼ cup plus 2 tablespoons **tomato paste**

2 tablespoons **all-purpose flour**

6 cups **vegetable broth**

1 tablespoon **fresh thyme leaves**

1 dried **bay leaf**

1 (28-ounce) can **whole peeled tomatoes,** crushed by hand

2 tablespoons finely chopped **fresh flat-leaf parsley**

# THAI-STYLE VEGGIE & NOODLE SALAD WITH PEANUT DRESSING

1 head **broccoli**, stemmed and broken into small florets

½ bunch **asparagus**, trimmed and halved crosswise

1 (8-ounce) package **Thai rice noodles**

½ small **red bell pepper**, finely chopped

½ small **yellow bell pepper**, finely chopped

## DRESSING

¼ cup **smooth peanut butter**

¼ cup **cider vinegar**

¼ cup **low-sodium soy sauce**

1 tablespoon plus 1 teaspoon **toasted sesame oil**

2 teaspoons **honey**

2 teaspoons grated **garlic**

2 teaspoons grated **fresh ginger**

2 teaspoons **toasted sesame seeds**

2 teaspoons **freshly ground black pepper**

## TO SERVE

1 cup **mung bean sprouts**

¼ cup chopped **salted roasted peanuts**

¼ cup coarsely chopped **fresh cilantro**

2 **scallions**, thinly sliced

Noodles, veggies, and peanutty dressing—you can't go wrong with this crowd-pleasing salad that has a wow-factor combination of flavors, textures, and colors. To trim the asparagus, bend each spear about an inch from the bottom until it snaps, then discard the woody, inedible part. Dropping broccoli in boiling water for a few minutes, then shocking them in ice, keeps them green and crispy. If you're pressed for time, broccoli florets can often be purchased in a bag.

1 Bring a large saucepan of water to a boil over high heat. Fill a large bowl with ice and water and set it nearby.

2 Add the broccoli florets to the boiling water and cook until bright green and easily pierced with the tip of a paring knife, about 2 minutes. Using a slotted spoon, transfer the broccoli to the ice water to stop the cooking. Scoop out the broccoli and dry on paper towels.

3 Add the asparagus to the boiling water and cook for 1½ minutes. Using tongs, transfer the asparagus to the ice water to stop the cooking, then remove and cut into 1-inch pieces.

4 Meanwhile, cook the noodles according to the package instructions, drain, and transfer to a large bowl. Add the broccoli, asparagus, and bell peppers and toss together.

5 Make the dressing: Whisk together the peanut butter, vinegar, soy sauce, sesame oil, honey, garlic, ginger, sesame seeds, and black pepper in a medium bowl until smooth.

6 Pour the dressing over the noodles and vegetables and toss to combine. Sprinkle the bean sprouts, peanuts, cilantro, and scallions over the top and serve immediately.

# LAYERED POTATO PANCAKE
## (POMMES ANNA)

This recipe is a testament to the heights a humble potato can reach with nothing more than a little butter, salt, and pepper. Crispy, crunchy, creamy, wowie, zowie. Serve with a salad or roasted vegetables on the side.

1 pound **Yukon Gold potatoes** (about 4), peeled

6 tablespoons (¾ stick) **unsalted butter**, melted

**Kosher salt** and **freshly ground black pepper**

**Flaky sea salt**

1 Preheat the oven to 400°F.

2 Using a mandoline or sharp knife, cut the potatoes crosswise into ¹⁄₁₆-inch-thick slices. Place the potato slices in a large bowl, add 3 tablespoons of the melted butter, and gently toss to coat.

3 Heat a large ovenproof nonstick skillet over the lowest heat for 2 minutes. Add just enough melted butter to coat the bottom **A** . Starting from the center **B** and working your way out **C** , arrange the potato slices around the bottom of the pan in concentric rings, overlapping them by ½ inch, to cover the bottom of the pan completely **D** . Drizzle the potatoes with some of the remaining melted butter and season with salt and pepper.

4 Continue arranging and overlapping the potato slices to create more layers, drizzling over more butter and seasoning with salt and pepper between each, until all the potatoes are in the skillet. Drizzle any remaining butter on top **E** .

5 Increase the heat to medium and cook, undisturbed, until the bottom of the potato pancake is golden brown, about 15 minutes.

6 Cover the skillet and transfer to the oven. Bake for 20 minutes.

7 Immediately and carefully uncover the skillet. Place a large plate over the skillet and, holding the skillet and the plate together, flip the skillet to invert the potato pancake onto the plate. Slide the potato pancake back into the skillet so the bottom is now on top **F** . Return the skillet to the oven and bake, uncovered, until the potato pancake is golden brown on the bottom and tender in the center, about 10 minutes.

8 Transfer the potato pancake to a cutting board and let cool slightly. Cut it into large wedges, sprinkle with sea salt, and serve warm.

recipe continues

TASTY ULTIMATE

# OLIVE & HERB FRENCH-STYLE FLATBREAD (FOUGASSE)

⅔ cup lukewarm **water** (105°F to 110°F)

1 teaspoon **active dry yeast**

½ teaspoon **sugar**

1 tablespoon **extra-virgin olive oil**, plus more for greasing and brushing

1 teaspoon **kosher salt**

2¼ cups **all-purpose flour**, plus more for dusting (see box, page 179)

Fine **cornmeal**, for dusting

½ cup finely chopped mixed **Mediterranean olives**

1 tablespoon finely chopped **fresh flat-leaf parsley**

1 tablespoon **fresh thyme leaves**

2 teaspoons finely chopped **fresh rosemary**

**Flaky sea salt** and **coarsely ground black pepper**

Show up at any party with this herb- and olive-studded bread and you'll be immediately crowned a VIFP (that is a Very Important Flatbread Person).

1   Whisk together the water, yeast, and sugar in a large bowl and let stand until foamy, about 10 minutes (see box, opposite). Stir in the olive oil and salt, then add the flour and stir until a dough forms.

2   Using a rubber spatula, scrape the dough out onto a lightly floured surface. Knead it until it becomes smooth and elastic, about 6 minutes (see box, page 250). Form the dough into a ball. Grease a large bowl with olive oil. Place the dough in the bowl and turn to coat in the oil. Cover the bowl with a kitchen towel or plastic wrap and let the dough rise in a warm, draft-free area until doubled in size, about 1 hour.

3   Preheat oven to 450°F. Line two baking sheets with parchment paper.

4   Turn the dough out onto a lightly floured surface. Cut the dough in half  **A**  and then flatten and stretch each piece into a roughly 12-inch-long by 8-inch-wide triangle. Transfer each triangle to a prepared baking sheet.

5   Using a paring knife, cut a slit lengthwise down the center of each triangle, leaving 1 inch of the dough attached at both ends  **B** . Cut 3 smaller (2- to 3-inch) slashes on each side of the long slash  **C** , angling them down toward the shorter side of the triangle; the slashes should resemble the veins of a leaf. Gently spread the slashes apart with your fingers. Cover each baking sheet with a damp kitchen towel or plastic wrap and let stand until the dough is slightly puffed, about 30 minutes.

6   Uncover the baking sheets. Gently brush the dough with more olive oil and sprinkle evenly with the olives, parsley, thyme, rosemary, sea salt, and pepper.

7   Bake the flatbreads, one at a time, until golden brown all over and crisp on the bottom, about 20 minutes. Transfer the baking sheet to a wire rack and let cool for at least 10 minutes before serving. The flatbreads will keep, wrapped in plastic wrap, at room temperature for up to 2 days.

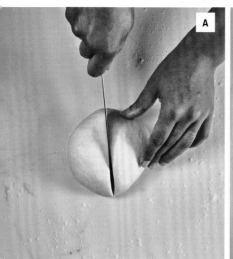

# Working with Yeast

Yeast—those tiny specks of live culture that give rise to breads and some pastries—come in two dry formulas, active dry and instant. Active dry yeast needs to be "activated" (hence the name), which you do by dissolving the granules in warm liquid along with a little sugar or honey. You'll know your active dry yeast is alive if, after 5 to 10 minutes, small bubbles start to form on the surface of the mixture. Instant yeast is ready to go as-is and can be added directly to the other dry ingredients in your recipe, without dissolving in liquid first. Regardless of which kind you use, yeast should be stored in a cool, dry, dark place (think your fridge or freezer) until the "best before" date on the packaging

# DESSERTS

# FUDGY BROWNIES

1 cup (2 sticks) **unsalted butter**, plus more for greasing

8 ounces **unsweetened chocolate**, coarsely chopped (1¼ cups)

1 cup packed **light brown sugar**

½ cup **granulated sugar**

2 teaspoons **vanilla extract**

1 teaspoon **kosher salt**

3 large **eggs**

12 ounces **semisweet chocolate chips** (2 cups)

¾ cup **all-purpose flour** (see box, page 179)

It's a tale as old as time: the showdown between the two undisputed champions of the brownie universe. In one corner, cakey brownies with their homey, crumby fluffiness achieved with the addition of baking powder. In the other corner: fudgy brownies, with their enviable moist texture and dense, squishy centers. These are so rich you'll need to cut them smaller than usual. Whichever brownie you try, use the best-quality chocolate you can find—it's worth it. We declare a tie, but try them both and decide for yourself.

1 Preheat the oven to 350°F. Grease a 9 by 13-inch baking dish with butter and line the bottom and sides with parchment paper.

2 In a small saucepan, combine the chocolate and butter over medium heat, stirring occasionally, until melted, combined, and smooth. Remove the pan from the heat and let cool for 5 minutes.

3 Whisk together the brown sugar, granulated sugar, vanilla, salt, and eggs in a large bowl until smooth and slightly foamy, at least 1 minute. Add the melted chocolate mixture and whisk until smooth.

4 Combine the chocolate chips and flour in a medium bowl and toss to coat evenly. Add to the batter and stir to combine. Transfer the batter to the prepared pan and smooth the top with a spatula. Bake until a toothpick inserted halfway between the center and one side of the pan comes out clean, 30 to 35 minutes (see box, page 187).

5 Transfer the pan to a wire rack and let the brownies cool slightly. Cut into 24 squares before serving.

# CAKEY BROWNIES

MAKES **16** BROWNIES

Preheat the oven to 350°F. Grease a 9 by 13-inch baking dish with butter and line the bottom and sides with parchment paper.

Whisk together the flour, cocoa powder, baking powder, and salt in a large bowl until smooth. Stir in the chocolate chips.

Combine the butter, sugar, and vanilla in a large bowl. Using a handheld mixer, beat on medium speed until pale and fluffy, about 2 minutes (see box, page 188). Add the eggs one at a time, being sure each is incorporated before adding the next. Beat in the milk. Add the flour mixture and beat on low speed until just combined.

Transfer the batter to the prepared pan and smooth the top with a spatula. Bake until a toothpick inserted into the center comes out clean, about 35 minutes (see box, page 187).

Transfer the pan to a wire rack and let the brownies cool slightly. Cut the brownie block into 16 squares before serving.

½ cup (1 stick) **unsalted butter**, plus more for greasing

1½ cups **all-purpose flour** (see box, page 179)

½ cup **unsweetened cocoa powder**

½ teaspoon **baking powder**

1 teaspoon **kosher salt**

12 ounces **bittersweet chocolate chips** (2 cups)

1½ cups **sugar**

1 teaspoon **vanilla extract**

5 large **eggs**

½ cup **whole milk**

# HOMEMADE CRÈME BRÛLÉE

4 cups **heavy cream**

2 teaspoons **vanilla extract**

½ cup plus 6 tablespoons **sugar**

6 large **egg yolks,**
(see box, page 149)

One of the dessert world's most outstanding contributions is actually the perfect make-ahead recipe. The custard needs to be chilled for four hours before torching, or let it chill for up to three days (just make sure to keep it covered tightly with plastic wrap so it doesn't absorb other fridge flavors). The name literally translates to "burnt cream," but you can just call it delicious.

1   In a small saucepan, warm the cream and vanilla over medium-high heat until the cream is just beginning to simmer at the edges—do not let it boil.

2   Meanwhile, whisk together ½ cup of the sugar and the egg yolks in a medium bowl until smooth.

3   While whisking, slowly pour a ladleful of the hot cream into the egg mixture to temper the eggs. Whisk until smooth and incorporated. Continue slowly whisking in the hot cream in this manner until all the cream has been added.

4   Arrange six 6- to 8-ounce ramekins in a large roasting pan. Divide the egg mixture evenly among the ramekins. Set the roasting pan on the oven rack and carefully pour enough hot water into the pan so it comes halfway up the sides of the ramekins. Bake until the custards are set but still jiggle slightly in the center when tapped, 45 to 60 minutes.

5   Carefully remove the roasting pan from the oven and transfer the ramekins to a wire rack. Let cool to room temperature. Cover each ramekin with plastic wrap and refrigerate for at least 4 hours and up to 3 days.

6   When ready to serve, remove the custards from the refrigerator and evenly sprinkle 1 tablespoon of the remaining sugar over the top of each. Using a kitchen torch, melt the sugar until it turns very dark amber and caramelizes into a crust on top of the custards. (If you don't have a torch, preheat the broiler, set the ramekins on a baking sheet, and broil until the sugar melts and caramelizes onto the custards.)

7   Let stand for 1 minute to let the sugar crust harden before serving.

# AQUARIUM COOKIES

MAKES
**10**
COOKIES

These are almost too awesome to eat—emphasis on *almost*. If you want to wow kids and big kids of all ages (ahem, adults), this is the recipe for you. Melting hard candies in the middle of the cookies creates colorful, edible window panes sandwiching sprinkles of fun.

½ cup (1 stick) **unsalted butter,**
at room temperature

½ cup **sugar**

1 large **egg**

2 cups **all-purpose flour,** plus
more for dusting (see box, below)

¼ teaspoon **kosher salt**

20 pieces **hard candy,** such as
Jolly Ranchers

**Multicolored sprinkles**

¼ cup **white chocolate chips**

1   Combine the butter and sugar in a large bowl and mix together with a wooden spoon until smooth. Add the egg and stir well to combine. Sift in the flour and salt and stir to incorporate (see box, page 219). Cover the bowl with plastic wrap and refrigerate for 30 minutes.

2   Preheat oven to 350°F. Line two baking sheets with parchment paper.

3   Turn the dough out onto a lightly floured surface and roll it out to ¼-inch thickness. Using a 3-inch round cookie cutter, cut out rounds of dough **A** . Using a 2-inch round cookie cutter, cut out the center of each cookie **B** . Combine the cookie dough scraps and centers, reroll, and continue cutting out more rounds until you have 20 rings of dough total.

4   Place the rings on the prepared baking sheets. Bake one sheet at a time until lightly browned on the bottom and set, about 10 minutes. Remove the baking sheet from the oven and place 1 hard candy in the center of each cookie ring **C** . Return the pan to the oven and bake until the hard candy melts and spreads out to fill the center of the cookie, 3 to 5 minutes **D** . If there are any gaps between the candy and the cookie ring, gently tilt the baking sheet to allow the melted candy to fill the space. Transfer the baking sheet to a wire rack and let cool until the candy centers harden. Repeat with the remaining cookies and candies.

5   Once they have hardened, pour some sprinkles onto the centers of 10 of the cookies. Flip the remaining 10 cookies bottom-side up.

6   Put the white chocolate chips in a small microwave-safe bowl and microwave in 30-second intervals, stirring between each, until melted and smooth. Spoon a thin line of melted white chocolate around the 10 upside-down cookies **E** , then immediately sandwich them on top of the sprinkle-garnished cookies, trapping the sprinkles inside.

7   Transfer the cookies to the refrigerator for about 15 minutes. Let the cookies come to room temperature before serving.

*recipe continues*

## 101 ▸ Measuring Flour

In the U.S., recipes generally call for dry ingredient measurements in cups (versus weight, as in Europe and most of the rest of the world), but depending on how you get your flour into the cup (scooping, packing, dipping, etc.), your results may be off. To get an accurate measurement, use the "spoon and level" or "scoop and sweep" method: Using a tablespoon, scoop your flour into your measuring cup itself, mounding it until it begins to spill over the side, then level off the excess with the end of the spoon or the flat back of a knife, making sure not to tap or knock the cup, which will cause the flour to settle and pack more tightly. For the most accurate measurement, you'll want to use a scale to get an exact number of grams, but the recipes in this book don't require such precision. *Phew!*

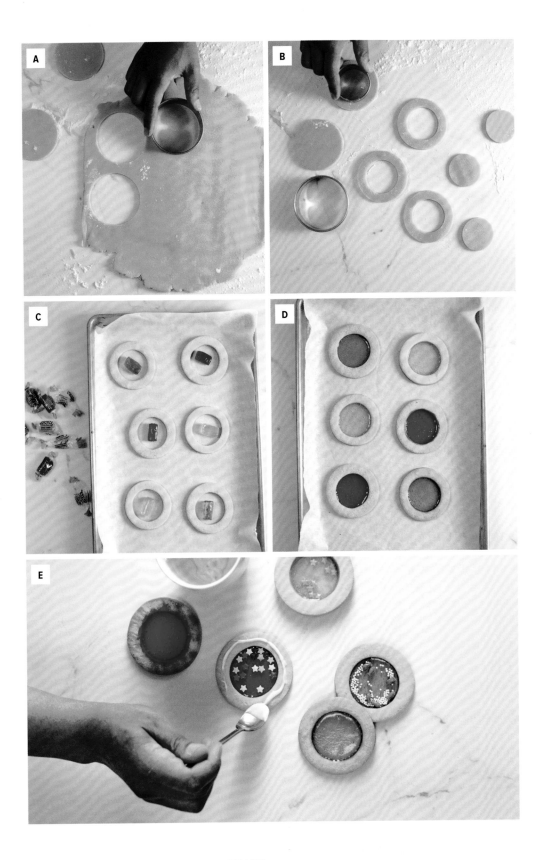

TASTY ULTIMATE

# SLOW COOKER APPLE SPICE CAKE

2 (20-ounce) cans **apple pie filling**

1 (15.25-ounce) box **spice cake mix**

1 cup (2 sticks) **unsalted butter**

**Vanilla ice cream**, for serving

Sometimes, the easiest recipes are the ones you'll make the most. But not because they're dead simple—more like because they darned delicious. You are just three ingredients away from a dreamy dessert that has all the flavors of a classic American Pie—no special technique. Vanilla ice cream is just the icing on this cake—try to get it on top of the cake while it's still warm!

1   Pour the apple pie filling into a 6-quart slow cooker and spread it out evenly. Sprinkle the cake mix evenly over the pie filling, then top with the whole sticks of butter, spaced equally apart. Cover and cook on High for 2 to 2½ hours, until the filling is bubbling and the butter and cake mix have formed a crumble layer on top.

2   Uncover and spoon into bowls. Serve hot, topped with a scoop of vanilla ice cream.

# THE ULTIMATE CHOCOLATE CAKE

SERVES
**12**

Three layers of otherworldly chocolate heaven make this the cake of special-occasion dreams. This is the one to break out whenever a showstopper dessert is needed. When the crowning beauty is complete, you can have fun quizzing your eating partners about the surprise secret ingredients (stout beer, espresso powder, and mayonnaise—who knew? *You* did).

1   Preheat the oven to 325°F. Grease three 8-inch round cake pans with butter **A** and line the bottoms with parchment paper cut to fit **B** .

2   Sift together the flour, cocoa powder, baking soda, salt, and baking powder into a large bowl (see box, page 219).

3   In a large liquid measuring cup, whisk together the stout, vanilla, and espresso powder.

4   Combine the butter and granulated sugar in a large bowl. Using a handheld mixer, beat on medium speed until pale and fluffy, about 5 minutes, scraping down the sides of the bowl with a spatula as needed (see box, page 188). With the mixer running on medium speed, add the eggs one at a time, making sure each is incorporated before adding the next. Add the mayonnaise and beat until the mixture is smooth and creamy.

5   With the mixer on low speed, alternate adding the flour mixture and the stout mixture in three additions, starting with the flour mixture, and beat until the batter just comes together. Using a rubber spatula, fold in the dark chocolate.

6   Divide the batter evenly among the prepared cake pans (about 2½ cups each) and smooth the tops with a spatula. Bake the cakes until a toothpick inserted into the center of each comes out clean, about 35 minutes (see box, page 187). Place the cake pans on a wire rack and let cool 10 to 15 minutes.

7   Working with one cake at a time, run a butter knife between the edges of the cake and the pan to loosen, then place a large plate over the pan and, holding the pan and plate together, invert them to release the cake from the pan. Repeat with the remaining cakes.

*recipe continues*

## CAKE

1 cup (2 sticks) **unsalted butter**, at room temperature, plus more for greasing

1½ cups **all-purpose flour** (see box, page 179)

1 cup **Dutch-processed cocoa powder**

1½ teaspoons **baking soda**

1 teaspoon **kosher salt**

½ teaspoon **baking powder**

1½ cups **stout beer**

1 tablespoon **vanilla extract**

1 tablespoon **instant espresso powder**

1½ cups **granulated sugar**

3 large **eggs**

½ cup **mayonnaise**

4 ounces **dark chocolate**, finely chopped

## BUTTERCREAM

1½ cups (3 sticks) **unsalted butter**, at room temperature

1 tablespoon **vanilla extract**

5 cups **confectioners' sugar**, sifted

½ cup **Dutch-processed cocoa powder**

¼ cup **whole milk**

Fresh **strawberries** and **raspberries**, for garnish (optional)

8   Remove the parchment paper from the bottoms of the cakes and slide the cakes back onto the rack to cool completely.

9   Meanwhile, make the buttercream: Combine the butter and vanilla in a large bowl and, using a handheld mixer, beat on medium speed until evenly incorporated.

10  With the mixer on low speed, gradually add spoonfuls of the confectioners' sugar and cocoa powder until both have been incorporated and the mixture is smooth. Add the milk and beat on medium speed until all the ingredients are incorporated and the buttercream is fluffy.

11  Place one cake layer on a parchment-lined cake stand and spread about ¾ cup of the buttercream on top. Place a second cake layer on the first and spread another ¾ cup of the buttercream over the top. Add the third cake layer, then spread the remaining frosting evenly over the top and sides of the cake **C** . Remove the parchment paper **D** .

12  Top the cake with fresh strawberries and raspberries **E** , if you like, then slice and serve.

## 101

## Frosting a Layer Cake

We know you want to get the cake into your mouth ASAP, but first we frost. To start, make sure your cake is completely cool—if it's still warm, your frosting will melt, and that's not the look we're going for here.

1   Lay down strips of parchment paper to keep your cake stand, plate, or platter clean as you work. (You can slide them out from underneath the cake afterward and—voilà!—your cake pan is spotless and ready for presentation.)

2   Start with a big blob of frosting centered on top of the cake stack, then using a small spatula (we love an offset spatula for this job because its offset blade helps keep your movements precise and steady for spreading) or a table knife, press down lightly on the icing to move it evenly out to the edges of the cake.

3   Repeat with more frosting on the top and the sides, working gently but firmly so you get consistent results. If this seems too daunting, you can also "crumb coat" your cake by applying a thin layer of frosting with this method first, without worrying about staying perfectly neat, then refrigerating the cake for 20 minutes to set it.

4   Afterward, apply the rest of the icing over the cake to make a final, thicker layer. The crumb coat ensures that no crumbs appear in the icing, which would make your cake look messy. Pro tip: Use more frosting than you think you need, it's much easier to take frosting off than it is to spread a too-thin layer.

5   When you are ready to serve, slide out the parchment paper to reveal a clean surface.

6   Run your knife under hot water, wipe it dry, then use it to get perfectly clean, straight slices.

7   Make sure to wipe the crumbs off in between each cut to keep each slice neat.

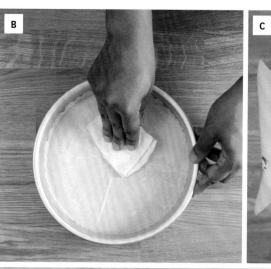

# COOKIES & CREAM CHEESECAKE BUNDT

Underneath this glossy glazed chocolate Bundt cake lies a luscious layer of cream cheese and cookie goodness, an effect that's shockingly easy to create courtesy of an ice cream scoop and chocolate sandwich cookies. It's all your cookies-and-cream fantasies wrapped up in one beautiful package.

½ cup **vegetable oil**, plus more for greasing

2 (8-ounce) packages **cream cheese**, at room temperature

½ cup **confectioners' sugar**

1 teaspoon **vanilla extract**

1 (15.25-ounce) box **chocolate cake mix**

3 large **eggs**

10 **chocolate sandwich cookies**, such as Oreos

1 pound **high-quality chocolate**, at least 60% cocoa, finely chopped

2 cups **heavy cream**

1  Preheat oven to 350°F. Grease a 10-cup Bundt pan with vegetable oil.

2  Using a rubber spatula, stir together the cream cheese, confectioners' sugar, and vanilla in a large bowl until smooth.

3  Prepare the chocolate cake batter according to the package instructions, using 1¼ cups water, the vegetable oil, and the eggs. Pour half the cake batter into the prepared pan, smoothing the top with a spatula.

4  Using a 2-ounce ice cream scoop, dollop the cream cheese mixture evenly onto the cake batter, making sure it does not touch the sides of the pan. Flatten the tops of the cream cheese dollops slightly by placing a chocolate sandwich cookie on top of each dollop.

5  Pour the rest of the chocolate cake batter into the pan, covering the cookies and cream cheese dollops, and smooth the top with a spatula. Bake until the cake rises and a toothpick inserted into the center comes out clean, about 45 minutes (see box, right). Transfer the cake to a wire rack set over a baking sheet and let cool for 20 minutes. Invert the pan onto the rack, letting the cake fall out onto the rack, and let cool completely (see box, page 290).

6  Meanwhile, make the glaze: Place the chocolate and the cream in a medium microwave-safe bowl and microwave in 30-second intervals, stirring between each, until the glaze is smooth and glossy.

7  Pour the glaze evenly over the cake, letting the excess drip off. Let the cake stand until the glaze has set, at least 30 minutes.

8  Transfer the cake to a serving plate. Slice and serve.

## Testing for Doneness

Cakes and brownies can sometimes look baked through when they may in fact still have a soft spot or two within. Any thin skewer can be used as a cake tester (think thin wooden kebab skewers, a toothpick, or even a fork or knife). If you insert it into the center of the cake, it should come out clean or with just a few dry crumbs attached; what you don't want is visible wet streaks of batter.

Nonstick cooking spray

2 cups **granulated sugar**

2 cups (4 sticks) **unsalted butter**

6 large **eggs**

1 **vanilla bean**, split lengthwise
and seeds scraped

3½ cups **all-purpose flour**
(see box, page 179)

1 teaspoon **kosher salt**

1 cup **confectioners' sugar**, sifted

2 tablespoons **whole milk**

## 101

## Creaming

You'll notice that many recipes call
for "creaming" butter and sugar
together with an electric mixer.
Doing so completely is an essential
step to a cake with structure; it
creates air pockets that help layers
maintain height and fluffy crumbs
once baked. From time to time,
scrape down the edges of the bowl
and keep beating until the butter
and sugar are cohesive, with barely
any sugar granules visible. The
mixture will be pale yellow and
fluffy. If you've forgotten to leave
time to bring your butter to room
temperature on the counter, no
biggie! Just microwave a glass bowl,
then turn it over on top of the butter.
The heat will slowly bring up the
temperature of the butter.

# CLASSIC POUND CAKE

Why *is* this classic dessert called a pound cake?
The amount of sugar, butter, eggs, and flour
needed equal a pound each. Make sure to properly
cream the butter and sugar together for
a good long time—this creates the sweet
snack's moist, crumbly texture.

1  Preheat the oven to 350°F. Grease a 10-cup Bundt pan with nonstick
cooking spray.

2  Combine the granulated sugar and butter in a large bowl. Using a
handheld mixer, beat on medium-high speed until very pale and fluffy,
at least 5 minutes, scraping down the sides of the bowl with a spatula
as needed (see box, left). With the mixer on medium speed, add the
eggs one at a time, making sure each is fully incorporated before
adding the next. Beat in the vanilla bean seeds.

3  Sift the flour and salt into the batter (see box, page 219) and beat on
low speed until just combined.

4  Transfer the batter to the prepared pan and smooth the top with a
spatula. Bake until the cake is golden brown on top and a toothpick
inserted into the center comes out clean, 1 hour to 1 hour 10 minutes
(see box, page 187). Transfer the cake pan to a wire rack set over a
baking sheet and let cool for 20 minutes. Invert the pan onto the rack,
letting the cake fall out, and let cool completely (see box, page 290).

5  Meanwhile, make the glaze: Whisk together the confectioners' sugar
and milk in a medium bowl until smooth.

6  Drizzle the glaze evenly over the cake, letting it drip into the grooves
and the excess drip off. Let the cake stand until the glaze has set, at
least 30 minutes.

7  Transfer the cake to a serving plate. Slice and serve.

# MISMATCHED LINZER COOKIES

MAKES
**12**
COOKIES

Who says you have to conform to be cool? These jam-filled cookies march to their own beat, and the hazelnut sugar really makes them special. Feel free to try other jam flavors here; apricot, strawberry, and orange marmalade are all swell.

½ cup **whole hazelnuts**

1 cup **granulated sugar**

1½ cups (3 sticks) **unsalted butter**, at room temperature

2 teaspoons **vanilla extract**

1 large **egg**

3 cups **all-purpose flour**, plus more for dusting (see box, page 179)

1 teaspoon **kosher salt**

**Confectioners' sugar**, for dusting

½ cup **raspberry jam**

1  Preheat the oven to 325°F.

2  Spread the hazelnuts over a rimmed baking sheet and bake until fragrant and toasted, about 8 minutes. Let cool completely, about 20 minutes.

3  Transfer the hazelnuts to a food processor, add the granulated sugar, and process until finely ground and mixed, about 30 seconds.

4  Transfer the hazelnut sugar to a large bowl. Add the butter and, using a handheld mixer, beat on medium speed until fluffy, about 2 minutes. Add the vanilla and egg and beat until smooth. Add the flour and salt and beat on low speed until just combined.

5  Transfer the dough to a floured surface, form it into a disc, and wrap it in plastic. Refrigerate the dough for at least 1 hour and up to 2 days.

6  Line two baking sheets with parchment paper. On a lightly floured surface, roll out the chilled dough disc to ¼-inch thickness. Using three 3-inch cookie cutters of different shapes, cut out an equal number of cookies of each shape and place them on the prepared baking sheets, spaced 2 inches apart. Reroll the scraps three times to get 24 cookies total. Refrigerate the cookies on the baking sheets for 30 minutes.

7  Using a 1-inch cookie cutter with a different shape from the one you used for the cookie itself, stamp out the centers of half the cookies; discard the centers (or bake them separately to enjoy later).

8  Bake the cookies until lightly browned at the edges, 12 to 14 minutes. Let the cookies cool on the baking sheets for 1 minute, then transfer to a wire rack and let cool, about 20 minutes.

9  Dust the centerless cookies generously with confectioners' sugar and set aside. Place about 2 teaspoons of the jam in the center of each whole cookie, spreading it to within ¼ inch of the edge. Top each whole cookie with a matching-shaped centerless cookie.

# MINI S'MORES ÉCLAIRS

This happy mashup showcases the petite cuteness of an éclair and the over-the-top decadence of a s'more. These should be served immediately after filling to keep the marshmallow center at its fluffy best. No need to purchase a box of crumbs—just give whole graham crackers a whirl in your food processor or seal them in a resealable plastic bag and whack away with a rolling pin (or any other solid object you have around the house). The éclair shells can be made the day before assembly and stored at room temperature in an airtight container.

½ cup (1 stick) **unsalted butter**, cubed

1 teaspoon **kosher salt**

1 cup **graham cracker crumbs** (from about 9 graham crackers), plus more for garnish

¾ cup **all-purpose flour** (see box, page 179)

5 large **eggs**

1 (14-ounce) jar **marshmallow creme**, such as Fluff

4 ounces **dark chocolate**, finely chopped

½ cup **heavy cream**

**Mini marshmallows**, for garnish

1  Preheat the oven to 425°F. Line two baking sheets with parchment paper.

2  In a medium saucepan, combine the butter, salt, and 1 cup water. Heat over medium heat to melt the butter and bring the mixture to a boil. Reduce the heat to medium-low and add the graham cracker crumbs and flour. Using a wooden spoon, mix thoroughly to combine. Cook, stirring, until the mixture forms a dough and easily pulls away from the sides of the pan, about 2 minutes.

3  Remove the pan from the heat and let the dough cool for 5 minutes.

4  One at a time, stir 4 of the eggs in the cooled dough, fully incorporating each before adding the next. (The eggs will initially be difficult to incorporate into the dough, but continue stirring vigorously and they will eventually blend in to form a smooth shiny dough.)

5  Transfer the dough to a piping bag fitted with a ½-inch round tip and pipe the batter into 2- to 3-inch-long logs on the prepared baking sheets (you should have about 32 logs; use additional baking sheets if needed). Using a wet fingertip, lightly smooth out any peaks or tails on the dough logs.

6  Beat the remaining egg with 1 tablespoon water to make an egg wash. Brush the dough with the egg wash.

7  Bake for 10 minutes, then, without opening the oven, reduce the oven temperature to 350°F and continue baking until the éclair shells are puffed and golden brown on the bottom, about 15 minutes more.

recipe continues

8  Remove the éclair shells from the oven and let cool for 1 minute. Using the tip of a knife, cut a small X into the bottom of each to allow steam to escape **A** . Set the éclair shells bottom-side up on a wire rack to cool completely, about 1 hour.

9  Fill a clean piping bag fitted with a ¼-inch round tip with the marshmallow creme and pipe the marshmallow creme into the cooled éclair shells (see box, below) **B** .

10  Put the chocolate in a small microwave-safe bowl. Pour the heavy cream into a separate small microwave-safe bowl and microwave until just beginning to simmer, 1 to 2 minutes. Immediately pour the hot cream over the chocolate. Let stand for 1 minute, then stir until the chocolate has melted and the mixture is smooth. (If, after stirring for a minute or so, the chocolate has not fully melted or the mixture isn't smooth, microwave the mixture in 10-second increments, stirring after each, until smooth.)

11  Dip the top side of each filled éclair shell in the melted chocolate **C** , letting any excess drip off **D** . Place the dipped éclairs back on the rack, chocolate-side up **E** , and sprinkle with graham cracker crumbs. While the chocolate is still wet, top each with 3 mini marshmallows, arranging them in a cluster.

12  If you have a kitchen torch, torch the mini marshmallows until lightly charred **F** . Serve the éclairs immediately.

## 101

# Piping

To make uniform lines of anything—whether it's the setup for eclairs or the icing on the top of a cake, piping is the way to go. When preparing a piping bag for the task at hand, use your hands to force the batter, dough, or frosting all the way down to the bottom of the corner (twist the bag from the top to easily do this) to get rid of any air bubbles. You might even want to stand the bag up in a glass to make it easier to fill. You can buy pastry bags and tips in various sizes at any crafts or kitchen store, but if you can't find one, no problem; just break out a heavy-duty resealable plastic bag, fill it, then cut off one corner. Voilà, now you can pipe!

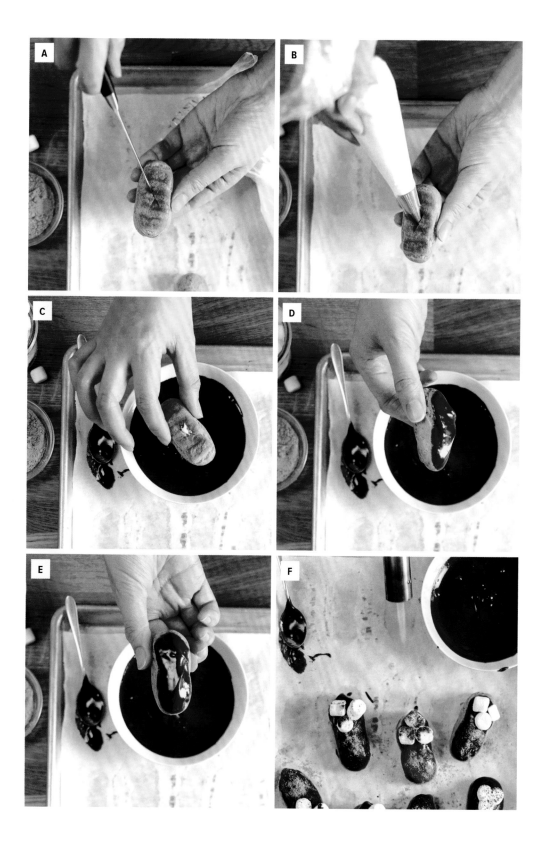

# TRIPLE-LEMON POPPY SQUARES

Easy, peasy, lemon squeezy. Lemon zest, lemon juice, and lemon liqueur join forces to take this dessert to sweet and tangy heights. If you are skittish around pastry crusts, this is a great recipe to start with because no rolling or shaping is necessary—you just press your way to success.

## CRUST

Nonstick cooking spray

1 cup (2 sticks) **unsalted butter**, at room temperature

½ cup **granulated sugar**

2 tablespoons **poppy seeds**

Finely grated zest of 1 **lemon** (see box, page 203)

2 cups **all-purpose flour** (see box, page 179)

½ teaspoon **kosher salt**

## FILLING

2 cups **granulated sugar**

¾ cup **all-purpose flour**

½ teaspoon **kosher salt**

6 large **eggs**

Finely grated zest of 3 **lemons**

¾ cup fresh **lemon juice** (from 4 to 6 lemons)

2 tablespoons **limoncello liqueur**

**Confectioners' sugar**, for dusting

1 Make the crust: Preheat the oven to 350°F. Coat a 9 by 13-inch metal baking pan with cooking spray, line the bottom and sides with foil, then coat the foil with cooking spray as well.

2 Combine the butter, granulated sugar, poppy seeds, lemon zest, and salt in a large bowl. Using a handheld mixer, beat on medium speed until pale and fluffy, about 2 minutes.

3 Add the flour and beat on low speed until the dough just comes together. Transfer the dough to the prepared pan and press it into an even layer on the bottom. Freeze the dough for 20 minutes.

4 Bake the chilled dough until light brown at the edges, 20 to 25 minutes. Transfer the pan to a wire rack and let the crust cool slightly. Leave the oven on.

5 Meanwhile, make the filling: Whisk together the granulated sugar, flour, and salt in a large bowl until evenly combined. Whisk in the eggs until smooth. Stir in the lemon zest, lemon juice, and limoncello.

6 Pour the filling over the cooled crust and bake until the filling is set and the edges are lightly browned, 30 to 35 minutes. Transfer the pan to a wire rack and let cool completely, about 1 hour.

7 Cut into 24 bars and dust the tops heavily with confectioners' sugar before serving.

# Preparing Cake Pans

You wouldn't build a house without a good foundation; treat your cake with the same respect! Rub down every bit of the cake pan with cooking spray or butter (yep, bottom *and* sides will make the cake brown nicely). Greasing and flouring the pan, then lining with parchment paper, allows for an even quicker release (plus easy pan cleanup). To create a perfect circle of parchment to fit your tin, take your parchment and fold it in half, and then in half again to create something resembling a square. Then, channel your paper airplane skills: Identify the point where all the folds meet and fold the parchment in half on a diagonal, then again one more time on a diagonal. Finally, measure the parchment from the middle to the outside and trim. Then unfold and flatten the circle in the bottom of the pan. Grease with more cooking spray or butter, then add a spoonful of flour and rotate the pan to coat the bottom and sides evenly with flour. Flip the cake pan and hover it over a trash can or sink and tap the bottom of the pan to knock out the excess flour. Now you're ready to bake!

# CHOCOLATE, CHERRY & PISTACHIO ICE CREAM CAKE (SPUMONI)

SERVES
8

*You can say* arrivederci *to your childhood ice cream cake—this grown-up version is living* la dolce vita. *For an upgrade, seek out Luxardo cherries, an Italian candied cherry in syrup that is insanely delicious and decadent.*

2 pints **pistachio ice cream**

1 pint **vanilla ice cream**

2 pints **cherry ice cream**

2 pints **chocolate ice cream**

½ cup **Dutch-processed cocoa powder**

½ cup **granulated sugar**

½ teaspoon **vanilla extract**

¼ teaspoon **kosher salt**

8 ice cream **sugar cones**

1 (6.5-ounce) aerosol container **dairy whipped topping**, such as Reddi-wip

**Rainbow and chocolate sprinkles**, for decorating

16 **maraschino cherries**, drained

1 Let the four flavors of ice cream stand at room temperature for about 10 minutes to soften.

2 Meanwhile, separate the bottom and the outer ring of an 8-inch springform pan. Line the bottom with plastic wrap, then attach the ring to the bottom, leaving the excess plastic wrap attached. Cut a 28-inch-long, 4-inch-wide strip of parchment paper and use it to line the inside of the pan, forming a "collar" that sticks up above the edge of the pan.

3 Using a rubber spatula, press and spread the pistachio ice cream into an even layer in the bottom of the prepared pan. Using a 2-ounce ice cream scoop, dollop 4 scoops of vanilla ice cream evenly over the pistachio ice cream, pressing them down into it lightly.

4 Using a rubber spatula, press and spread the cherry ice cream into an even layer over the pistachio and vanilla ice creams. Dollop 4 more scoops of vanilla ice cream evenly over the cherry ice cream, pressing them down into it lightly.

5 Using a rubber spatula, press and spread the chocolate ice cream into an even layer over the cherry and vanilla ice creams.

6 Cover the ice cream cake with plastic wrap and freeze until set, at least 4 hours or preferably overnight.

7 While the cake is chilling, make the chocolate sauce: In a small saucepan, whisk together the cocoa powder and granulated sugar, then stir in the vanilla, salt, and ⅓ cup water. Bring to a boil over medium-high heat and cook, stirring, until thick, about 3 minutes. Transfer the sauce to a small bowl (you should have about ⅔ cup) and let cool completely.

recipe continues

8   Drizzle half the chocolate sauce decoratively over a round serving platter. Remove the outer ring of the springform pan from the base, then peel the parchment paper off the cake. Use the overhanging plastic wrap to lift the cake off the pan base. Use a large metal spatula to set the cake in the middle of the serving plate. Drizzle the remaining chocolate sauce evenly over the cake.

9   When ready to serve, lightly press the sides of the sugar cones face up evenly around the edge of the cake. Fill each cone with whipped topping to look like an ice cream cone, then pipe 8 mounds of whipped topping on top of the cake, evenly spacing them around the outside edge (see box, page 192). Sprinkle the mounds of whipped topping with the sprinkles, alternating between rainbow and chocolate. Top each mound with a cherry.

10  Cut the cake into slices. Serve each portion with an ice cream cone.

# PUMPKIN SPICE LATTE BARS

MAKES
**12**
BARS

If you eagerly await fall's first pumpkin spice latte, raise your hands in the air and wave 'em like you just don't care (no shame in your game here). You already know the perfect drink to accompany this dessert, so hop to it—a little jar of pumpkin spice mix evokes everything you love about autumn, one teaspoon at a time.

**Nonstick cooking spray**

1 cup **granulated sugar**

½ cup (1 stick) **unsalted butter**

1 teaspoon **vanilla extract**

5 large **eggs**

1½ cups **all-purpose flour** (see box, page 179)

1 cup **gingersnap crumbs** (from about 18 cookies)

1 tablespoon **baking powder**

½ teaspoon **kosher salt**

2 cups plus 2 tablespoons **confectioners' sugar**

¼ cup **strong brewed espresso** or **coffee,** cooled

1 tablespoon plus ½ teaspoon **pumpkin pie spice mix**

2 (8-ounce) packages **cream cheese,** at room temperature

1  Preheat the oven to 350°F. Line a 9 by 13-inch baking dish with parchment paper and coat it with cooking spray.

2  Combine the granulated sugar and butter in a large bowl. Using a handheld mixer, beat on medium speed until fluffy, about 2 minutes (see box, page 188). Add the vanilla and 1 egg and beat on medium speed until smooth. Add the flour, gingersnap crumbs, baking powder, and salt and beat on low speed until just combined.

3  Transfer the dough to the prepared pan and press it evenly over the bottom.

4  Combine the remaining 4 eggs, 2 cups of the confectioners' sugar, the espresso, 1 tablespoon of the pumpkin pie spice mix, and the cream cheese in a food processor. Process until smooth.

5  Pour the cream cheese filling over the dough and smooth out the top with a spatula. Bake until the filling is lightly browned on top and set in the center, about 25 minutes. Transfer the pan to a wire rack and let the bars cool completely, about 1 hour. Wrap the pan in plastic wrap and refrigerate for at least 4 hours or preferably overnight.

6  When ready to serve, sift the remaining 2 tablespoons confectioners' sugar and ½ teaspoon pumpkin pie spice mix over the bars until completely coated (see box, page 219).

7  Cut into 12 bars and serve.

# NO-BAKE BLUEBERRY RIPPLE CHEESECAKE

10 **graham crackers**, crushed

7 tablespoons **unsalted butter**, melted

3 (8-ounce) packages **cream cheese**, at room temperature

1½ cups **confectioners' sugar**, sifted (see box, page 219)

1 teaspoon **vanilla extract**

½ cup **whole milk**

2 teaspoons **unflavored powdered gelatin**

2 cups fresh **blueberries** (11 ounces)

½ cup **blueberry jam**

This recipe is especially welcome on steamy summer days when turning on the oven just won't do. The hardest part here will be waiting the four hours while it chills—but you can work on your tan, and we promise it will make the final product taste that much better.

1 Combine the graham cracker crumbs and melted butter in a food processor and pulse until moistened. Press the crumbs evenly over the bottom of a 9-inch springform cake pan to make a crust.

2 Wipe out the food processor and return it to its base. Combine the cream cheese, confectioners' sugar, and vanilla in the processor and process until smooth.

3 Pour the milk in a small microwave-safe bowl, then sprinkle the gelatin over the top. Let stand for 5 minutes to hydrate the gelatin. Microwave the milk until hot to the touch, about 30 seconds, then stir to dissolve the gelatin. Pour the milk-gelatin mixture into the food processor and process until the filling is completely smooth.

4 Pour the blueberries over the graham cracker crust, pressing them gently into a single layer. Pour the cream cheese filling over the berries and smooth the top using a spatula.

5 Put the jam in a small microwave-safe bowl and briefly microwave it to loosen. Dollop spoonfuls of the jam evenly over the filling. Use a toothpick to gently swirl the jam and cheesecake filling together. Cover the cheesecake with plastic wrap and refrigerate until completely set, at least 4 hours or preferably overnight.

6 When ready to serve, run a knife between the pan and the cake to loosen it, then remove the outer ring of the pan and set the cake on a serving plate. Slice and serve.

# ORANGE CREAM TRUFFLES

MAKES
**54**
TRUFFLES

Skip the freezer and have a ball with these truffles—no ice cream truck required. They've got all the flavors of your favorite frozen treat-on-a-stick, but put any ideas about a labor-intensive dessert in the deep-freeze; these come together lickety split.

4½ cups **white chocolate chips**
(about 20 ounces)

½ cup **heavy cream**

Finely grated zest of 2 **oranges**
(see box, below)

6 drops of **orange gel food coloring**

1   In a medium saucepan, combine 3 cups of the white chocolate chips, the heavy cream, and the orange zest and cook over low heat, stirring, until the chocolate has melted and the mixture is completely smooth. Pour the mixture into a 9 by-5-inch loaf pan, cover with plastic wrap, and refrigerate until firm, at least 4 hours or preferably overnight.

2   Line a rimmed baking sheet with parchment paper. With a small ice cream scoop, scoop out 1-inch balls of the chocolate mixture and arrange them on the baking sheet. (If any of the truffles begin to melt, place the baking sheet in the freezer for 10 minutes.)

3   Put the remaining 1½ cups white chocolate chips in a small microwave-safe bowl and microwave in 30-second intervals, stirring after each, until melted and smooth.

4   One at a time, dunk the truffles into the melted white chocolate, lifting them out with the tines of a fork and letting any excess chocolate drip back into the bowl. Return the coated truffles to the parchment-lined baking sheet and refrigerate to harden the chocolate.

5   Stir the food coloring into the remaining melted white chocolate. Using a fork, drizzle it over the truffles.

6   Refrigerate the truffles for at least 1 hour and up to 3 days before serving.

## 101

## Zesting

If you've ever rolled an orange or lemon between your hands, you've smelled the glorious citrus oils it releases. Zesting citrus and adding it to marinades, pasta, desserts, and many other dishes adds a fresh hint of flavor. Use your microplane or the smallest holes on your box grater for fine zest, or a vegetable peeler to pare off strips of zest to put them in seafood soups (remove before serving!) and marinades or to thinly slice into thin strips for garnishing cakes or cocktails.

# SUPER-CREAMY & TALL SOUR CREAM CHEESECAKE

## CRUST

45 **vanilla wafer cookies**

6 tablespoons (¾ stick) **unsalted butter**, melted

⅓ cup **confectioners' sugar**

## FILLING

5 (8-ounce) packages **cream cheese**, at room temperature

1½ cups **granulated sugar**

1 cup **sour cream**

3 tablespoons **all-purpose flour**

1 teaspoon **vanilla extract**

1 teaspoon **kosher salt**

5 large **eggs**

2 large **egg yolks**
(see box, page 149)

More is more here (yes, we said *five* blocks of cream cheese), but part of the preparation is a story of less: This press-in wafer cookie crust is as simple as it gets. You'll be tempted to overbake this baby, since it will still be getting jiggly with it when it comes out of the oven, but follow the instructions—when it cools it firms up *jussst* the right amount.

1 Preheat the oven to 450°F. Set a 9-inch springform pan on a rimmed baking sheet.

2 Make the crust: Combine the vanilla wafers, melted butter, and confectioners' sugar in a food processor and pulse until the cookies are ground to crumbs and moistened with the butter, about 10 pulses. Press the crumbs evenly over the bottom and ½ inch up the sides of the springform pan.

3 Make the filling: Wipe out the food processor and return it to its base. Combine the cream cheese, granulated sugar, sour cream, flour, vanilla, salt, eggs, and egg yolks in the food processor and process until completely smooth.

4 Pour the filling over the crust and smooth the top with a spatula. Bake the cake for 10 minutes, then reduce the oven temperature to 250°F and bake until the filling is almost set but still slightly loose in the center when the pan is tapped, about 1 hour more. Turn the oven off and leave the cake in the oven until completely cooled, 2 to 3 hours.

5 Cover the cake with plastic wrap and refrigerate for at least 8 hours or up to overnight.

6 When ready to serve, remove the outer ring of the springform pan and set the cake on a serving plate. Cut the cake into thin wedges and serve.

# CHERRY "OLD-FASHIONED" PIE

SERVES
8

You can have your pie . . . and a cocktail too. This pie might be appear to be as classic as your grandma's, but it's got all sorts of hidden tricks inside. A little bit of whiskey, a couple dashes of Angostura bitters, and a dab of orange marmalade aren't just a gimmick; they all serve to deepen and highlight that cherry flavor. You can make the dough ahead of time, wrap it in plastic, and freeze it for up to two months, then thaw it in the refrigerator for twenty-four hours before using.

## CRUST

3 cups **all-purpose flour**, plus more for dusting (see box, page 179)

1 tablespoon **granulated sugar**

2 teaspoons **kosher salt**

1 cup (2 sticks) **unsalted butter**, cut into ½-inch cubes and chilled

½ cup **ice-cold water**

## FILLING

½ cup **orange marmalade**

⅓ cup **cornstarch**

⅓ cup plus 1 tablespoon **turbinado sugar**, such as Sugar In The Raw

3 tablespoons **whiskey**

1 tablespoon **lemon juice**

1 teaspoon **vanilla extract**

1 teaspoon **kosher salt**

2 pounds pitted whole fresh or thawed frozen **sour cherries** (about 5 cups)

8 dashes **Angostura bitters**, plus more for serving

1 large **egg**, lightly beaten

**Whipped cream**, for serving

8 strips **candied orange peel**

8 **maraschino cherries** with stems

1   Make the crust: Combine the flour, butter, granulated sugar, and salt in a food processor and pulse until pea-size crumbles form, at least 10 pulses. Drizzle in the water, then pulse again until the dough forms large clumps, about 10 more pulses.

2   Turn the dough out onto a clean surface and shape it into a ball. Cut the ball in half, then shape each half into a ½-inch-thick disc. Wrap each disc separately in plastic and refrigerate for at least 1 hour and up to 2 days.

3   Preheat the oven to 375°F.

4   On a lightly floured surface, roll out one disc of the chilled dough into a 12-inch circle, ¼ inch thick. Transfer the dough to a 9-inch deep-dish pie pan, letting it settle into the bottom and up the sides.

5   Roll out the second disc of dough into a 12-inch circle, ¼ inch thick. Using a knife or pizza cutter, cut the circle into 1-inch-wide strips.

6   Make the filling: Whisk together the marmalade, cornstarch, ⅓ cup of the turbinado sugar, the whiskey, lemon juice, vanilla, and salt in a large bowl. Add the cherries and toss to coat evenly.

7   Transfer the cherry filling to the pie pan and smooth the top with a spatula. Dash the bitters evenly over the filling.

8   Arrange the strips of dough in a lattice pattern over the filling (see box, page 207). Trim the edges of the strips and the dough lining the pan so they overhang the pan by ½ inch. Lift up and then fold under the dough edge to form a thick crust, then press to seal or crimp as desired.

recipe continues

9   Brush the lattice and any exposed dough with the beaten egg, then sprinkle liberally with the remaining 1 tablespoon turbinado sugar.

10  Bake the pie until the crust is golden brown and the filling is bubbling in the center, about 1 hour 25 minutes to 1 hour 30 minutes. Transfer the pie to a wire rack and let cool completely, about 4 hours.

11  Put the whipped cream in a large bowl and add dashes of bitters to taste. Fold gently to combine.

12  Skewer 1 strip of orange peel and 1 cherry with a toothpick and repeat with the remaining orange peel and cherries.

13  Cut the pie into slices and garnish each with a dollop of the bitters whipped cream. Top each slice with a maraschino cherry—orange peel skewer and serve.

## Lattices & Crimping

What's more American than pie? The beauty queen known as lattice-crust pie. Pie decoration, lattices, and crimping are where you can show off your creative skills in the kitchen. Even if you don't have your MFA, you too can get crafty. Here's how you lattice.

1 Since this is essentially a double-crust pie, your first step is to line a pie plate with one of the two crusts **A** .

2 On a lightly floured work surface, roll out your pie dough to a 12-inch disc. Using a sharp knife or pizza cutter **B** , cut the dough into strips about 1¼ inches thick to yield 8 to 10 strips **C** .

3 Fill your pie **D** , then arrange 4 or 5 of the strips across the pie, leaving even space between each strip. Fold back every other strip, then lay a new strip in the center of the pie perpendicular to the other strips and unfold the folded strips over the new strip **E** .

4 Now fold back the strips you didn't fold last time and arrange a second strip of dough across the pie and unfold the folded strips over it **F** . Repeat with the remaining dough strips.

5 Using a pair of kitchen shears, trim the strips so there is still a slight overhang over the pie.

6 After that, to crimp the edge of a pie crust, use the tines of a fork or your fingers to pinch the edge of the crust together to seal it and create a decorative edge.

# TROPICAL FRUIT PAVLOVA

## LIME CURD

½ cup **granulated sugar**

1 large **egg**

Finely grated zest and juice of 2 **limes** (see box, page 203)

2 tablespoons **unsalted butter**, cut into ½-inch cubes and chilled

## MERINGUE

¼ cup **cornstarch**

1 tablespoon **distilled white vinegar**

1 tablespoon **vanilla extract**

½ teaspoon **kosher salt**

2½ cups **granulated sugar**

8 **egg whites**, at room temperature (see box, page 149)

1 cup **heavy cream**, chilled

½ cup **coconut cream**, chilled

1¾ pounds mixed **pineapple**, **papaya**, **mango**, and **kiwi**, cut into 1-inch pieces (about 4 cups total)

¼ cup **toasted unsweetened flaked coconut**

You put the lime (curd) in the coconut (meringue) and you get a tropical vacation masquerading as this dessert. Only ripe pineapple, papaya, mango, and kiwi need apply here: Since the fruit will be served uncooked, search for fruit at its peak of beauty and ripeness.

1  Make the lime curd: In a small saucepan, whisk together the granulated sugar, the egg, three-quarters of the lime zest, and all the lime juice until smooth. Cook over medium heat, stirring often, until thickened, about 8 minutes. Remove the pan from the heat and whisk in the butter until it has melted completely and the curd is smooth.

2  Pour the lime curd through a fine-mesh strainer set over a small bowl. Stir in the remaining lime zest. Cover the curd with plastic wrap and refrigerate until thickened, at least 2 hours and up to 1 week.

3  Make the meringue: Preheat the oven to 350°F. Line a baking sheet with parchment paper and place a 9-inch round cake pan in the center. Use a pencil to trace a dark circle around the outside of the pan onto the parchment; remove the pan and flip over the parchment. The circle should still be visible.

4  Stir together the cornstarch, vinegar, vanilla, and salt in a small bowl until smooth.

5  Combine the granulated sugar and egg whites in a large bowl. Using a handheld mixer, beat on medium-high speed until the egg whites hold soft peaks.

6  Stir the cornstarch mixture again to smooth it out, then add it to the egg whites and beat until the egg whites are thick and glossy and hold stiff peaks. Scrape the meringue onto the parchment paper into the center of the circle. Use a spatula to shape the meringue into a disc, following the outline of the circle. Smooth the top and sides.

7  Transfer the meringue to the oven and immediately reduce the oven temperature to 215°F. Bake the meringue until it looks dry on the outside but is not browned at all, about 1 hour 15 minutes. Without opening the door, turn the oven off and let the meringue cool completely, at least 3 hours.

8   Using two metal spatulas, gently remove the meringue from the parchment paper and set it on a cake stand or serving plate.

9   Combine the **heavy cream** and coconut cream in a large bowl. Using a handheld mixer, beat on medium-high speed until the cream holds stiff peaks. Spoon the coconut whipped cream onto the center of the meringue and spread it evenly over the top, leaving a 1-inch border.

10  Arrange the fruit pieces all over the whipped cream. Stir the chilled **lime** curd again until smooth, then drizzle it all over the pavlova. Sprinkle the toasted coconut on top. Slice and serve within 30 minutes.

# PART 2

# IMPRESS YOUR FRIENDS

# BRUNCH

# SILVER-DOLLAR PANCAKES WITH VANILLA BEAN SUGAR

Sometimes, size isn't everything—that's certainly the case with these lil' silver-dollar pancakes, which cook quickly thanks to their size, and get a flavor boost from a seriously genius vanilla sugar. On the other side of the spectrum: a Dutch Baby pancake (sometimes known as German pancake), which is like a single large poofy eggy crêpe you start on the stovetop and finish in the oven. Ours is topped with caramelized bananas and white chocolate, making your choice between these two master recipes even harder. Our solution? Make both and ask questions later.

¾ cup plus 1 tablespoon **all-purpose flour** (see box, page 179)

¼ cup plus 2 tablespoons **confectioners' sugar**

2 tablespoons **cornstarch**

1½ teaspoons **baking powder**

½ teaspoon **kosher salt**

⅛ teaspoon **baking soda**

½ cup plus 2 tablespoons **milk**

3½ tablespoons **unsalted butter**, melted, plus more for greasing

½ teaspoon **vanilla extract**

1 large **egg**

2 tablespoons **superfine sugar**

½ **vanilla bean**, split lengthwise and seeds scraped

1  Preheat the oven to 200°F.

2  Sift the flour, 2 tablespoons confectioners' sugar, the cornstarch, baking powder, salt, and baking soda into a medium bowl (see box, page 219); whisk until smooth. Add the milk, 1½ tablespoons of the melted butter, the vanilla, and egg and whisk until the batter just comes together (there will be some lumps). Let the batter rest for 5 minutes.

3  Meanwhile, combine the superfine sugar and vanilla bean seeds in a small bowl and rub with your fingers until the seeds are evenly distributed. Stir in the remaining ¼ cup confectioners' sugar.

4  Heat a large nonstick skillet over medium heat. Grease the skillet generously with some butter, then pour 1 heaping tablespoon of the batter into the pan to make a silver-dollar-size pancake; repeat with the remaining batter just to fill the skillet. Cook until the pancakes are golden brown on the bottom and bubbly on top, 45 to 60 seconds. Using a spatula, flip the pancakes and cook until the batter is cooked through, 30 to 45 seconds more.

5  Transfer the pancakes to a serving plate, cover with a kitchen towel, and keep warm in the oven while you make the remaining pancakes. Once all the pancakes are made, arrange them on the warm serving plate and drizzle with the remaining 2 tablespoons melted butter. Sprinkle the vanilla bean sugar over the pancakes and serve.

# PEANUT BUTTER DUTCH BABY PANCAKE WITH CARAMELIZED BANANA & WHITE CHOCOLATE

MAKES
1
PANCAKE

¾ cup **all-purpose flour**
(see box, page 179)

¾ cup **milk**

3 tablespoons **natural peanut butter**

½ teaspoon **kosher salt**

3 large **eggs**

1 large **banana**

¼ cup **sugar**

5 tablespoons **unsalted butter**

3 ounces **white chocolate**, finely chopped

¼ cup chopped **salted roasted peanuts**

1  Preheat the oven to 425°F.

2  Combine the flour, milk, peanut butter, salt, and eggs in a medium bowl and whisk until smooth (some lumps are okay). Let the batter rest for 5 minutes.

3  Meanwhile, peel the banana, cut in half crosswise, then cut each piece in half lengthwise. Spread the sugar on a plate and press the cut side of each banana piece in the sugar, pressing to adhere.

4  In a 10-inch ovenproof nonstick skillet, melt 2 tablespoons of the butter over medium-high heat until foaming. Add the banana, sugar-side down, and cook until caramelized on the bottom, 3 to 4 minutes. Using tongs, transfer the banana to a cutting board, sugar-side up. Leave the skillet over medium-high heat.

5  Melt the remaining 3 tablespoons butter in the skillet. Pour in the batter and then immediately, and carefully, transfer the skillet to the oven and bake until puffed and golden around the edges, 18 to 20 minutes.

6  Meanwhile, cut the banana into ½-inch pieces. Put the white chocolate pieces in a small microwave-safe bowl and microwave in 15-second intervals, stirring between each, until just melted.

7  Immediately slide the pancake onto a large serving plate and arrange the caramelized banana pieces in the center. Drizzle the white chocolate over the top and sprinkle with the chopped peanuts. Serve immediately.

# HAM & EGG BAKE WITH HOLLANDAISE SAUCE

1 (16-ounce) can **refrigerated biscuit dough**

1 cup chopped **deli-style ham**

1½ cups **whole milk**

¼ cup finely chopped **fresh chives,** plus more for serving

1 teaspoon **kosher salt**

1 teaspoon **freshly ground black pepper**

8 large **eggs**

### HOLLANDAISE

1 tablespoon **fresh lemon juice**

½ teaspoon **kosher salt**

2 large **egg yolks** (see box, page 149)

Pinch of **cayenne**

4 tablespoons (½ stick) **unsalted butter,** melted and kept hot

To upgrade your brunch game, stop right here. Hollandaise sauce might sound like something only a pro chef can whip up, but a blender or food processor makes it foolproof. Before you know it, you'll be pouring buttery sauce over your very own biscuit, ham, and egg creation.

1   Preheat the oven to 350°F.

2   Open the can of biscuits and cut each round into 9 pieces. Evenly spread the pieces over the bottom of a 9 by 13-inch baking dish (they won't cover the entire bottom of the dish), then distribute the ham among the pieces.

3   Stir together the milk, chives, salt, pepper, and eggs in a large bowl. Pour the egg mixture over the biscuit pieces and ham.

4   Bake until everything is puffed and set in the middle, about 35 minutes.

5   Meanwhile, make the hollandaise: Combine the lemon juice, salt, egg yolks, and cayenne in a blender or food processor. With the motor running, gradually pour in the hot melted butter until fully emulsified and smooth.

6   Slice the egg bake into 12 squares and set each one on a plate. Pour some hollandaise sauce over the top and sprinkle with chives before serving.

# BISCUITS & GRAVY BAKE

Southern comfort has arrived at your doorstep. Premade biscuit dough helps this dish come together quickly. Learn to make gravy here and you'll be all set come Thanksgiving. Dry run complete!

**GRAVY**

4 tablespoons (½ stick) **unsalted butter**

¼ cup **all-purpose flour**

2 cups **whole milk**

**Kosher salt** and **freshly ground black pepper**

1 (12-ounce) can **refrigerated biscuit dough**

2 cups crumbled cooked **breakfast sausage** (1 pound)

1 cup shredded **Cheddar cheese** (8 ounces)

½ cup **whole milk**

6 large **eggs**

½ teaspoon **kosher salt**

½ teaspoon **freshly ground black pepper**

1   Preheat the oven to 350°F.

2   Make the gravy: In a small saucepan, melt the butter over medium heat. Stir in the flour and cook, stirring, for 1 minute (see box, page 263). Slowly whisk in the milk and bring to a simmer. Cook, stirring, until thickened to the consistency of gravy, about 6 minutes. Season the gravy with salt and pepper.

3   Meanwhile, open the tube of biscuits and cut each biscuit into 8 pieces. Evenly spread the pieces over the bottom of a 9 by 13-inch baking dish (they won't cover the entire bottom of the dish). Distribute the sausage among the biscuit pieces, then sprinkle on the cheese.

4   Whisk together the milk, eggs, salt, and pepper in a large bowl until smooth. Pour the egg mixture over the biscuit pieces, sausage, and cheese in the baking dish, then drizzle with the gravy.

5   Bake until the eggs on the bottom of the dish are cooked and the top is golden brown, 35 to 45 minutes. Transfer the dish to a wire rack to cool slightly.

6   Spoon onto plates and serve hot.

# PERFECT FLUFFY PANCAKES

MAKES
**6**
LARGE
PANCAKES

Egg whites are the heroes of these pancakes—whipping them and gently folding them into the batter takes these cakes to new heights. Focus on the words "folding" and "gentle"—the less you mess with the batter, the more air will remain inside. More air equals more fluff. You get the picture. To keep pancakes warm, place the cooked pancakes on a baking sheet lined with a kitchen towel. Cover with another kitchen towel and place the sheet in the oven heated to its lowest setting for up to two hours.

4 cups **all-purpose flour**
(see box, page 179)

¼ cup **baking powder**

3 large **eggs**

1 large **egg white**

4 cups **whole milk**, at room
temperature

¾ cup (1½ sticks) **unsalted butter**,
melted

**Butter** and **maple syrup**,
for serving

1 Sift together the flour and baking powder in a large bowl (see box).

2 Separate the eggs, putting the yolks in one large bowl and the whites in another (see box, page 149). Whisk the milk and melted butter into the egg yolks until smooth.

3 Add the single egg white to the bowl with the others. Using a handheld mixer, beat the egg whites on medium-high speed until they hold soft peaks.

4 Pour the milk mixture into the flour mixture and stir with a rubber spatula until just combined. Add the beaten egg whites and gently fold to combine.

5 Heat an 8-inch nonstick skillet over low heat. Pour about 1½ cups of the pancake batter into the skillet, smooth the top, then cover with a lid. Cook until golden brown on the bottom and a toothpick inserted into the center comes out clean, about 20 minutes (see box, page 187). Transfer the pancake to a plate and repeat with the remaining batter to make 5 more pancakes.

6 Serve the warm pancakes on individual plates, with butter and maple syrup alongside.

## 101

## Sifting

We know sifting can seem like an unnecessary extra step, but trust us, for truly stellar baked goods it's totally worth it. Sifting aerates certain dry ingredients that are powdery and tend to clump, like flour, cocoa powder, or powdered sugar, and helps them more evenly incorporate into liquids and other ingredients. That way you can really take the cake. Bonus: It can help mix things together evenly, too!

# CINNAMON ROLLS

## DOUGH

½ cup (1 stick) **unsalted butter**, melted, plus more for greasing

2 cups **whole milk**, heated to 115°F

½ cup **granulated sugar**

1 (¼-ounce) packet **active dry yeast** (see box, page 173)

6 cups **all-purpose flour**, plus more for dusting (see box, page 179)

2 teaspoons **kosher salt**

1 teaspoon **baking powder**

## FILLING

¾ cup (1½ sticks) **unsalted butter**, at room temperature

¾ cup packed **light brown sugar**

2 tablespoons **ground cinnamon**

## GLAZE

½ (8-ounce) package **cream cheese**, at room temperature

1 cup **confectioners' sugar**

3 tablespoons **whole milk**

2 tablespoons **unsalted butter**, melted

1 teaspoon **vanilla extract**

You've never truly experienced bliss until you've smelled a pan of homemade cinnamon rolls baking in your oven. To slice each roll cleanly and evenly, try using plain dental floss. Slide the dental floss under the roll, cross the two ends and lift. Ta-da! The rolls will stay straight and won't pinch, which even a sharp knife can cause.

1 Generously grease two 8-inch round cake pans with butter.

2 Make the dough: Whisk together the melted butter, warm milk, and granulated sugar in a large bowl. Sprinkle the yeast evenly over the milk mixture and let stand until foamy, about 10 minutes.

3 Add the flour, salt, and baking powder to the milk mixture and mix with a wooden spoon until a dough forms. Turn it out onto a clean surface and knead until tight and elastic, 6 to 8 minutes (see box, page 250).

4 Grease a large bowl with some butter and add the dough. Cover the bowl with a kitchen towel or plastic wrap and let the dough rise in a warm, draft-free area until doubled in size, about 1 hour.

5 Uncover the dough and turn it out onto a well-floured surface. Using a floured rolling pin, roll the dough into a large rectangle, about ½ inch thick. Position the dough so one long edge is facing you. Stretch out the corners to ensure that they are sharp and even.

6 Fill the dough: Using a spatula, spread the softened butter evenly over the dough, then sprinkle the brown sugar evenly over the butter, followed by the cinnamon. Roll the rolling pin over the cinnamon and sugar to press them into the butter.

7 Beginning from the long edge closest to you, roll up the dough into a log. Pinch the dough at the seam to seal it. Flip the log seam-side down and trim the short ends so they are even. With a sharp knife or plain dental floss (see headnote), slice the log crosswise in half, then slice each half into 7 evenly sized rolls, each about 1½ inches thick.

8 Place 7 cinnamon rolls, cut-side up, in each prepared pan, arranging them with one in the center and six around the sides. Cover both pans with a kitchen towel or plastic wrap and let the rolls rise in a warm, draft-free area until slightly puffed, about 30 minutes.

9 Preheat the oven to 350°F.

10   Uncover the cinnamon rolls and bake until golden brown on top,
     25 to 30 minutes.

11   Meanwhile, make the glaze: Whisk together the cream cheese,
     confectioners' sugar, milk, melted butter, and vanilla in a medium
     bowl until smooth.

12   Transfer the pans to a wire rack. Immediately drizzle the cinnamon
     rolls in both pans with the glaze, dividing it evenly. Let the cinnamon
     rolls stand until they have cooled slightly and the glaze has set
     somewhat, about 20 minutes. Serve warm.

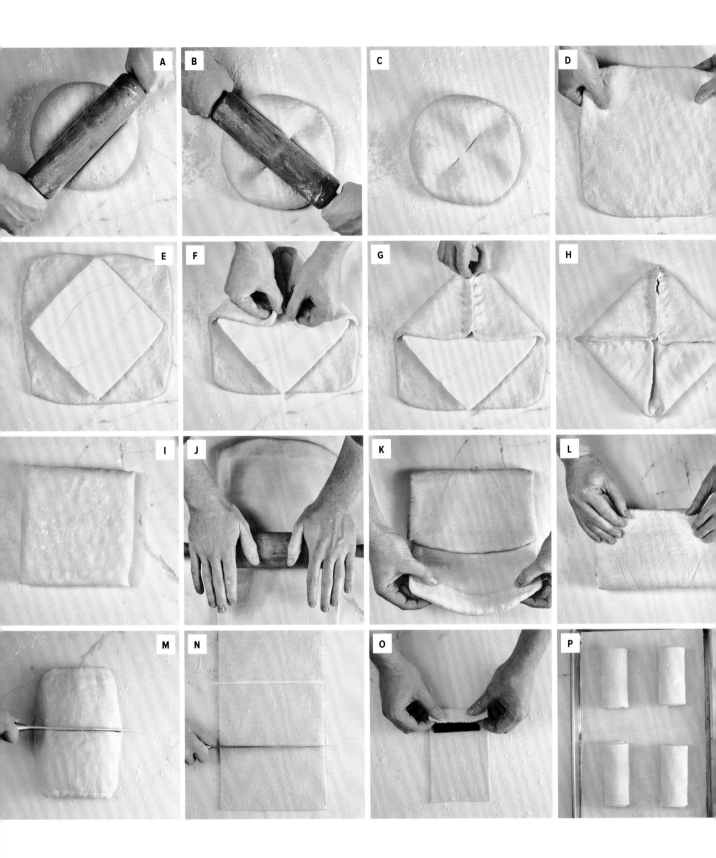

# CHOCOLATE CROISSANTS
## (PAINS AU CHOCOLAT)

Think of us as your personal cooking coach when it comes to an epic (but doable) baking project like preparing your own chocolate croissants. Make sure you bring your patience along with your rolling pin because this recipe requires overnight chilling. The turns of the dough are essential to make the 27 layers (count 'em!) of flaky pastry. If you have A/C, keep it on when working with this dough; colder temperatures make for happy, buttery layers.

4 cups **all-purpose flour** (see box, page 179)

½ cup **whole milk**

¼ cup **sugar**

2 teaspoons **kosher salt**

1 (¼-ounce) packet **instant yeast**

1½ cups (3 sticks) **unsalted butter**, chilled, plus 3 tablespoons at room temperature

1 pound **dark chocolate**, broken into 3-inch pieces

1 large **egg**, lightly beaten

1 Combine the flour, milk, sugar, salt, yeast, ¾ cup water, and the 3 tablespoons room-temperature butter in a large bowl and stir together with a wooden spoon until a dough forms.

2 Turn the dough out onto a clean surface and knead until tight and elastic, 6 to 8 minutes (see box, page 250). Shape the dough roughly into a ball. Wrap in plastic and refrigerate for 1 hour.

3 Cut each stick of cold butter in half lengthwise. On a sheet of parchment paper, lay the butter pieces on their wider sides next to one another to form a rectangle. Cover with another piece of parchment. Tap all over with a rolling pin to flatten slightly, then use the rolling pin to roll the butter into a 7-inch square, ½ inch thick. If needed, use a knife to trim the edges, place the trimmings back on top of the butter, and roll again. Transfer the butter block to the refrigerator.

4 Unwrap the dough on a lightly floured surface. Dust the rolling pin with flour and push the pin into the dough once, diagonally from one corner to the opposite corner **A** , then repeat with the two opposite corners **B** to form an "X" indentation on the dough **C** . Roll out each quadrant of the dough, starting from the center, to form a 10-inch square **D** .

5 Place the chilled butter block on top of the dough so you have a diamond of butter on top of the square of dough **E** . Fold the corners of the dough over the butter **F** to meet in the middle **G** , enclosing the butter block completely. Pinch the edges of the dough together to seal the seams **H** . Flip the dough seam-side down and flatten it with the rolling pin slightly to further seal the seams **I** .

recipe continues

6   Transfer the dough to a baking sheet and cover with plastic wrap. Refrigerate for 1 hour.

7   Unwrap the dough on a floured surface and roll it into an 8 by 18-inch rectangle with one short edge facing you **J** . Fold the top third down to the middle and brush off any excess flour. Fold the bottom third over the middle **K** so the dough is folded like a letter **L** . Turn the dough 90 degrees clockwise to the left so now a long edge is facing you. This completes the first turn. Cover the dough with plastic wrap and refrigerate for 1 hour.

8   Repeat rolling out the dough and turning it two more times, refrigerating for 1 hour in between each turn, to complete three turns total. If at any time the dough or butter begins to soften, stop and transfer it to the refrigerator for 20 minutes before continuing. After the final turn, cover the dough with plastic wrap and refrigerate overnight.

9   Line two baking sheets with parchment paper. Cut the chilled dough in half crosswise **M** ; return one half to the refrigerator and set the other on a floured surface. Roll out the dough to an 8 by 20-inch rectangle. Trim the edges with a knife so they're even, then cut the dough crosswise into 4 smaller 8-by-5-inch rectangles **N** . Place a piece of chocolate on one short edge of a dough rectangle. Beginning from that edge, roll the dough tightly around the chocolate **O** . Place the croissant seam-side down on one of the baking sheets and repeat to make 4 croissants total **P** . Remove the other half of the dough from the refrigerator and repeat to make 4 more croissants, setting them on the second baking sheet as you roll them.

10  Loosely drape a kitchen towel over the baking sheets and let the croissant rise in a draft-free area until slightly puffed, about 1 hour.

11  Preheat the oven to 400°F.

12  Brush the croissants with the beaten egg. Bake until they are golden brown and cooked through, 25 to 30 minutes. Transfer the baking sheets to a wire rack and let the croissants cool for 20 minutes before serving.

# GLAZED ORANGE PULL-APART BREAD

SERVES
12

We think of this recipe in terms of a TV-style makeover show. A glossy orange glaze completes this pull-apart bread's transformation from duckling to swan. Cue the reveal!

1 Preheat the oven to 325°F. Grease a 10-cup Bundt pan with butter.

2 Open the cans of biscuits and cut each round into quarters. Place them in a large bowl. Add the melted butter, granulated sugar, brown sugar, vanilla, salt, and orange zest and toss to coat the biscuit pieces evenly.

3 Transfer the mixture to the prepared pan and roughly smooth the top. Bake until golden brown, puffed, and a toothpick inserted into the center comes out clean, 50 to 55 minutes (see box, page 187). Transfer the pan to a wire rack set over a baking sheet and let cool for 10 minutes. Invert the monkey bread onto the rack and let cool for 20 minutes (see box, page 290).

4 Meanwhile, stir together the confectioners' sugar and orange juice in a small bowl to form a thick glaze. Drizzle the glaze evenly over the cooled bread and let stand for 10 minutes to set, then transfer the bread to a serving dish. Serve the bread whole and let your guests pull it apart.

1 cup (2 sticks) **unsalted butter**, melted and cooled, plus more for greasing

2 (16-ounce) cans **refrigerated biscuit dough**

½ cup **granulated sugar**

½ cup packed **light brown sugar**

1 teaspoon **vanilla extract**

½ teaspoon **kosher salt**

Finely grated zest of 2 **oranges** (see box, page 203)

1½ cups **confectioners' sugar**, sifted (see box, page 219)

2 to 3 tablespoons **orange juice**

# SAUSAGE, APPLE & CHEDDAR MONKEY BREAD

1 tablespoon **vegetable oil**, plus more for greasing

12 ounces **breakfast sausage**

2 sweet-tart **apples**, such as Granny Smith or Gala (about 12 ounces), peeled, cored, and cut into ½-inch cubes

1 (16-ounce) can **refrigerated biscuit dough**

1½ cups shredded white **Cheddar cheese** (8 ounces)

½ cup (1 stick) **unsalted butter**, melted and cooled

2 teaspoons minced **fresh rosemary** leaves

2 teaspoons **garlic powder**

1 teaspoon **onion powder**

Anything that gives a piece of kitchen equipment new life is a recipe we love. Case in point: this pull-apart bread, which recruits your standard Bundt pan for duty. Gather a crowd, because the moment you invert this masterpiece, everyone is going to go crazy grabbing their own personal piece of bliss.

1 Preheat the oven to 400°F. Grease a 10-cup Bundt pan with vegetable oil.

2 In a large nonstick skillet, heat the vegetable oil over medium-high heat. Crumble in the sausage and cook, stirring, until cooked through and no longer pink, about 5 minutes. Add the apples and cook, stirring, until the sausage is browned and the apples are soft, 15 to 17 minutes minutes. Transfer the sausage and apples to a large bowl and let cool completely, about 20 minutes.

3 Open the can of biscuits and cut each round in quarters. Add the biscuit pieces to the bowl with the apples and sausage, then add the Cheddar, melted butter, rosemary, garlic powder, and onion powder and toss to combine.

4 Transfer the mixture to the prepared pan and bake until the biscuit dough is puffed and golden and the cheese has melted, 20 to 25 minutes.

5 Let the monkey bread cool for 5 minutes, then invert it onto a serving platter and serve (see box, page 290).

TASTY ULTIMATE

# WESTERN OMELET & HASH BROWN BREAKFAST CASSEROLE

Pretty much everything under the sun that makes breakfast delicious is included in this casserole, and two key ingredients—cornflakes and hash browns—are store-bought to save you time without sacrificing glory. You can serve this right in the baking dish, meaning fewer dishes when cleanup time rolls around.

6 tablespoons (¾ stick) **unsalted butter**, melted

1 small **yellow onion**, finely chopped

1 small **green bell pepper**, finely chopped

**Kosher salt** and **freshly ground black pepper**

2 cups **diced cooked ham** (10 ounces)

12 large **eggs**, lightly beaten

2 cups **whole milk**

2 cups shredded **American cheese** (8 ounces)

30 ounces frozen cubed **hash brown potatoes**

2 cups **cornflake cereal** (3 ounces)

1 Preheat the oven to 350°F (175°).

2 In a large nonstick skillet, melt 2 tablespoons of the butter over medium-high heat. Add the onion and bell pepper, season with salt and black pepper, and cook, stirring, until soft and beginning to brown, about 8 minutes. Stir in the ham, then remove the skillet from the heat **A** .

3 Combine the eggs, milk, cheese, potatoes, 2 teaspoons salt, and 1 teaspoon black pepper in a large bowl and stir until evenly incorporated. Add the vegetable-ham mixture **B** and stir to combine. Pour the mixture into a 9 by 13-inch baking dish and roughly smooth the top.

4 Combine the remaining 4 tablespoons butter and the cornflakes in a large bowl and stir to coat. Sprinkle the cornflakes evenly over the casserole **C** . Bake until golden brown on top and bubbling in the middle, 1 hour 15 minutes to 1 hour 20 minutes.

5 Transfer the baking dish to a wire rack and let cool for 10 minutes before serving **D** .

# BLUEBERRY-PEACH SHEET PANCAKE

4 cups **pancake mix**

2 cups **whole milk**

4 large **eggs**

1 ripe **peach**, peeled, pitted, and cut into 12 wedges

1 cup **fresh blueberries**

**Butter** and **maple syrup**, for serving

Breakfast is meant to be a good time—not a demonstration of you slaving over the stove doling out pancakes one by one to a hungry crowd. Sheet pan pancakes to the rescue! For some make-ahead magic you can even slice the pancakes into portions, seal them in a resealable bag, and freeze them for up to one month. If blueberries and peaches aren't in season, you can swap them out for strawberries, bananas, or even chocolate chips.

1 Preheat the oven to 425°F. Line a rimmed baking sheet with parchment paper.

2 Whisk together the pancake mix, milk, and eggs in a large bowl until smooth. Pour the batter onto the prepared baking sheet and use a spatula to spread it to the edges.

3 Arrange the peach slices on top of the batter, spacing them evenly, followed by the blueberries.

4 Bake until the pancake is golden brown and cooked through, about 15 minutes. Transfer the baking sheet to a wire rack and let the pancake cool slightly.

5 Cut the pancake into 12 squares and place 3 squares on each plate. Serve hot, with butter and maple syrup alongside.

# LATTE COFFEE CAKE

If your beloved morning latte had a hot-and-heavy affair with a cake, this would be the prodigious result. If you can't find espresso powder (also called instant espresso), instant coffee makes a fine substitute. The final touch of dusting confectioners' sugar in a heart shape will make you look like you can go head-to-head with the best baristas in town.

Nonstick cooking spray

### CRUMB TOPPING

½ cup plus 2 tablespoons **granulated sugar**

½ cup (1 stick) **unsalted butter**, melted and cooled

1 tablespoon **espresso powder** or **instant coffee**

½ teaspoon **kosher salt**

1½ cups **all-purpose flour**

### CAKE

2¼ cups **all-purpose flour** (see box, page 179)

2½ teaspoons **baking powder**

1 cup **granulated sugar**

1 tablespoon **espresso powder** or **instant coffee**

½ teaspoon **kosher salt**

1 cup strong **brewed coffee**, cooled

½ cup (1 stick) **unsalted butter**, melted and cooled

¼ cup plus 2 tablespoons **sour cream**

2 teaspoons **vanilla extract**

2 large **eggs**

**Confectioners' sugar**, for dusting (optional)

Preheat the oven to 325°F. Coat a 9-inch round springform pan with cooking spray, line the bottom with a round of parchment paper cut to fit, then coat the parchment with cooking spray as well.

Make the crumb topping: Combine the granulated sugar, melted butter, espresso powder, and salt in a medium bowl and stir until smooth. Add the flour and stir with a fork until crumbly. Refrigerate the crumb topping until ready to use.

Make the cake: Combine the flour, baking powder, granulated sugar, espresso powder, and salt in a large bowl and whisk until smooth.

In a separate medium bowl, whisk together the coffee, melted butter, sour cream, vanilla, and eggs to combine. Pour the butter mixture over the flour mixture and whisk gently until just combined.

Pour the cake batter into the prepared pan and smooth the top with a spatula. Sprinkle the chilled crumb topping over the top, taking care not to pack it down. Bake until a toothpick inserted into the center of the cake comes out clean, 1 hour 30 minutes to 1 hour 40 minutes (see box, page 187). Transfer the cake to a wire rack and let cool for 20 minutes. Carefully unmold the cake from the pan and remove the parchment paper. Transfer the cake to a serving plate and let cool completely, about 1 hour.

If you like, cut a heart shape out of the middle of a piece of parchment paper and center the cut-out over the cake. Dust the top of the cake with a thick layer of confectioners' sugar, then remove the parchment to show the heart on top before serving.

# BAKED PEANUT BUTTER & JELLY FRENCH TOAST

Bet you can already imagine the melted peanut butter and warm jam in every single bite of this achingly good French toast, which has *peanut butter in the batter!* Chopped roasted, salted peanuts are sprinkled on at the last minute for that extra-crunchy peanutty touch.

1 (12-ounce) loaf day-old **white country** or **french bread**, cut into 1-inch cubes (about 6 cups)

2 cups **whole milk**

1 cup packed **light brown sugar**

½ cup plus 2 tablespoons **smooth peanut butter**

1 teaspoon **vanilla extract**

6 large **eggs**

½ cup **raspberry jam**

½ cup **maple syrup**

Chopped **roasted salted peanuts**, for serving

1 Preheat the oven to 350°F.

2 Spread the bread over the bottom of a 9 by 13-inch baking dish.

3 Combine the milk, brown sugar, ½ cup of the peanut butter, the vanilla, and the eggs in a large bowl and whisk until smooth. Pour the mixture evenly over the bread in the baking dish. Let stand for 10 minutes to allow the bread to soak up the custard.

4 Dollop spoonfuls of the jam evenly over the bread and custard.

5 Bake until golden brown and puffed, 40 to 45 minutes. Transfer the pan to a wire rack and let cool for 5 minutes.

6 Meanwhile, whisk together the remaining 2 tablespoons peanut butter with the maple syrup in a small bowl. Drizzle the mixture over the French toast.

7 Cut the French toast into squares. Sprinkle each square with chopped peanuts and serve.

# THE ULTIMATE WAFFLE

It's a lot of gumption to call something "the ultimate," but we stand behind it when it comes to these waffles. Their superiority shines through in a supernatural lightness and an extra-crispy texture. Even better, you don't need a special waffle iron to make them; your standard waffle iron will do the trick—just make sure it's nice and hot every time you pour in the batter.

2 cups **all-purpose flour** (see box, page 179)

2 teaspoons **baking powder**

1 teaspoon **kosher salt**

1 cup **whole milk**

½ cup **buttermilk**

4 tablespoons (½ stick) **unsalted butter**, melted and cooled

½ teaspoon **vanilla extract**

2 large **eggs**, separated (see box, page 149)

⅓ cup **sugar**

**Butter** and **maple syrup**, for serving

1 Preheat a waffle iron to medium-high.

2 Whisk together the flour, baking powder, and salt in a large bowl, then form a well in the center. Pour in the milk, buttermilk, melted butter, vanilla, and egg yolks and whisk until the batter just comes together (there will be some lumps).

3 Place the egg whites in a small bowl and beat until foamy. While beating, sprinkle in the sugar and continue beating until the egg whites hold soft peaks. Gently fold the egg whites into the batter until just combined.

4 Ladle a heaping ½ cup of the batter into the heated waffle iron, close the lid, and cook according to manufacturer's instructions until the waffle is golden brown and crisp, usually 5 to 6 minutes. Transfer the waffle to a plate and repeat with the remaining batter.

5 Serve the waffles hot, with butter and maple syrup alongside.

# GAME DAY

# EASY ONE-POT MAC 'N' CHEESE

5 cups **whole milk**

1 (1-pound) box **elbow macaroni**

2 cups shredded white **Cheddar cheese** (8 ounces)

½ cup (1 stick) **unsalted butter**

**Kosher salt** and **freshly ground black pepper**

Finely chopped fresh **flat-leaf parsley**, for serving

There's never enough mac, which is why we offer you two. The lure of a one-pot dish is real (just think of all those pots you don't have to wash!); the smart trick here is cooking the elbow macaroni directly in the milk. Those who swear by a crunchy-topped baked version will flip for our Ultimate Mac 'n' Cheese; this one ratchets up the stakes by adding bacon and five (yes, five!) types of cheese.

1  In a large pot, bring the milk to a simmer over medium-high heat.

2  Stir in the elbow macaroni and cook, stirring constantly, until the pasta is al dente, 7 to 10 minutes (see box, page 158).

3  Remove the pot from the heat. Add the Cheddar and butter and stir until both are melted, the sauce is smooth, and the pasta is coated. Season with salt and pepper.

4  Spoon into bowls and sprinkle each with parsley. Serve hot.

# ULTIMATE MAC 'N' CHEESE

SERVES
**12**

1 Preheat the oven to 350°F.

2 In a large pot, cook the bacon over medium heat, stirring, until the bacon is crispy and the fat has rendered, 10 to 12 minutes.

3 Add the bread crumbs, chives, parsley, and garlic and cook, stirring often, until the bread crumbs are toasted, 5 to 8 minutes. Transfer the mixture to a medium bowl.

4 Wipe the pot clean and return it to medium heat. Melt the butter in the pot. Stir in the flour and cook for 1 minute (see box, page 000). Stir in the evaporated milk and bring to a simmer. Stir in the dry mustard and cayenne and season with salt and black pepper.

5 Stir the pasta into the sauce. Add the cubed Cheddar, the Colby Jack, Provolone, Gruyère, and Gouda and stir until the cheeses have just melted into the sauce and coat the pasta.

6 Pour the mixture into a large baking dish and top with the shredded Cheddar and the mozzarella. Bake until the mac 'n' cheese is golden brown on top and bubbling in the center, 40 to 45 minutes. Transfer the dish to a wire rack. Sprinkle the bread crumb mixture over the top. Spoon into bowls while hot.

8 ounces **bacon**, diced

2 cups **panko bread crumbs**

½ cup finely chopped **fresh chives**

½ cup finely chopped **fresh flat-leaf parsley**

5 **garlic cloves**, minced

4 tablespoons (½ stick) **unsalted butter**

¼ cup **all-purpose flour**

1½ cups canned **evaporated milk**

2 teaspoons **dry mustard**

½ teaspoon **cayenne**

**Kosher salt** and **freshly ground black pepper**

1 (1-pound) box **elbow macaroni**, cooked to al dente (see box, page 158)

2 ounces yellow **Cheddar cheese**, cubed, plus 1 cup shredded (4 ounces)

2 ounces **Colby Jack cheese**, cubed

2 ounces **Provolone cheese**, cubed

½ cup shredded **Gruyère cheese** (2½ ounces)

½ cup shredded smoked **Gouda cheese** (2½ ounces)

1 cup shredded low-moisture **mozzarella cheese** (4 ounces)

# CHICKEN PARM BITES

**MAKES**
**18**
**BITES**

1 pound **chicken tenders**, halved crosswise

6 ounces low-moisture **mozzarella cheese**

**Vegetable oil**, for frying

2 cups **panko bread crumbs**

½ cup grated **Parmesan cheese** (2 ounces), plus more for serving

1 tablespoon **garlic powder**

1 tablespoon **dried basil**

1 tablespoon **dried parsley**

1 tablespoon **kosher salt**

½ cup **all-purpose flour**

2 large **eggs**, lightly beaten

1 cup prepared **marinara sauce**

What's not to like about chicken stuffed with mozzarella cheese and then deep fried? Whip out your sharpest knife here, as it's important to make a precise cut in the chicken tender so stuffing the cheese is as easy as possible.

Using a sharp paring knife, carefully cut slits in the "core" of the chicken pieces, making sure to not cut all the way through to the opposite side **A**.

Cut the mozzarella into pieces that will fit inside the slits, then stuff them inside the chicken pieces **B**.

Fill a large pot with vegetable oil to a depth of 1 inch. Attach a deep-fry thermometer to the side and heat the oil over medium-high heat to 350°F (see box, page 81).

Meanwhile, whisk together the bread crumbs, Parmesan, garlic powder, basil, parsley, and salt in a medium bowl. Place the flour in one shallow dish and the eggs in another **C**.

5 Working one at a time, dredge the chicken pieces in the flour (see box, page 247), shaking off any excess **D**, then dip in the egg, allowing any excess to drip off **E**, and finally dredge in the bread crumb mixture **F**, pressing to coat all over **G**. Set the coated chicken on a wire rack and repeat to coat the remaining pieces.

6 Working in batches, fry the chicken pieces, turning once, until fully cooked and golden brown, about 4 minutes total **H**. Transfer the chicken pieces to paper towels to drain. Repeat with the remaining chicken, letting the oil return to temperature after each batch.

7 Arrange the chicken on a platter. Sprinkle with more Parmesan and serve hot, with marinara sauce alongside for dipping **I**.

# PESTO CHICKEN GARLIC KNOT SLIDERS

Nonstick cooking spray

3 pounds **prepared pizza dough**

3 cups shredded **rotisserie chicken**

1 (8-ounce) jar **basil pesto**

2 cups shredded low-moisture **mozzarella cheese** (8 ounces)

3 tablespoons **unsalted butter**, melted

2 tablespoons finely chopped **fresh flat-leaf parsley**

3 **garlic cloves**, minced

Think of your classic garlic knot. Now upgrade them with a delectable rotisserie chicken and pesto filling, and don't forget the melty mozzarella cheese—it's almost too much goodness to handle. Pro tip: When cutting, it's helpful to hold the knots together with a towel on top while cutting them horizontally, as the motion of the knife might cause some of them to pull apart. Use a serrated knife for the cleanest slicing results.

1   Preheat the oven to 400°F. Grease a 9 by 13-inch baking dish with cooking spray.

2   Cut the pizza dough into 16 equal pieces, about 3 ounces each. Using your hands, roll each piece of dough into a 7- to 8-inch-long rope. Carefully tie each rope into a knot, tucking the ends underneath.

3   Arrange the knots in the prepared baking dish, nestling them close together in a 4-by-4 grid. Cover with a kitchen towel or plastic wrap and let rest until slightly puffed, about 20 minutes.

4   Uncover the knots and bake until they are light golden brown on top, about 25 minutes. Transfer the knots to a wire rack and let cool for 20 minutes. Reduce the oven temperature to 350°F.

5   Cut the grid of knots horizontally, creating 1 large top piece and 1 large bottom piece.

6   Return the bottom half of the knot grid to the baking dish. In this order, evenly layer the chicken, pesto, and mozzarella over the bread. Place the top half of the knot grid on top.

7   Stir together the melted butter, parsley, and garlic in a small bowl. Brush the mixture all over the top of the knots.

8   Bake until the tops of the knots are golden brown and the cheese has melted, 10 to 15 minutes. Transfer the baking dish to a wire rack and let cool for 5 minutes. Pull apart the knots into individual sliders and serve warm.

# CHEESY POTATO NEST

SERVES
**6 to 8**

Spiralizers have been cranking out a storm of zoodles (zucchini noodles), but it's time that this kitchen gadget met the potato for something a touch more indulgent. If you don't have Monterey Jack cheese, go ahead and substitute Colby or Cheddar. Either way, you're going to want to nest your appetite right in the center of this treat.

2 large **russet potatoes**

**Vegetable oil**, for frying

1 teaspoon **kosher salt**

1 teaspoon **onion powder**

½ teaspoon **garlic powder**

½ teaspoon **freshly ground black pepper**

¼ teaspoon **cayenne**

2 cup shredded **Monterey Jack cheese** (8 ounces)

1 cup shredded yellow **Cheddar cheese** (4 ounces)

2 tablespoons finely chopped **fresh chives**

**Ketchup**, for serving

1  Preheat the oven to 450°F. Line a baking sheet with foil.

2  Using a spiralizer, spiralize the potatoes  A . Transfer them to a large bowl of cold water to rinse off excess starch  B . Drain the potatoes in a colander, then transfer them to paper towels and let air-dry for 10 minutes.

3  Meanwhile, fill a large pot with vegetable oil to a depth of 2 inches. Attach a deep-fry thermometer to the side and heat the oil over medium-high heat to 375°F (see box, page 81).

4  While the oil heats, whisk together the salt, onion powder, garlic powder, black pepper, and cayenne in a small bowl. Toss together the Monterey Jack and Cheddar cheeses in a medium bowl.

5  Gather one-quarter of the potato spirals into a roughly 6- to 7-inch nest and, using tongs, slowly lower them into the oil all at once  C . Fry the potato nest, flipping once halfway through, until golden brown and crisp, about 5 minutes total. Using two long metal spatulas or tongs, reach underneath the nest on opposite sides and lift it out of the oil  D . Transfer the nest to the prepared baking sheet and immediately sprinkle with one-quarter of the spice blend. Repeat with the remaining potatoes to make 3 more nests, letting the oil return to temperature after each. Stack each seasoned potato nest on top of the last as the batches are finished  E .

6  Shower the stacked potato nest with the cheese mixture  F . Bake until the cheeses are completely melted and bubbling on top, 5 to 7 minutes.

7  Sprinkle the potato nest with chives and serve with ketchup.

recipe continues

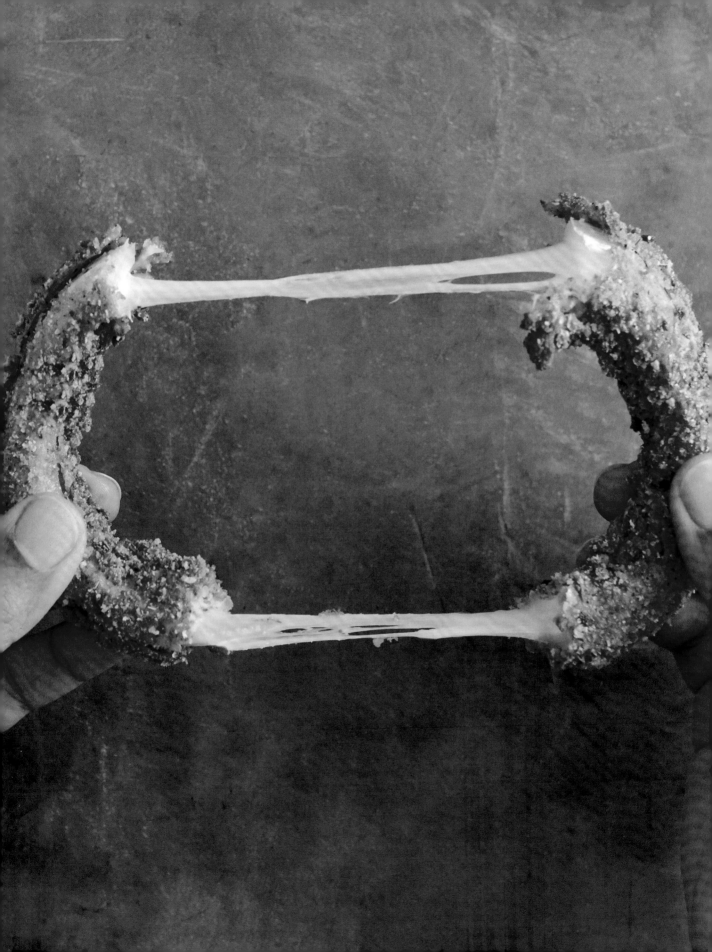

# MOZZARELLA STICK ONION RINGS

MAKES
**26**
ONION
RINGS

If there ever was a couple that was fated in the stars, it was mozzarella sticks and onion rings. Mozzarella stick onion ring heaven at home is nigh. It's crucial to fry in batches so that the rings don't get crowded and are able to crisp up nicely.

2 large **white onions** (about 13 ounces each)

12 ounces deli-sliced low-moisture **mozzarella cheese** (about 16 slices)

2 cups **all-purpose flour**

6 large **eggs**, lightly beaten

3 cups **plain bread crumbs**

**Kosher salt** and **freshly ground black pepper**

**Vegetable oil**, for frying

Thinly sliced **fresh basil leaves** and store-bought **marinara sauce**, for serving

1 Cut the onions crosswise into ½-inch-thick rings and separate the rings. Stack the mozzarella slices on top of each other in two large stacks, then cut the stacks into ½-inch-wide strips.

2 Working on a cutting board, place a smaller onion ring in the center of a larger one, creating concentric circles. Using as many mozzarella strips as necessary and cutting them to fit as needed, fill the gap between the rings with the cheese so that everything fits snugly together. You may need more than one layer of cheese, depending how large a gap is between the rings. Repeat with the remaining onion rings and cheese to make about 26 stuffed onion rings. Place the stuffed rings on a baking sheet and freeze until firm, about 1 hour.

3 Set up a dredging station: Place the flour, eggs, and bread crumbs in three separate shallow dishes. Season each with salt and pepper.

4 Coat a frozen ring in the flour, shaking off the excess, then dip it into the beaten egg, letting any excess drip back into the bowl (see box, right). Dredge the onion ring in the bread crumbs, then back into the egg, and finally back in the bread crumbs, pressing to coat completely. Return the ring to the baking sheet to dry. Repeat to coat the remaining onion rings. Place the baking sheet in the freezer and chill the rings until firm, at least 1 hour or up to 1 week.

5 Fill a large pot with vegetable oil to a depth of 2 inches and attach a deep-fry thermometer to the side. Heat the oil over medium-high heat to 350°F (see box, page 81).

6 Fry the onion rings 2 to 3 at a time, turning occasionally, until golden brown, about 2 minutes. Be careful not to fry them for too long to avoid having the cheese ooze out. Using tongs, transfer the rings to a wire rack set over paper towels to drain.

7 Once all the rings are fried, scatter basil leaves over the top. Serve hot with marinara sauce for dipping.

## 101 Dredging

Coating your onion rings (or chicken or shrimp or really anything) with flour before frying is a shortcut to a deliciously crispy exterior and perfectly moist interior. For a classic dredge, also known as SBP (Standard Breading Procedure), you need flour, eggs, and some sort of crumb—plain or panko bread crumbs, crushed chips or cornflakes, etc. The process of dipping in flour, then egg, creates a layer of edible glue that makes the crumbs stick to food like magic. And if you go back and forth more than once, you get extra crunch. Make sure to designate one hand for the wet ingredients (eggs) and one hand for the dry (flour and crumbs) to avoid sticky mixing.

1 bunch **kale** (about 8 ounces), stemmed, leaves torn into bite-size pieces

2 tablespoons **olive oil**

2 tablespoons **seasoning mix of your choice** (recipes follow)

**Kosher salt** and **freshly ground black pepper**

# KALE CHIPS FOUR WAYS

Forget the fact that the whole world went gaga for kale as a super ingredient; these chips are just damn good, any which way you prepare them—especially when you layer in flavors from around the world.

1   Preheat the oven to 350°F. Line a baking sheet with parchment paper.

2   Combine the kale, olive oil, seasoning mix of your choice, and salt and pepper in a medium bowl and toss to coat completely. Arrange the kale in a single layer on the baking sheet. Bake until the edges are browned, about 15 minutes. Transfer the baking sheet to a wire rack and let the kale chips cool for 10 minutes before serving.

## MOROCCAN PEPPER SEASONING MIX

1 tablespoon plus 1 teaspoon **Aleppo pepper**

¾ teaspoon **smoked paprika**

¾ teaspoon **ground coriander**

¾ teaspoon **ground cumin**

¾ teaspoon **garlic powder**

⅛ teaspoon **cayenne**

⅛ teaspoon **citric acid** (sold in most grocery stores in the canning aisle)

Combine all the ingredients in a small bowl and stir together.

## JERK SEASONING MIX

2 teaspoons **dried thyme**

1½ teaspoons **ground allspice**

1 teaspoon **garlic powder**

1 teaspoon **onion powder**

½ teaspoon **ground ginger**

¼ teaspoon **Scotch bonnet chile powder** or **cayenne**

Combine all the ingredients in a small bowl and stir together.

## DRY BBQ SEASONING MIX

1½ teaspoons **dark brown sugar**

1½ teaspoons **sweet paprika**

½ teaspoon **garlic powder**

½ teaspoon **onion powder**

½ teaspoon **poultry seasoning**

¼ teaspoon **dry mustard**

Combine all the ingredients in a small bowl and stir together.

## JAPANESE "7 SPICE" SEASONING MIX

1½ teaspoons **crushed red pepper flakes**

1½ teaspoons **freshly ground black pepper**

1½ teaspoons **dried orange peel**

¾ teaspoon **white sesame seeds**

¾ teaspoon **ground ginger**

¾ teaspoon finely crumbled **dried nori seaweed**

¾ teaspoon **poppy seeds**

Combine all the ingredients in a spice grinder and process until finely ground.

# HOMEMADE SOFT PRETZELS

MAKES
**8**
PRETZELS

As something best eaten fresh out of the oven, a pretzel is a prime candidate for home baking versus store taking. Dipping the pretzels in a solution of baking soda and water gives them that glossy pretzel sheen when they emerge from the oven. Make sure to seek out coarse or large-grained kosher salt for the topping—it gives the pretzels an extra authentic touch.

1½ cups **lukewarm water** (110°F)

1 tablespoon **granulated sugar**

1 (¼-ounce) packet **active dry yeast**

4½ cups **all-purpose flour**

2 tablespoons **vegetable oil**, plus more for greasing

1 tablespoon **kosher salt**

⅔ cup **baking soda**

2 large **eggs**, lightly beaten

**Coarse salt**, for sprinkling

1 Preheat the oven to 450°F. Cut eight 8-inch squares of parchment paper. Line a baking sheet with one whole sheet of parchment paper.

2 Whisk together the water and granulated sugar in a large bowl. Add the yeast and let stand until foamy, about 10 minutes.

3 Add the flour, vegetable oil, and kosher salt and stir until a dough forms. Turn the dough out onto a clean surface and knead until a smooth, elastic dough forms, about 6 minutes (see box, page 250).

4 Grease a large bowl with a little bit of oil. Add the dough and turn to coat with oil. Cover the bowl with a kitchen towel or plastic wrap and let the dough rise in a warm, draft-free area until doubled in size, about 1 hour.

5 Turn the dough out onto a clean surface and cut it into 8 equal pieces. Working with one piece of dough at a time, roll the dough into a thin rope, then twist the ends together and fold them onto the middle of the rope to form a pretzel shape A . Place each formed pretzel on an individual square of parchment paper.

6 Bring a large pot of water to a boil over high heat. Stir in the baking soda. Using the squares of parchment paper to handle the pretzels, lower them one at a time into the boiling water B and cook, pressing lightly with a slotted spoon to submerge in the water, for 30 seconds.

7 Using a slotted spoon, lift the pretzels from the water C and transfer them to the prepared baking sheet. Brush the pretzels with the beaten egg and sprinkle with coarse salt D . Bake until the pretzels are golden brown, 10 to 15 minutes. Transfer the pretzels to a wire rack and let cool for 5 minutes before serving.

recipe continues

**101**

## Kneading

If you want to get your homemade bread on, you're going to need to knead. Gluten, the protein in flour that gives bread its structure and texture, needs to be developed—courtesy of a little elbow grease from you—before your loaves can get all the love. To knead, sprinkle a clean, dry work surface minimally with flour (the more flour you use, the more you risk of stiffening and toughening your dough). If needed, you can flour the dough lightly, too. Use the heel of your hand to press it away from your body, then fold it over and rotate it a quarter turn between each knead. Follow the recipe's instructions to determine how smooth your dough should be.

# DEEP-FRIED DEVILED EGGS

Vegetable oil, for frying

12 large **hard-boiled eggs**
(see box, page 118)

1 cup **all-purpose flour**

3 large **eggs**

2 cups **panko bread crumbs**

**Kosher salt** and **freshly ground
black pepper**

¼ cup **mayonnaise**

2 tablespoons **dill pickle relish**

2 tablespoons **yellow mustard**

1 teaspoon **hot sauce**,
such as Tabasco

**Sweet paprika**, for garnish

The devil is most certainly in the details here—
you've probably fried chicken or fish, but what
about an egg? Don't panic if you don't have a
"proper" piping bag designed for pastry.
A plastic sandwich bag with the corner
snipped off works just as well.

1   Fill a medium saucepan with vegetable oil to a depth of 2 inches. Attach a deep-fry thermometer to the side and heat the oil over medium heat to 350°F (see box, page 81).

2   Halve the hard-boiled eggs lengthwise and separate the whites and yolks. Set the whites on a plate; put the yolks in a medium bowl and set aside.

3   Place the flour, raw eggs, and bread crumbs in three separate shallow dishes and season each with salt and pepper. Dip the cooked egg whites in the flour, shaking off any excess, then dip them in the raw eggs, allowing any excess to drip off, and finally dredge in the bread crumbs, pressing to coat (see box, page 247).

4   Working in batches, drop the breaded egg whites in the hot oil and fry until golden brown and crisp, 2 to 3 minutes. Remove the egg whites with a slotted spoon and drain on a paper towels. Repeat with the remaining egg whites, letting the oil return to temperature after each batch.

5   In a medium bowl, combine the cooked egg yolks, mayonnaise, relish, mustard, and hot sauce. Season with salt and pepper. Mash until smooth. Transfer the yolk mixture to a piping bag fitted with a ½-inch round tip. (See box, page 192; alternatively, use a plastic sandwich bag and snip off the corner.)

6   Arrange the fried egg whites on a serving platter, cut-side up, and pipe the yolk mixture into the centers. Dust the deviled eggs with paprika before serving.

# COCKTAIL NUTS FOUR WAYS

1 cup **raw cashews**

1 cup **raw pecan halves**

1 cup **raw walnut halves**

1 cup **raw almonds**

¼ cup **olive oil**

2 teaspoons **kosher salt**

2 tablespoons **seasoning mix of your choice** (recipes follow)

Preparing your own cocktail nuts is simple, cheap, and easy, and serving these to guests will make you feel like you're running a high-end cocktail lounge. Cheers!

1 Preheat the oven to 350°F. Line a rimmed baking sheet with foil.

2 Combine all the nuts, the olive oil, salt, and seasoning mix of your choice in a large bowl. Toss to coat completely.

3 Transfer the nuts and seasonings to the prepared baking sheet and spread them into an even layer. Bake, stirring once halfway through, until golden brown and toasted, about 15 minutes.

4 Transfer the cocktail nuts to a serving bowl and serve warm, or let cool completely and store in an airtight container at room temperature for up to 2 weeks.

MEDITERRANEAN

FRENCH

## MEDITERRANEAN HERB AND SEED MIX

1½ teaspoons **dried thyme**

1½ teaspoons **dried marjoram**

1½ teaspoons **sumac**

1 teaspoon **toasted sesame seeds**

¾ teaspoon **dried oregano**

½ teaspoon **ground cumin**

Combine all the ingredients in a small bowl and stir together.

## FRENCH HERB SEASONING MIX

½ **dried bay leaf**, crumbled

1½ teaspoons **dried thyme**

1 teaspoon **dried summer savory**

1 teaspoon **dried marjoram**

1 teaspoon **dried rosemary**

½ teaspoon **dried oregano**

½ teaspoon **dried lavender**

Process the bay leaf in a spice grinder until finely ground. Transfer to a small bowl and stir in the remaining ingredients.

## INDIAN-STYLE SEASONING MIX

1 teaspoon **cumin seeds**

1 teaspoon **coriander seeds**

1 teaspoon **fennel seeds**

¾ teaspoon **black Himalayan salt** (kala namak) or **Hawaiian black sea salt**

½ teaspoon **amchoor** (dried mango powder)

½ teaspoon **ground ginger**

½ teaspoon **dried mint**

½ teaspoon **freshly ground black pepper**

¼ teaspoon **ajwain (carom) seeds**

¼ teaspoon **garam masala**

⅛ teaspoon **cayenne**

Combine the cumin, coriander, and fennel seeds, and black salt in a spice grinder and process until finely ground. Stir in the remaining ingredients.

## ETHIOPIAN-STYLE SEASONING MIX

1 tablespoon **dried onion flakes**

½ teaspoon **coriander seeds**

¼ teaspoon **fenugreek seeds**

¼ teaspoon **whole black peppercorns**

⅛ teaspoon **allspice berries**

2 **green cardamom pods**, crushed

1 **whole clove**

1 **dried chile de árbol**, seeded

1½ teaspoons **sweet paprika**

⅛ teaspoon freshly **grated nutmeg**

⅛ teaspoon **ground ginger**

⅛ teaspoon **ground cinnamon**

Combine the onion flakes, coriander, fenugreek, peppercorns, allspice, cardamom, clove, and árbol chile in a spice grinder and process until finely ground. Transfer to a bowl and stir in the paprika, nutmeg, ginger, and cinnamon.

**ETHIOPIAN**

**INDIAN**

255

# CAESAR SALAD POTATO SKINS

Hold up! Wait a minute! How does classic Caesar salad combine with potato skins to make one spectacular dish? Read on to find out. Keep your attention on your oven when you are broiling the potato skins—you want the cheese to be golden brown, not scorched.

8 small **russet potatoes**, preferably the same size and shape

6 tablespoons **olive oil**

**Kosher salt** and **freshly ground black pepper**

3 tablespoons fresh **lemon juice**

1½ tablespoons **Dijon mustard**

1½ tablespoons **garlic paste** (see box, opposite)

1½ tablespoons **anchovy paste**

⅓ cup grated **Parmesan cheese** (2 ounces)

2 tablespoons plus 2 teaspoons **panko bread crumbs**

16 **romaine lettuce leaves**, ribs removed, thinly sliced into ribbons

2 **lemons**, cut into 8 wedges each, for serving

1   Preheat the oven to 400°F.

2   Brush the potatoes with 3 tablespoons of the olive oil and season with salt and pepper. Place them on a baking sheet and bake until tender and golden brown, 40 to 50 minutes. Transfer the potatoes to a cutting board and let cool for 5 minutes.

3   Halve the potatoes lengthwise. Using a small spoon, scoop out the potato flesh and discard, leaving a ⅛-inch-thick shell of potato and skin on all sides. Return the potato shells to the baking sheet. Turn on the broiler.

4   In a large bowl, whisk together the remaining 3 tablespoons olive oil, the lemon juice, mustard, garlic, and anchovy paste until smooth. Brush some of the dressing over the insides of the potato shells. Sprinkle each with 1 teaspoon of the Parmesan and ½ teaspoon of the bread crumbs.

5   Broil the potato skins until the outsides are crisp and the cheese is browned, 5 to 10 minutes (see box, page 57).

6   Meanwhile, add the lettuce to the bowl with the remaining dressing and toss to coat well.

7   Transfer the hot potato skins to a serving platter. Divide the lettuce among the potatoes and serve each with a small wedge of lemon for squeezing.

# Garlic Paste

Good garlic paste doesn't require a run to the grocery store. All you need is garlic, salt, and a sharp knife. First, peel the garlic by smashing the cloves against a cutting board. Finely chop the cloves, then sprinkle them with a pinch of salt. Using the side of your knife, press and mash the garlic together with the salt, scraping and mincing, too, until they form a fine paste. By mashing the salt against the cloves as you cut, moisture is drawn out from the garlic, taming its sharp bite—this is particularly desirable when mixing the garlic into preparations where it won't be cooked, like vinaigrettes, dips, and other sauces. As a bonus, garlic is also super easy to measure once it reaches a paste consistency.

gin negroni vs.
whiskey manhattan 260
bacon avocado caesar salad 262
truffle mac 'n' cheese 263
scalloped potatoes 264
green shrimp cocktail 266

# DATE NIGHT

baked lobster tails 267
molten lava brownies 271
seared pork chops with mushroom
& white wine sauce 272
salted caramel macchiato tiramisu
for two 275

# GIN NEGRONI

2 ounces **dry gin**

2 ounces **bitter red liqueur**, such as Campari

2 ounces **sweet vermouth**

2 **orange peels** (without pith), for garnish

A tale of two cocktails, one bitter and one sweet. The Negroni gets its bitterness from Campari, an Italian spirit made from a secret blend containing orange and spices. The bitterness is tempered with sweet vermouth, a kind of fortified wine. The drink is served over ice in a lowball, or rocks glass, with a twist of aromatic orange rind. For those looking for a sweeter cocktail, we present the Manhattan. It gets its main alcoholic punch from rye whiskey. Angostura bitters, a potion of herbs and spices, gives just the right hint of bitterness, and the lovely sweetness comes from Italian candied cherries. Serve this cocktail chilled and strained into a martini glass.

1  Place a large ice cube in each of 2 short lowball glasses.

2  In each glass, add 1 ounce each of the gin, Campari, and vermouth. Stir until chilled, about 15 seconds.

3  Garnish each glass with an orange peel and serve.

# WHISKEY MANHATTAN

SERVES
2

1  Place 2 martini glasses in the freezer to chill while you make the cocktails.

2  Combine the whiskey, vermouth, and bitters in a cocktail shaker filled with crushed ice. Stir or shake until chilled, about 15 seconds.

3  Strain half the mixture into each chilled glass. Garnish each with a cherry and serve.

4 ounces **rye whiskey**

2 ounces **sweet vermouth**

4 dashes **Angostura bitters**

2 **maraschino cherries**, such as Luxardo or Amarena, for garnish

SERVES
2

# BACON AVOCADO CAESAR SALAD

¼ cup store-bought or homemade **Caesar dressing**

1 head **romaine lettuce**, cored and chopped into 1-inch pieces

½ cup **croutons**

½ cup shaved **Parmesan cheese** (2 ounces), plus more for serving

4 **bacon slices**, cooked and coarsely crumbled

1 ripe **avocado**, diced

Picture the perfect classic Caesar—now add bacon crumbles and diced avocado and say "upgrade" ten times fast. We've provided you with a twofer: Flip back to the Caesar Salad Potato Skins recipes on page 256 and use the Caesar dressing recipe listed there, or, even easier, keep the prep light and use a store-bought dressing.

1 Put the dressing in the bottom of a salad bowl. Add the lettuce, croutons, Parmesan, bacon, and avocado. Toss to combine and coat.

2 Sprinkle more shaved Parmesan on top to serve.

# TRUFFLE MAC 'N' CHEESE

SERVES
4

Just when you thought mac 'n' cheese couldn't possibly get any better, here comes truffle mac 'n' cheese. The addition of thinly sliced cremini or button mushrooms plays up the truffle oil's heavenly, earthy flavor. Just remember—a little bit of that oil goes a *looong* way, so use sparingly.

3 tablespoons **unsalted butter**

1 cup **cremini** or **button mushrooms**, thinly sliced

2 tablespoons **all-purpose flour**

1 cup **whole milk**

1 cup grated **Parmesan cheese** (4 ounces)

1 cup shredded **Cheddar cheese** (8 ounces)

**Kosher salt** and **freshly ground black pepper**

2 cups cooked **pasta shells**

Minced **fresh chives** and **truffle oil**, for serving

1  In a medium saucepan, melt 1 tablespoon of the butter over medium heat. Add the mushrooms and cook, stirring, until soft, about 6 minutes. Transfer the mushrooms to a medium bowl and return the pan to medium heat.

2  Make a roux (see box, below) by melting the remaining 2 tablespoons butter in the pan, then stir in the flour and cook, whisking continuously for 1 to 2 minutes. Slowly pour in the milk, whisking continuously to avoid lumps. Cook, stirring, until the sauce comes to a boil, 3 to 5 minutes. Add the Parmesan and Cheddar cheeses and stir until melted and smooth. Season the cheese sauce with salt and pepper and remove the pan from the heat.

3  Add the mushrooms and cooked pasta to the sauce and stir to coat completely.

4  Spoon the pasta into bowls and sprinkle with chives. Drizzle with truffle oil and serve hot.

## 101

## Roux

Think of a roux as slurry's dry cousin (see page 289). While also used as a thickening agent for gravy, soups, stews, and sauces, a roux is typically made from flour and fat, instead of flour and water, and browned in a pan until golden and toasty before adding the liquid. It lends color, flavor, and thickness to whatever it graces. Regular butter, clarified butter, leftover bacon drippings, or rendered fat (see page 90) are all perfect candidates for the fat portion of a roux.

1 tablespoon **unsalted butter**

2 **garlic cloves**, minced

1 tablespoon **all-purpose flour**

1 cup **whole milk**

1 teaspoon **kosher salt**

½ teaspoon **freshly ground black pepper**

1¼ pounds **Yukon Gold potatoes** (about 3 large), peeled

2 tablespoons grated **Parmesan cheese**

Finely chopped **fresh flat-leaf parsley**, for serving (optional)

# SCALLOPED POTATOES

This recipe is a great one for showing off your knife skills: Keep those potato slices as uniform as possible and aim for ⅛-inch-thick slices (we'll wait here while you bust out a ruler). The parsley garnish is optional, but the sprightly color it adds to the gorgeous golden brown crust is GOALS.

1 Preheat the oven to 350°F.

2 In a small saucepan, melt the butter over medium heat. Add the garlic and cook, stirring, until it is just beginning to brown, about 2 minutes. Stir in the flour and cook, stirring, until there are no more lumps, about 1 minute.

3 While whisking continuously to keep the mixture smooth, slowly drizzle in the milk. Season with the salt and pepper. Stirring steadily, bring the sauce to a boil, then remove the pan from the heat and let cool.

4 Using a knife or mandoline, cut the potatoes crosswise into ⅛-inch-thick slices. Arrange them in the bottom of a small (1½- to 2-quart) baking dish, overlapping them as needed to fit them all in. Pour the white sauce evenly over the potatoes, then sprinkle with Parmesan.

5 Bake until the sauce is bubbling, the top is golden brown, and the potatoes are tender, 1 hour. Transfer the dish to a wire rack and let cool slightly. Sprinkle with chopped parsley, if using. Serve hot.

# GREEN SHRIMP COCKTAIL

2 pounds large (12/15-count) peeled (tail-on) and deveined **raw shrimp** (see box, page 116)

2 tablespoons **olive oil**

**Kosher salt** and **freshly ground black pepper**

8 ounces **tomatillos**, husked and well rinsed

1 cup packed **fresh cilantro leaves**

2 tablespoons **green hot pepper sauce**

1 tablespoon **prepared horseradish**

2 teaspoons **minced garlic**

Eaten raw, tomatillos—a tomato-like veggie commonly found in Mexican sauces—can be a little acidic and sharp-tasting, but when cooked their flavor mellows out. This green sauce, packed with horseradish, cilantro, garlic, and those tomatillos, is the perfect foil for the roasted pink shrimp, letting their sweeter side shine. When you remove the husks from the tomatillos, they'll feel a little sticky—don't fret, this is their natural state, and will disappear during cooking.

1  Preheat the oven to 400°F.

2  Spread the shrimp over a rimmed baking sheet, drizzle with the olive oil, and season with salt and pepper. Toss to coat, then arrange the shrimp in an even layer. Roast until opaque, pink, and cooked through, 12 to 15 minutes.

3  Meanwhile, fill a medium saucepan halfway with water and bring to a boil over high heat. Add the tomatillos and cook until bright green, about 3 minutes. Drain the tomatillos and transfer to a blender or food processor. Add the cilantro, pepper sauce, horseradish, and garlic and blend until smooth. Pour the sauce into a small bowl, season with salt and pepper, and let cool.

4  Serve the shrimp warm with the sauce.

# BAKED LOBSTER TAILS

Lobster hardly needs any additions to reach epic Tasty proportions, but brush the tails with a mix of melted butter, garlic powder, paprika, lemon juice, and parsley and you'll ratchet up the delicious factor like, woah. After boiling the lobster tails, you can store the cooled, par-cooked lobsters in the refrigerator for up to one day in advance.

2 (8-ounce) **raw lobster tails**

3 tablespoons **unsalted butter**, melted

1 teaspoon **kosher salt**

1 teaspoon **freshly ground black pepper**

1 teaspoon **garlic powder**

1 teaspoon **sweet paprika**

1 teaspoon fresh **lemon juice**

1 teaspoon finely chopped **fresh flat-leaf parsley**

**Lemon wedges**, for serving

1   Preheat the oven to 450°F. Line a baking sheet with parchment paper.

2   Bring a large pot of water to a boil over high heat.

3   Holding a lobster tail upside down and starting at the base, insert a long wooden or metal skewer lengthwise through the lobster meat. Repeat with the second lobster tail **A**.

4   Add the lobsters to the boiling water and cook, covered, for exactly 5 minutes, until the shells are dark red. (The meat will not be fully cooked, but you'll be finishing them in the oven.). Using tongs, transfer the lobster tails to a cutting board and let cool to room temperature **B**.

5   Remove the skewers. Holding one lobster tail right-side up and starting at the opposite end from the fin, use a clean pair of scissors or kitchen shears to cut a slit down the center of the shell, making sure to cut in a straight line and avoid cutting through the lobster meat inside as much as possible **C**. Stop cutting before you reach the fin.

6   Insert the tip of a spoon facedown between the shell and the meat. Run it along the length of the slit you created to separate the meat from the shell **D**. Holding the shell open with one hand **E**, lift the meat up and out of the shell in one piece **F**. Press the two sides of the shell back together, then lay the meat over the seam in the shell.

7   Make a shallow cut down the center of the top of the lobster meat with kitchen shears and peel back the thin, red-mottled layer to reveal the white meat underneath to give the lobster tails their signature look. Place the lobster tails on the prepared baking sheet.

8   Stir together the butter, salt, pepper, garlic powder, paprika, lemon juice, and parsley in a small bowl. Brush the butter mixture evenly over both lobster tails. Bake until the lobster meat is cooked through and fragrant, 5 to 10 minutes.

9   Transfer each lobster tail to a plate and serve hot, with lemon wedges.

recipe continues

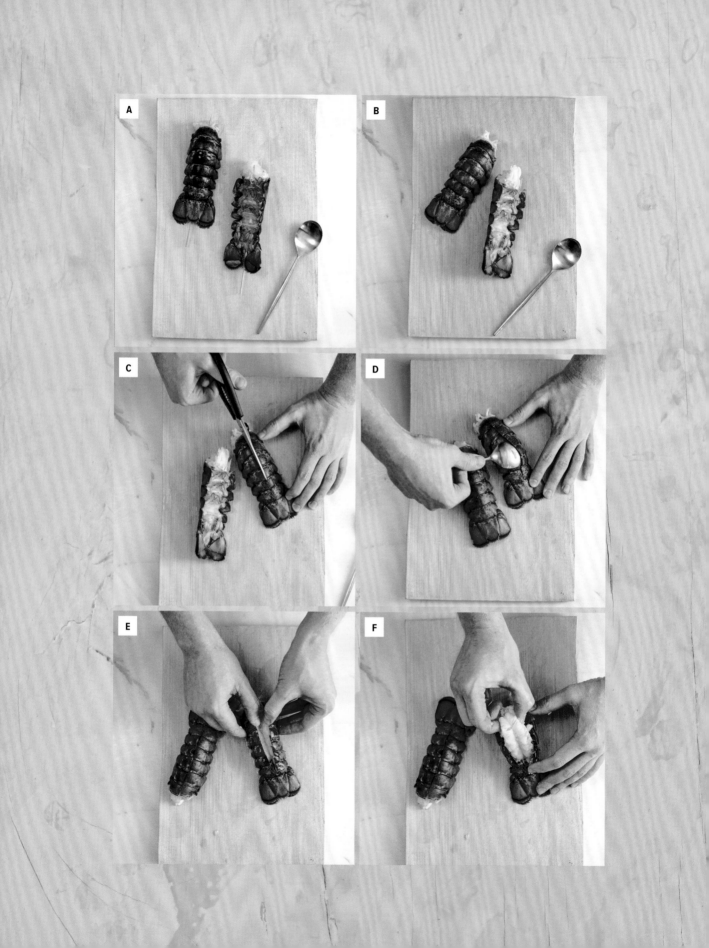

# MOLTEN LAVA BROWNIES

SERVES
2

Dark chocolate truffles are the secret hack behind these guaranteed-wow individual lava cakes. This recipe will leave you with excess brownie batter. Oh, what a terrible problem to have, right? We suggest that you make a small tray of brownies with the leftover batter, freeze the brownies, then crumble them over ice cream for a sundae whenever it strikes your fancy. Think of it as having brownies in the bank.

Nonstick cooking spray

1 (18.3-ounce) box **brownie mix**

½ cup **vegetable oil**

2 large **eggs**

4 **milk chocolate** or **dark chocolate truffles**, such as Lindt

**Mixed fresh berries, vanilla ice cream**, and **chocolate sauce**, for serving

1   Preheat the oven to 350°F. Grease two 6-ounce ramekins with cooking spray.

2   Prepare the brownie mix according to the package instructions, using the vegetable oil, eggs, and ¼ cup water. Measure out 1½ cups of the brownie batter; discard the remainder or save it for another use.

3   Spoon ½ cup of the brownie batter in each ramekin, then press 2 chocolate truffles side by side into the center of each. Spoon ¼ cup of the remaining brownie batter over the top of the truffles in each ramekin and smooth the tops with the back of the spoon.

4   Bake the brownie cakes until the batter is set and dry on top, about 25 minutes. Transfer the ramekins to a wire rack and let the cakes cool slightly, about 5 minutes.

5   Run a knife around the edge of each ramekin, then invert each cake onto a serving plate.

6   Top the cakes with fresh berries and serve warm with ice cream and drizzled with chocolate sauce.

# SEARED PORK CHOPS WITH MUSHROOM & WHITE WINE SAUCE

2 tablespoons **olive oil**

2 (10-ounce) bone-in **pork chops**, frenched (see box, page 55)

**Kosher salt** and **freshly ground black pepper**

4 tablespoons (½ stick) **unsalted butter**

10 ounces **cremini mushrooms**, thinly sliced

6 **garlic cloves**, smashed

4 **thyme sprigs**

1 cup **dry white wine**, such as sauvignon blanc

1 tablespoon **Dijon mustard**

1 tablespoon fresh **lemon juice**

Finely chopped **fresh flat-leaf parsley**, for serving

Mushrooms, wine, and pork . . . there's no need to hit the restaurant ever again. Frenching is a technique where the rib bone is exposed and all meat is removed; ask your butcher to do this for a beautiful finished dish.

1 In a large cast-iron skillet, heat the olive oil over medium-high heat. Season the pork chops with salt and pepper. Add them to the skillet and cook, flipping once halfway through, until golden brown on both sides (see box, below) and an instant-read thermometer inserted in the side registers 155°F, 12 to 15 minutes total. Transfer the pork chops to individual plates and return the skillet to medium-high heat.

2 Melt the butter in the skillet. Add the mushrooms, garlic, and thyme and cook, stirring occasionally, until the mushrooms begin to brown, about 6 minutes. Pour in the wine and cook, scraping up any browned bits from the bottom of the skillet, until the wine has reduced by half, about 5 minutes (see box, page 33). Stir in the mustard and lemon juice, then season with more salt and pepper. Pick out and discard the garlic cloves and thyme stems.

3 Spoon the sauce over the pork chops and sprinkle with parsley.

### 101

## Searing

To seal in flavor and juices and develop crust on protein or even vegetables, nothing beats a sear. Achieve sear status by heating a heavy-bottomed skillet or pot over high heat, then swirling in a small amount of oil. Once it's hot and shimmery, add the goods. You can flip it halfway through cooking, but don't move it around in the pan as it cooks—stillness ensures a nice crust. You'll know your food has been properly seared when it releases easily from the pan and has a gorgeous golden brown color.

# SALTED CARAMEL MACCHIATO TIRAMISU FOR TWO

Three words: Salted. Caramel. Tiramisu. This dish becomes a legend most when it has time to sit for twenty-four hours, which gives the cookies ample time to soak up all the delicious moisture, but it can also be served after being refrigerated for only two.

2 tablespoons **granulated sugar**

2 large **egg yolks,**
room temperature (see box, page 149)

8 ounces **mascarpone cheese**

2 tablespoons **prepared caramel sauce**, plus more for drizzling

9 **Italian ladyfingers** (savoiardi)

½ cup strong **brewed espresso,**
cooled

**Whipped cream** and **flaky sea salt**, for serving

1 Put the sugar and egg yolks in a small bowl and whisk vigorously until the mixture thickens and falls back on itself in a ribbon when the whisk is lifted out, 6 to 8 minutes. Fold in the mascarpone and caramel sauce to combine evenly.

2 Break each ladyfinger in half crosswise. Dunk each half briefly in the espresso and arrange 3 halves, side by side, in the bottom of each of two cocktail glasses. (You may need to squish them together tightly to fit.) Top each with 3 heaping tablespoons of the caramel-mascarpone mixture and smooth the tops with the back of the spoon. Continue layering the ladyfinger halves and the caramel-mascarpone mixture to make three layers. Discard any remaining espresso. Cover the glasses with plastic wrap and refrigerate for at least 2 hours and up to 24 hours. (The longer it sits, the better it gets.)

3 When ready to serve, top each glass with a dollop of whipped cream. Drizzle with more caramel sauce and sprinkle with a pinch of sea salt.

# HOLIDAY

## PIE DOUGH

2 cups **all-purpose flour**, plus more for dusting (see box, page 179)

2 teaspoons **granluated sugar**

1 teaspoon **kosher salt**

10 tablespoons (1¼ sticks) **unsalted butter**, cut into ½-inch cubes and chilled

⅓ cup ice-cold **water**

## FILLING

1¾ cups **granluated sugar**

2 teaspoons **cream of tartar**

½ teaspoon **ground cinnamon**

Finely grated zest and juice of 1 **lemon** (see box, page 203)

2 cups coarsely broken **buttery crackers**, such as Ritz (4 ounces)

2 tablespoons **unsalted butter**, cut into ½-inch cubes and chilled

1 large **egg**

# MOCK APPLE PIE

There's nothing more American than apple pie—except two apple pies. The Traditional Mile-High Apple Pie is the one your mom made (or maybe you wish your mom had made): a double-crusted buttery crust piled high with sweet-tart apples. The Mock Apple Pie contains no apples (shocker!). Born of the thrifty ingenuity of America's Great Depression years, broken crackers and cinnamon disguise themselves convincingly as the real thing.

1 Make the pie dough: Sift the flour, sugar, and salt into a large bowl (see box, page 219). Add the butter and use your fingers to pinch the butter into the flour until it forms pea-size crumbles. Add the water and stir with a fork until the dough is moistened evenly.

2 Turn the dough out onto a clean surface and knead briefly until it comes together (see box, page 250). Shape the dough into a mound, cut it in half, then shape each half into a ½-inch-thick disc. Wrap each disc separately in plastic and refrigerate for at least 1 hour and up to 2 days.

3 Make the filling: In a medium saucepan, combine the sugar, cream of tartar, and 1½ cups water and bring to a boil over high heat. Reduce the heat to medium and simmer until slightly reduced, about 15 minutes. Remove the pan from the heat and stir in the cinnamon, lemon zest, and lemon juice. Let the syrup cool completely.

4 Preheat the oven to 400°F.

5 On a lightly floured surface, roll out one disc of chilled dough to ⅛-inch thickness. Transfer the dough to a 9-inch metal pie plate, letting it settle into the bottom and up the sides, and letting the excess hang over the sides of the pan.

6 Fill the pie plate with the crackers, then drizzle the syrup over the top. Dot the butter evenly over the crackers and syrup.

7 Roll out the second dough disc to ⅛-inch thickness and place it over the filling. Trim the edges of the top and bottom crusts, leaving 1 inch of overhang, then tuck the overhang underneath and press it against the lip of the pie dish. Use a fork to crimp the edge of the dough.

8 Beat the egg with 1 tablespoon water in a small bowl. Brush the egg wash all over the top of the pie. Cut four slits in the top of the pie. Bake until the crust is golden brown and the filling is bubbling in the center, about 35 minutes. Transfer the pie to a wire rack and let cool completely, about 3 hours, before slicing and serving.

# TRADITIONAL MILE-HIGH APPLE PIE

1  Make the pie dough: Sift the flour, granulated sugar, and salt into a large bowl (see box, page 219). Add the butter and use your fingers to pinch the butter into the flour until it forms pea-size crumbles. Add the water and stir with a fork until the dough is moistened evenly.

2  Turn the dough out onto a clean surface and knead briefly until it comes together (see box, page 250). Shape the dough into a mound, cut it in half, then shape each half into a ½-inch-thick disc. Wrap each disc separately in plastic and refrigerate for at least 1 hour and up to 2 days.

3  Preheat the oven to 425°F.

4  Make the filling: Combine the flour, granulated sugar, brown sugar, lemon juice, salt, cinnamon, and nutmeg in a large bowl and stir until smooth. Add the apples and toss to coat completely.

5  On a lightly floured surface, roll out one disc of chilled dough to ⅛-inch thickness. Transfer the dough to a 9-inch deep-dish pie dish, letting it settle into the bottom and up the sides, and letting the excess hang over the sides of the dish.

6  Stir the apples once more to evenly combine, then pour them into the pie dish, mounding them in the center. Dot the remaining butter evenly over the apples.

7  Roll out the second dough disc to ⅛-inch thickness and place it over the filling. Trim the edges of the top and bottom crusts, leaving 1 inch of overhang, then tuck the overhang underneath and press it against the lip of the pie dish. Use your fingers to crimp the edge of the dough as desired.

8  Beat together the egg with 1 tablespoon water in a small bowl. Brush the egg wash all over the top of the pie. Cut four slits in the top of the pie. Bake for 30 minutes, then reduce the oven temperature to 350°F and bake until the crust is golden brown and the filling is bubbling in the center, 1½ hours more.

9  Transfer the pie to a wire rack and let cool completely, about 4 hours, before slicing and serving.

## PIE DOUGH

3 cups **all-purpose flour**, plus more for dusting (see box, page 179)

1 tablespoon **granulated sugar**

2 teaspoons **kosher salt**

1½ cups (3 sticks) **unsalted butter**, cut into ½-inch cubes and chilled

⅔ cup **ice-cold water**

## FILLING

¼ cup **all-purpose flour**, plus more for dusting

½ cup **granulated sugar**

½ cup packed **light brown sugar**

2 tablespoons fresh **lemon juice**

1 teaspoon **kosher salt**

1 teaspoon **ground cinnamon**

½ teaspoon freshly **grated nutmeg**

8 sweet-tart **apples** (about 4 pounds), such as Granny Smith, Gala, Fuji, or Honeycrisp, peeled, cored, and cut into ⅛-inch-thick slices

2 tablespoons **unsalted butter**, cut into ½-inch cubes and chilled

1 large **egg**

# ULTIMATE THANKSGIVING ROAST TURKEY

1 (12- to 16-pound) **whole turkey**, giblets removed

¼ to ⅓ cup **kosher salt**, plus more to taste

1 cup (2 sticks) **unsalted butter**, at room temperature

½ cup fresh **sage leaves**, minced, plus whole leaves for serving

1 tablespoon **dried thyme**

1 tablespoon **dried rosemary**

4 **garlic cloves**, minced

**Freshly ground black pepper**

1 large **yellow onion**, cut into 8 wedges

½ **lemon**, cut into wedges, plus more for serving

1 large **carrot**, cut into 3-inch pieces

1 large **celery stalk**, cut into 3-inch pieces

5 cups **chicken stock**

You'll need to get a day's head start on this turkey, but it is well worth the extra time. This recipe uses a dry brining technique, different from wet brining in that you don't need to submerge the turkey in a water solution (or find a pot big enough to do it in). Instead, just rub the turkey all over with salt and let it rest in the fridge. This recipe also includes instructions for the perfect gravy, so we've got you (and this turkey) covered from start to finish.

1  Using a knife, remove the wishbone and wing tips from the turkey; put them in a small bowl in the refrigerator. Trim any excess fat and skin from the turkey and discard.

2  Place the turkey on a wire rack set over a roasting pan. Rub the turkey all over with the salt (use 1 teaspoon salt per 1 pound of turkey). Transfer to the refrigerator, uncovered, and let dry brine for 24 hours.

3  When ready to cook the turkey, preheat the oven to 325°F.

4  Stir together the butter, sage, thyme, rosemary, and garlic in a small bowl until smooth. Season with salt and pepper.

5  Remove the turkey from the refrigerator and use your fingers to gently loosen the skin from the meat over the breasts and thighs. Stuff the butter mixture evenly underneath the skin over the breasts and thighs. Smear any remaining butter over the entire outside of the turkey.

6  Stuff the cavity of the turkey with 2 onion wedges and the lemon wedges. Toss the remaining 6 onion wedges, the carrot, and the celery into the roasting pan underneath the turkey. Add 4 cups of the stock to the pan.

7  Roast the turkey until golden brown, an instant-read thermometer inserted into the thigh registers 165°F, and the juices run clear, 1½ to 2 hours.

8  Transfer the pan to a separate wire rack and set the turkey (still on the wire rack) on a cutting board. Tent the turkey loosely with foil and let rest for 30 minutes.

9  Meanwhile, pour the pan drippings through a fine-mesh strainer into a medium saucepan and bring to a simmer over medium heat. Cook until reduced to about 3 cups, 10 to 12 minutes.

10  Whisk together the remaining 1 cup stock and the flour in a medium bowl until smooth (see box, page 289). Add the mixture to the pan and cook, stirring constantly, until thickened and smooth, about 5 minutes. Season with salt and pepper. Pour the gravy into a serving vessel.

Carve the turkey (see box, below) and arrange the pieces on a serving platter. Place sage leaves and lemon wedges around the turkey and serve warm, with the gravy alongside.

## 101

## Carving a Turkey

First, transfer your turkey to a large cutting board with a lip to catch any juices. Release the full legs from the body by finding where the large end of the drumstick (or the turkey's "knee," if you will) meets the breast, cutting through that line, then prying the leg outward from the body where it connects to the backbone at the hip joint (it should pop out fairly easily). With the whole leg resting skin-side down, cut along the line that appears between the drumstick and thigh to separate the two parts. Next, find the turkey's breastbone and cut straight down either side, staying flush against and following the line of the breastbone, to remove the breast meat in one large piece (removing the wishbone before roasting helps make this step particularly easy). Slice the breast against the grain so each piece gets some crispy skin. To release the wings, find where the shoulder meets the breast and give the wing a twist with your hands to find where it separates, then use a knife to free it from the carcass. Finish your platter of sliced meat with some fresh sage, lemon slices, and sprigs of fresh rosemary. Although the carcass is most likely looking decidedly less majestic at this point, you can save it to make an epic turkey soup later on.

# HONEY MUSTARD–GLAZED HAM

1 cup **orange juice**

¼ cup **cider vinegar**

¼ cup **stone-ground mustard**

10 **garlic cloves**

10 **whole cloves**

1 large **yellow onion**, coarsely chopped

1 bone-in **cured picnic ham** (about 10 pounds)

1 cup packed **light brown sugar**

½ cup **honey**

½ cup **Dijon mustard**

1 tablespoon **Worcestershire sauce**

Everyone's holiday favorite just got easier. This knockout dish starts with a whole bone-in cured picnic ham dressed up with a brown sugar, honey, Dijon mustard, and Worcestershire sauce glaze. A silicone pastry brush makes quick work of all the basting that you'll need to do for maximum shiny glaze status. Dibs on the leftovers!

1  Preheat the oven to 400°F.

2  Combine the orange juice, vinegar, stone-ground mustard, garlic, cloves, and onion in a large roasting pan and stir to mix evenly.

3  Trim off any tough outer skin from the ham, then score the remaining fat in a crosshatch pattern, spacing the cuts 1 inch apart. Place the ham on a roasting rack and set the rack in the roasting pan over the liquid and aromatics. Cover the pan with foil and bake for 1 hour. Transfer the roasting pan to a wire rack. Leave the oven on.

4  Uncover the ham and transfer it to a cutting board. Pick out and discard the whole cloves from the pan liquid, then pour the liquid and remaining solids into a medium saucepan. Return the ham to the roasting rack and the rack to the roasting pan.

5  Stir the brown sugar, honey, Dijon mustard, and Worcestershire into the pan liquid and bring the mixture to a boil over medium-high heat. Reduce the heat to medium to maintain a simmer and cook, stirring occasionally, until the mixture has thickened and reduced to the consistency of a glaze, about 15 minutes. Remove the pan from the heat.

6  Brush some glaze all over the ham and return it to the oven. Bake, occasionally basting the ham with more glaze (see box, left), until the glaze is caramelized and an instant-read thermometer inserted into the thickest part of the ham registers 145°F, 30 to 45 minutes.

7  Transfer the pan to a wire rack. Let the ham cool in the pan for 20 minutes, then move it to a cutting board and thinly slice. Serve warm.

## 101

## Basting

Basting—the act of pouring, splashing, or spooning liquid or a glaze over meat during cooking—flavors and tenderizes meat like few other techniques can. Oven basting refers to occasionally moistening a piece of roasting protein (think Thanksgiving turkey, page 280) with its own juices; this is usually done with a baster with a bulb on the end. But we like to forgo that and stick with a good ol' serving spoon to scoop and pour the flavorful liquid or glaze over whatever we're basting.

# DUO OF ROASTED VEGGIES

EACH SERVES **4**

It's the holidays and it's hectic, so save your sanity by focusing on these two super-simple roasted veggies that use one brilliant, easy technique. A quick toss with seasonings and a blast of heat from the oven and you've got burnished, deeply flavorful vegetables in less time than it takes to carve the ham.

## PAPRIKA & HERB ROASTED CARROTS

4 large **carrots** (1 pound), cut on an angle into ¼-inch-thick slices

¼ cup **olive oil**

¼ cup finely chopped **fresh flat-leaf parsley**

2 teaspoons **sweet paprika**

1 teaspoon **kosher salt**

½ teaspoon **freshly ground black pepper**

1 Preheat the oven to 400°F.

2 Combine the carrots, olive oil, parsley, paprika, salt, and pepper on a rimmed baking sheet and toss to coat evenly. Roast, stirring once halfway through, until the carrots are tender and caramelized, 20 to 25 minutes total.

3 Transfer the baking sheet to a wire rack and let cool for 5 minutes before serving.

## HONEY-BALSAMIC ROASTED BRUSSELS SPROUTS

1½ pounds **Brussels sprouts**, trimmed and halved lengthwise

2 tablespoons **olive oil**

2 tablespoons **balsamic vinegar**

2 teaspoons **honey**

1 teaspoon **kosher salt**

½ teaspoon **freshly ground black pepper**

1 Preheat the oven to 425°F.

2 Combine the Brussels sprouts, olive oil, balsamic, honey, salt, and pepper on a rimmed baking sheet and toss to coat evenly. Roast, stirring once halfway through, until the sprouts are tender and caramelized, 15 to 20 minutes total.

3 Transfer the baking sheet to a wire rack and let cool for 5 minutes before serving.

# SHOWSTOPPING BEEF WELLINGTON

When you really need to pull out all the stops, Wellington gets the job done! A gorgeously rosy cut of beef wrapped in pastry you get to dramatically slice in front of your guests? *Yessss.* When buying the meat for this dish, it's ideal to strike up a friendly convo with your butcher and ask him or her for a single whole piece of center-cut beef tenderloin—not several pieces tied together into a roast. Think of the puff pastry as your canvas: You can score a decorative design onto the surface with a fork and decorate the top with additional puff pastry cut into shapes, if you like.

2 pounds **cremini or button mushrooms**

1 (3-pound) piece center-cut **beef tenderloin**, about 9 inches long, at room temperature (see box, page 55)

**Kosher salt** and **freshly ground black pepper**

2 tablespoons **vegetable oil**

1 tablespoon **unsalted butter**

5 **garlic cloves**, minced

2 **shallots**, minced

¼ cup prepared **English mustard**, such as Colman's

8 ounces thinly sliced **prosciutto**

1 large (9 by 11-inch) **sheet puff pastry** (plus additional pastry for garnish, if desired), thawed if frozen, such as Dufour (see box, page 288)

2 large **eggs**, lightly beaten

1  Pulse the mushrooms in a food processor until finely minced; set aside.

2  Season the beef tenderloin all over with salt and pepper.

3  In a large skillet, heat the vegetable oil over high heat. When the oil is smoking, add the tenderloin and cook, undisturbed, until a dark brown crust forms on the bottom, about 3 minutes (see box, page 272). Using tongs, rotate the tenderloin, and repeat, searing it on all sides, including the ends, until completely dark brown A . Transfer the tenderloin to a cutting board or wire rack and let cool for 30 minutes B .

4  In the same skillet, melt the butter over medium-high heat. Add the minced mushrooms, garlic, and shallots and cook, stirring occasionally, until all the liquid released by the mushrooms has evaporated and the mixture becomes a thick paste, about 30 minutes. Remove the skillet from the heat and let the mushroom mixture cool for 30 minutes.

5  Remove and discard any kitchen twine from the tenderloin. Brush the mustard all over the meat C .

6  On a clean surface, arrange a layer of overlapping sheets of plastic wrap, longer side facing you and twice the length and width of the tenderloin. Arrange overlapping strips of prosciutto in an even 10-inch square in the center of the plastic wrap D . Spread the mushroom mixture evenly over the prosciutto, then place the tenderloin on top of the mushrooms, with one long side of the tenderloin facing you.

recipe continues

7  Using the plastic wrap as an aid, tightly roll up the tenderloin and mushrooms in the prosciutto. Tie the ends of the plastic wrap together tightly, like you're wrapping a piece of hard candy, to hold the roll's shape  E . Place in the refrigerator, seam-side down, to chill for 30 minutes.

8  Arrange another double layer of plastic wrap on a clean surface. Lay a sheet of puff pastry on top with one long edge facing you and, using a rolling pin, roll the sheet into a roughly 12 by 15-inch rectangle.

9  Remove and discard the plastic wrap from the prosciutto-wrapped tenderloin. Set the meat on top of the puff pastry, lining it up so the long side of the roll is facing you. Using the plastic as an aid, roll the meat in the pastry  F   G . Gently pinch the pastry to seal the seam. Tuck any extra puff pastry into the ends and wrap the whole roll tightly in the plastic wrap. Refrigerate for 15 minutes.

10  Preheat the oven to 400°F. Line a baking sheet with parchment paper.

11  Remove and discard the plastic from the pastry-wrapped meat and place the roll on the prepared baking sheet. Brush the surface with the beaten eggs. Using a fork, score a decorative design onto the surface of the puff pastry  H , and decorate the top with additional puff pastry, cut into shapes, if you like.

12  Bake until the puff pastry is a dark golden brown and an instant-read thermometer inserted into the center of the tenderloin registers 135°F for medium-rare, about 40 minutes. Transfer the baking sheet to a wire rack and let the beef Wellington cool for 20 minutes.

13  Transfer the beef Wellington to a serving plate, cut it crosswise into 1-inch-thick slices  I , and serve.

## 101

# Working with Puff Pastry

A type of so-called laminated dough (where the butter and dough are sealed together through lots of rolling and folding), high-quality frozen puff pastry (and its dozens of crispy layers) will make you look like a genius-level baker. Once puff pastry is defrosted, it can't be refrozen, so take out only as many sheets as you need. Always work with one sheet of defrosted puff pastry at a time, keeping the rest covered with a damp towel. Roll the sheets out gently on a lightly floured surface. If any cracks or tears occur in the pastry, just pinch it back together. If the pastry gets too soft while you're rolling or cutting it, return it to the fridge or freezer to firm up. A sharp knife or a pizza cutter will make the cleanest cuts.

# PRIME RIB WITH GARLIC & HERB BUTTER

SERVES
**8 to 10**

Prime rib is a rite of passage for a cook—and one that helps you achieve that holiday "wow" moment with surprisingly little effort behind the scenes. It's important to remove the rib roast from the fridge and have it come fully to room temperature (give the meat an hour on the counter) before sliding it into the oven for this specific roasting technique to work its magic. When you turn off the heat, resist the urge to open the oven door. Otherwise, the residual heat that is needed to finish cooking the roast will escape.

1 cup (2 sticks) **unsalted butter**, at room temperature

2 tablespoons finely chopped **fresh rosemary leaves**

2 tablespoons finely chopped **fresh thyme leaves**

2 tablespoons **kosher salt**

1 tablespoon **freshly ground black pepper**

7 **garlic cloves**, minced

1 (5- to 7-pound) **boneless rib eye roast**, trimmed of excess fat, at room temperature (see box, page 55)

2 tablespoons **all-purpose flour**

2 cups **beef stock**

1 Preheat the oven to 500°F.

2 Combine the butter, rosemary, thyme, salt, pepper, and garlic in a medium bowl and stir together until smooth.

3 Place the rib roast on a rack set in a roasting pan. Using your hands, rub the herb butter all over the roast. Bake the roast for 5 minutes per pound, until the outside is golden brown and crisp, 25 to 35 minutes for medium-rare, depending on the weight of your roast. Without opening the oven, turn off the heat and let the roast stand in the oven for exactly 2 hours.

4 Transfer the roast to a cutting board. Remove the rack from the pan and pour the pan drippings into a small saucepan.

5 To make a slurry, whisk the flour into the stock until there are no lumps (see box, right). Set the saucepan over medium heat and bring to a simmer. Pour in the slurry and cook, stirring, until the sauce bubbles and thickens, about 5 minutes. Remove the pan from the heat and pour the sauce through a fine-mesh strainer into a gravy dish.

6 Carve the roast into ¾-inch-thick slices and serve warm, with the gravy alongside.

## 101

## Slurry

Made up of a liquid plus a thickener like flour or cornstarch, slurries are your best pal when you need to thicken up a gravy, soup, stew, or sauce. By creating a slurry, you avoid the lumps you'd get if you added the powdery dry stuff straight to a larger amount of liquid. Just make sure that once you add the slurry to your recipe you thoroughly cook the mixture for several minutes to eliminate the raw taste of the thickener.

# CRANBERRY & BRIE HOLIDAY PULL-APART BREAD

Nonstick cooking spray

1 pound rind-on **Brie cheese**, cut into 1-inch cubes

2 (16-ounce) cans **refrigerated biscuit dough**

1 teaspoon coarsely chopped fresh **thyme leaves**

1 teaspoon coarsely chopped fresh **rosemary**

1 (14-ounce) can **whole-berry cranberry sauce**

Each dough ball in this bread/dessert hides a surprise "present" of Brie, making it holiday perfection. Thyme, rosemary, and cranberry sauce ensure no holiday ingredient— or slice of this bread—gets left behind

1   Preheat the oven to 350°F. Coat a 10-cup Bundt pan with cooking spray.

2   Open the can of dough and separate the individual biscuits. Using your hands, tear each round in half. Flatten a piece of torn dough in your palm and place 1 cube of Brie in the center. Pinch the dough around the cheese to enclose it, then roll it into a small ball. Repeat with the remaining dough and Brie.

3   Place a layer of the cheese-filled dough balls in the bottom of the prepared pan, spacing them out evenly. Sprinkle this layer with one-third each of the thyme and rosemary leaves, then spoon about one-third of the cranberry sauce evenly over the top. Repeat this layering until all the ingredients have been added to the pan, finishing with the cranberry sauce.

4   Bake until the dough is golden brown and the cranberry sauce is bubbling on top, about 40 minutes. Transfer the pan to a wire rack and let cool for 10 minutes. Invert the monkey bread onto a serving plate (see box, below), and serve warm.

## 101

## Inverting Baked Goods

To invert a cake or this spectacular monkeybread, let it cool until it's easy to handle but still warm. Place a rimmed baking sheet or serving platter over the top of the pan. Grab the pan and the baking sheet together (hold on tight, *wheee!*) and flip it all upside down. Remove the pan. Voilà! If you need to invert again (so the cake or bread is facing the same direction it was when it was in the pan), repeat with another plate or baking sheet.

MAKES
**16**
CUPS

# HOLIDAY SPICED CIDER

1 **orange**

2 teaspoons **whole cloves**

1 teaspoon **allspice berries**

1 **sweet-tart apple**, such as Granny Smith, Gala, or Fuji

1 gallon **apple cider**

½ cup packed **light brown sugar**

1 teaspoon freshly **grated nutmeg**

4 **cinnamon sticks**

**Whiskey** or **rum**, for serving (optional)

Picture yourself with your hands wrapped around a mug of this sweetly spiced hot apple cider (spiked with a shot of whiskey or rum, natch). Now, try to imagine just how insanely good your house will smell. Whatever you are picturing, the reality (laden with allspice, cloves, and nutmeg) is even better. Time to break out the slow cooker!

1 Pierce the orange all over with the cloves, embedding them in the skin so they stay put. Push the allspice berries through the skin of the apple, into the flesh.

2 Place the orange and apple in a slow cooker. Add the apple cider, brown sugar, nutmeg, and cinnamon sticks. Cover and cook on High for 2 hours, until the cider is infused with the flavors of the fruit and spices. Switch the setting to Warm or Low to keep the cider hot.

3 To serve, ladle the cider into mugs and finish each with a shot of whiskey or rum, if you like.

# GINGERBREAD CHOCOLATE TRUFFLES

MAKES
**30**
TRUFFLES

Ginger, cinnamon, and gingersnap cookie bits make the perfect contrast to these dark chocolate truffles. Tip: The gingersnap crumbs can be easily made with a quick pulse in a food processor, or bashed to bits in a resealable plastic bag with a rolling pin. If the chocolate mixture becomes too warm while you are working, just pop it back into the fridge and chill for a few minutes. Thankfully, the recipe yields about thirty truffles—enough to take a dozen to the office for that holiday cookie swap.

¾ cup plus 2 tablespoons **heavy cream**

10 ounces **bittersweet chocolate**, coarsely chopped (about 1¾ cups)

1 tablespoon **ground ginger**

1 tablespoon **ground cinnamon**

2½ ounces **gingersnap crumbs** (from about 10 cookies)

1 In a small saucepan, bring the cream to a bare simmer over medium heat. Remove the pan from the heat and add the chocolate. Let stand for 1 minute, then stir the chocolate and cream together until combined and smooth. Stir in the ginger and cinnamon until combined evenly.

2 Pour the chocolate mixture into a shallow baking dish and refrigerate until completely set, about 3 hours.

3 Spread the gingersnap crumbs over a shallow plate. Using a small spoon, scoop and roll the chilled chocolate into 1-inch balls. Roll the balls through the gingersnap crumbs to coat, then transfer to a plate, cover with plastic wrap, and refrigerate until ready to serve, for up to 5 days.

# KITCHEN SINK HOLIDAY COOKIES

1½ cups **all-purpose flour** (see box, page 179)

1½ teaspoons **baking powder**

1½ teaspoons **baking soda**

1 teaspoon **kosher salt**

¾ cup (1½ sticks) **unsalted butter**, at room temperature

¾ cup **granulated sugar**

¾ cup packed **light brown sugar**

2 large **eggs**

2 teaspoons **vanilla extract**

¾ to 1 teaspoon **peppermint extract**

1 cup **rolled oats**

1 cup chopped **chocolate-covered mint thins**, such as Andes (from one 4.67-ounce package)

¾ cup **sweetened shredded coconut**

¾ cup broken **pretzel sticks**

½ cup **white chocolate chips**

½ cup mixed **red and green candy-coated milk chocolate candies**, such as M&M's

Prepare to venture out on a choose-your-own-cookie adventure. If you're crazy about mint, go for the full teaspoon of mint extract—otherwise dial it down to ¾ teaspoon. For a dozen large cookies that will make a big impact, use a ⅓ cup measure to scoop the dough and bake, four to a baking sheet, for 22 to 25 minutes.

1  Preheat the oven to 350°F. Line two baking sheets with parchment paper.

2  Whisk together the flour, baking powder, baking soda, and salt in a large bowl.

3  In a separate large bowl, using a handheld mixer, beat together the butter and both sugars on medium speed until smooth and fluffy, about 2 minutes (see box, page 188). With the mixer on medium speed, add the eggs one at a time, making sure each is incorporated before adding the next. Beat in the vanilla and peppermint extracts.

4  Add the flour mixture, followed by the oats, mint thins, coconut, pretzels, chocolate chips, and milk chocolate candies and stir with a rubber spatula until everything is combined evenly.

5  Using a 1½-ounce ice cream scoop or two tablespoons, portion and roll the dough into 24 balls. Arrange 8 balls on each prepared baking sheet, spacing them 2 inches apart. Press on the balls to flatten them slightly. Bake the cookies one sheet at a time, turning the baking sheet halfway through, until golden brown and set, about 15 minutes total.

6  Let the cookies cool on the baking sheet for 1 minute, then transfer to a wire rack to cool for 20 minutes more before serving. Repeat to bake the remaining 8 dough balls.

# THANKS TO

### Producers

Kiano Moju

Hector Gomez

Matthew Johnson

Tiffany Lo

Rie McClenny

Nathan Ng

Claire Nolan

Ochi Scobie

Greg Perez

Hitomi Aihara

Adam Bianchi

Jody Tixier

Katie Melody

Julie Klink

Mel Boyajian

Cedee Sandoval

Isabel Castillo

Alix Traeger

Andrew Ilnyckyj

Joey Firoben

Crystal Hatch

Ryan Panlasigui

Rachel Gaewski

Kahnita Wilkerson

Daysha Edewi

Betsy Carter

Katie Aubin

Chris Salicrup

Cyrus Kowsari

Diana Lopez

Scott Loitsch

Merle O'Neal

Vaughn Vreeland

Jordan Kenna

Brenda Blanco

Gwenaelle Le Cochennec

Pierce Abernathy

Alvin Zhou

Marie Telling

Andrew Gauthier

Frank Tiu

Matthew Ciampa

### Production / Operations / Social / Adaptations / VidStats

Ashley McCollum

Angela Ruffin

Maíra Corrêa

Tanner Smith

Nick Guillory

Bryanna Duca

Stephen Santayana

Matt Ford

Lauren Weitz

Gabi D'Addario

Stevie Ward

Ryan Mei

## Food

Claire King

Alexis deBoschnek

Chloe Morgan

Carrie Hildebrand

Angie Thomas

## Branded

Dee Robertson

Kate Staben

Sami Promisloff

Mike Goodman

Camille Bergerson

Swasti Shukla

Hannah Williams

Becca Park

Allex Tarr

Jess Maroney

Mike Price

Dylan Keith

Tracy Raetz

Ryan Panlasigui

Grace Lee

Robert Gilstrap

Ken Orlino

Liza Kahn

Katie Schmidbauer

Nora Campbell

Melissa Ng

Sarah Freeark

Leigh Riemer

Brendan Kelly

## International

Jordan Ballantine

Matt Cullum

Ellie Holland

Evelyn Liu

Toby Stubbs

Gaspar Jose

Isadora Manzaro

Suria Rocha

Guta Batalha

Vitor Hugo Tsuru

Agatha Da Hora

Leticia Almeida

Nicolas Vendramini

Vanessa Hernandez

Lucia Plancarte

Karla Agis

Gus Serrano

Erich Mendoza

Javier Aceves

Thilo Kasper

Dani Beck

Sebastian Fiebrig

Pierre d'Almeida

Pierre Michonneau

Jun Tsuboike

Yui Takahashi

Saki Yamada

Daisuke Furuta

Daiki Nakagawa

Rumi Yamazaki

Ryo Yamaguchi

Sonomi Shimada

## Tech

Sam Balinghasay

Sara Gulotta

Randy Karels

Swati Vauthrin

Graham Wood

Ryan Inman

Will Kalish

Jeremy Back

Edgar Sanchez

Jess Anastasio

Caitlin Osbahr

Amir Shaikh

Meghan Heintz

Emma Byrne

Shema Kalisa

Sami Simon

Kiyana Salkeld

Paul Marino

Dan Tann

Steve Peterson

Charlyn Buchanan

Jay Henry

## Edit

Jessie Gaynor

Emmy Favilla

Jessica Probus

*Bloggers, chefs, and recipe developers who inspired some of the recipes in this book*

Alton Brown, *Good Eats* (Homemade Soft Pretzels, page 249)

Serious Eats (Cheesy French Onion Chicken, page 75)

The Gunny Snack (Easy Orange Chicken, page 84)

The Kitchn (The Best Crispy Chicken Parmesan, page 79)

Alyona's Cooking (Pepperoni Pizza Pull, page 34)

Handle the Heat (Cookies & Cream Cheesecake Bundt, page 187)

Feeling Foodish (Roasted Ratatouille, page 155)

Fine Cooking (Chocolate Croissants, page 223)

Hello, Wonderful (Blueberry-Peach Sheet Pan Pancake, page 230)

Food Network (Potato-Crusted Quiche, page 133)

Gordon Ramsey (Showstopping Beef Wellington, page 286)

Food Wishes (Honey Mustard-Glazed Ham, page 282)

Allrecipes (Easy Chickpea Curry, page 154, and Fresh Corn Chowder, page 160)

Kevin Is Cooking (Honey-Balsamic Roasted Brussels Sprouts, page 283)

Ina Garten, *Barefoot Contessa* (Paprika & Herb Roasted Carrots, page 283)

*Everyone at Clarkson Potter*

Amanda Englander

Gabrielle Van Tassel

Stephanie Huntwork

Jan Derevjanik

Catherine Casalino

Marysarah Quinn

Chloe Aryeh

Mark McCauslin

Ivy McFadden

Philip Leung

Merri Ann Morrell

Alexandria Martinez

Linnea Knollmueller

Derek Gullino

Aislinn Belton

Kate Tyler

Carly Gorga

Natasha Martin

Aaron Wehner

Doris Cooper

Jill Flaxman

Katie Ziga

Christine Edwards

John Dawson

David Sanford

*Original recipe developer*

Ben Mims

*Recipe testers*

Susan Phuong My Vu

Veronica Spera

Megan Cornell

Lukas Volger

*Our photography team*

Lauren Volo

Molly Schuster

Maeve Sheridan

Christina Zhang

Joy Howard

Greg Wright

Erika Iroff

Andie McMahon

Jennifer En

# INDEX